The Historical Series of the Reformed Church
in America

No. 9

FROM STRENGTH TO STRENGTH: A HISTORY OF NORTHWESTERN 1882–1982

by

GERALD F. DE JONG

Wm. B. Eerdmans Publishing Co.
Grand Rapids, Michigan

Library of Congress Cataloging in Publication Data

De Jong, Gerald Francis, 1921-
  From strength to strength.

  (The Historical series of the Reformed Church in
America; no. 9)
    Includes index.
    1. Northwestern College (Orange City, Iowa)—History.
I. Title. II. Series.
LD4016.D4 1982   378.777'13   82-8736
ISBN 0-8028-1944-3   AACR2

To Dr. Jacob Heemstra
President of Northwestern 1928-1951

Professor Jacob Heemstra

"In the year 1928 Professor Jacob Heemstra of Central College was called to take up the leadership of the new college. For twenty-three years—and these the best years of his life—he has invested in this enterprise. Most skillfully did he manage to pilot the youthful institution between the cliffs of depression and opposition. He experienced the years of the five loaves and the two little fishes with which to feed the multitudes. During these years the financial support came, to some extent, from the small change scraped together and deposited in empty cigar boxes. He has known the years when the institution was, so to speak, hidden as a kind of Cinderella in the kitchen. But he has also been the prince who found the golden slipper which did fit her foot only, and he has given the young college a worthy position among her sister institutions." (Translated from *De Volksvriend*, June 7, 1951; written on the occasion of Dr. Heemstra's retirement from the presidency.)

The Historical Series of the Reformed Church in America

This series has been inaugurated by the General Synod of the Reformed Church in America, acting through its Commission on History, for the purpose of encouraging historical research and providing a medium wherein this knowledge may be shared with the academic community and with the members of the denomination in order that a knowledge of the past may contribute to right action in the present.

It is an especial pleasure to present to the church this volume to celebrate the Centennial of Northwestern, 1882-1982.

Editor

The Rev. Donald J. Bruggink, Ph.D., Western Theological Seminary

Contents

Illustrations

Foreword

The Northwestern of the 1980's is the lens through which the Northwestern of yesterday is projected upon the screen of the future. With this volume, the opportunity exists to observe a century in perspective concerning the trials, tribulations and growth of Northwestern from infancy through adolescence, and on to maturity. This history also focuses on the challenge of the next century as the college looks forward to strengthen, to progress, to innovate and to provide greater service for future generations.

It is indeed appropriate that Dr. Gerald De Jong has prepared this significant history. As a highly-recognized and respected historian—especially in the field of Dutch-American and Reformed Church history—he is eminently qualified. His firsthand experience at Northwestern as a student, faculty member and administrator, give Dr. De Jong's account the advantage of a direct personal involvement in the development of the institution.

Appropriately this history does not present a mere chronology, but describes the forces prevalent in the development of Northwestern as well as the interactions among the institution, its constituency and its environment. Moreover, through careful research Dr. De Jong has caught the pioneer vision of those who established and promoted Northwestern as a strong Christian educational institution.

In a history of this nature, key personalities are inevitably portrayed as playing important roles. In this light, it is most appropriate that this publication is specifically dedicated to Dr. Jacob Heemstra, who made significant contributions to the total life of Northwestern. His administration was the key link from the Academy era to the Junior College level to the establishment of the four-year college, and without his forceful, dedicated leadership, there may not have been the thriving Northwestern of today.

It was my personal privilege to have served with Dr. Heemstra as a colleague. Following his 23 years of distinguished service as president of Northwestern Jr. College and Academy, I greatly appreciated the opportunity to serve the institution as president while he continued on the staff as president emeritus and also professor. His wise counsel was an inspiration to me. Never interfering in administrative matters, he remained a "Tower of Strength" with advice that was profound and helpful. I always looked upon this relationship as that of a "father guiding his son"! Dr. Heemstra was sincerely dedicated to the steady growth of the institution as it evolved into the four-year college. We all owe a debt of gratitude to him and to his vision.

On May 8, 1981, it was my special privilege to serve as keynote speaker for Northwestern's Heritage Day. Once again I was reminded of the deep dedication of Northwestern students, alumni, faculty, administration and members of the Board of Trustees. With this continued sincere commitment, the future of Northwestern is certainly well-established and secure.

As I mentioned in my presidential inaugural address on October 19, 1955, there is a continuing challenge in "Our Changeless Task in Times of Change" steadfastly to maintain the highest quality of Christian higher education at Northwestern College. To the reader of this history, it will become clear that the heritage of this institution will inevitably guide and inspire future constituencies of the college, as its history continues to unfold.

Preston J. Stegenga, Ph.D.
President, Northwestern
College (1955-1966)

Preface

It was one hundred years ago that a small group of men met in the consistory room of the First Reformed Church of Orange City, Iowa, to draw up articles of incorporation establishing Northwestern Classical Academy. The founders of the school were men of vision who had arrived with others in northwest Iowa only a few years earlier when it was still largely unbroken prairie. They saw that with hard work and perseverence the area could be converted into prosperous farm land and thriving communities. From the beginning, they also saw the need for a preparatory school that would offer more than was available in the elementary grades and would prepare young people for college—especially young men who wanted to enter the ministry. Events since that time have demonstrated that these men were not idle dreamers.

A hundred years is a long time and the educational institution established in 1882 has undergone several significant changes. A junior college program was added in 1928 and a senior college program in 1961, at which time the Academy was dissolved. These developments involved numerous changes in matters of staff, curriculum, extracurricular activities, physical plant, and, of course, budget, which increased from a few thousand dollars to over five million dollars. In one significant respect, however, the institution has not changed. It was founded for the purpose of providing a good education based on Christian principles, and it has not wandered a single step from this path—hence, the title of this history *From Strength to Strength*.

To make the account more understandable, it has been divided into three historical periods as follows: "The Academy: 1882-1928," "The Academy and Junior College: 1928-1961," and "Northwestern as a Four-Year College: 1961-1982." Similarly, the various elements that are an essential part of any educational institution (faculty, curriculum, physical plant, and finances) are generally treated separately within each time frame. A division of the subject matter along those lines is necessary to give each element a sense of continuity. It must be realized, of course, that they are not independent of one another, but were frequently intertwined—that is, developments in one area of Northwestern's growth

1

often affected other areas. For example, because not all staff members had the same philosophy of education, changes in staff (especially those involving principals, presidents, and deans) were certain to have an effect on curriculum. Similarly, a new addition to the physical plant, like Zwemer Hall or Ramaker Library, had an effect on academic life, as did the Multi-Purpose Auditorium and the Rowenhorst Student Center on extracurricular activities.

I am grateful to many persons who in one way or another have offered constructive criticisms as this manuscript progressed. Particular thanks in this regard are due various members of Northwestern's Centennial Committee: especially George De Vries, Nella Kennedy, Ralph Mouw, and Lyle Vander Werf. President Friedhelm Radandt and former President Preston Stegenga have also been helpful in offering suggestions. A word of thanks is also due Donald J. Bruggink, general editor of the Historical Series of the Reformed Church in America, for his careful editorial work. In addition, I appreciate the numerous courtesies extended by Arthur Hielkema and Marcia Vis of Northwestern's library staff.

Last but far from least, gratitude is expressed to the members of my family for not complaining about my neglecting them during the last year and a half while I carried on my research and did my writing. A special word of thanks must go to my wife Jeanne who typed and retyped the manuscript during its several revisions, and to my eldest son Owen who was of considerable help in matters of grammar and organization.

Gerald F. De Jong
University of South Dakota

PART ONE
THE ACADEMY: 1882-1928

I

The Ethnic and Religious Setting

Northwestern has gone through several phases of development since it was founded in 1882. The institution began as a preparatory school known as Northwestern Classical Academy, and in 1928, a junior college curriculum was added. Beginning in the late 1950's, the preparatory program was phased out and the college program was expanded to four years. Developments such as these make it difficult to write a simple and orderly account of the school's history. Faculty turnover and major modifications in the curriculum add to the confusion at times. Two factors, however, have helped give the school a degree of continuity, namely, the Dutch ethnic make-up of the community in which the school was founded and the Reformed religious faith of its constituency. The former was particularly important during the early period, while the latter has remained significant to the present day. A study of Northwestern's history must therefore begin with a brief account of how northwest Iowa, the school's locale, came to be settled by persons of this background.

The people of the Netherlands have until recent times shown only a limited interest in leaving their homeland as emigrants. Even during the closing decades of the nineteenth century and the beginning of the twentieth, when the idea of emigration seemed to pervade the air of all Europe, the percentage of Hollanders who left their' homeland for America was small in comparison to that of most European countries. Although lacking in numbers, Dutch immigrants nevertheless made their influence felt in some parts of the United States because of their tendency to locate near one another. In 1930, for example, when the total Holland-born population in the United States was at its peak for any decennial census year, almost two-thirds were located in only five states. Ranking first was Michigan, followed by New York, Illinois, New Jersey, and Iowa. Distinct Dutch communities were founded in each of these states and still exist to this day.

Among the various causes for Dutch emigration to America, religion was a significant factor for a brief period during the mid-nineteenth century and was one of the principal causes for bringing the first large group of immigrants to Iowa. The religious factor stemmed primarily from the determination of the Netherlands government to force conformity on a group of orthodox Calvinists who refused to abide by certain royal decrees aimed at placing ecclesiastical bodies under closer state supervision. Some critics also claimed the government was trying to keep the Bible out of the public schools. Finally, a religious awakening, known as the *réveil*, was highly critical of ministers for being too rationalistic in their preaching. Supporters of the *réveil* advocated a return to the strict views of the early Dutch Reformed fathers and upbraided the national state church, the so-called *Hervormde Kerk*, for becoming too formalistic and complacent in its ways.

The controversy over church reorganization and other religious problems finally culminated in the so-called Secession of 1834, when congregations began seceding from the state church and holding meetings of their own. Within a year, the number of such congregations had reached sixteen. The government attempted to break the morale of the Seceders by arresting persons attending their meetings, especially the ministers, and by billeting hardened and obnoxious soldiers in their homes. Seceders also frequently found themselves discriminated against by non-dissenting employers and ostracized at social gatherings. The government, however, was unable to break the spirit of the dissenters and gradually showed a willingness to compromise. The abdication of the conservative King William I in 1840 and the adoption of a more liberal constitution in 1848, practically brought the persecution to an end.

The relaxation of the laws against the Seceders came too late for many Hollanders who in the meantime had decided to "become the salt of the earth in some new settlement in America." By the time persecution had diminshed, a kind of emigration psychosis had taken such a firm hold on the minds of many dissenters that it would have been virtually impossible to reverse the trend. As reported by the Reverend Albertus Van Raalte, one of the seceding ministers, in answer to a question on the matter: "You will not be able to stop this emigration any more than you can stop the Rhine in its course." In several instances, almost entire congregations of Seceders, with their ministers, decided to find new homes in America.

One of the largest groups of immigrants, totaling about eight hundred, located in Marion County in southeastern Iowa, where on July 29, 1847, they purchased about eighteen thousand acres of government land and partially developed farms. Their leader was the Reverend Hendrik Pieter Scholte, who helped organize the orthodox Calvinists in the church-state struggle of the 1830's and 1840's and was one of the first ministers to secede from the state church of Holland. The new arrivals called their community Pella, signifying "refuge," after the town to which some of the Christians had fled when Jerusalem was destroyed by the Romans in 70 A.D. A visitor from the Netherlands reported in 1873 that "though the men who have settled here [at Pella] have thus far not yet become capitalists, [nevertheless] with industry, thrift, and perserverance nearly all have achieved a fairly large measure of prosperity, and their own appearance as well as that of their houses supports this contention."

News about the prosperity of the Iowa Hollanders quickly brought in more settlers. In this respect, it must be noted that although religion was a factor for a brief period in influencing Dutch emigration, economic considerations soon became more important. Adverse economic conditions in the Netherlands included unemployment, low wages, and high taxes. These problems were aggravated from time to time by floods, diseases among the livestock, and blights in the potato crops. A rapid growth in population also made it difficult for young men of rural background to obtain farms on reasonable terms, while the lack of industrialization made it equally difficult to find employment in the cities. In view of these considerations, it is not surprising that the rapidly expanding economy of the United States acted like a magnet in attracting discontented Hollanders to her shores. Factories and handicraft industries provided employment for Dutch immigrants in the towns and cities, while the liberal land policy of the government and the availability of millions of acres for sale by the railroad companies proved attractive for persons of rural background.

Emigration to America was further encouraged by the glowing reports sent to relatives and friends in Holland by those who had emigrated. Such reports must have been numerous. The postmaster of Orange City, Iowa reported in 1882 that an average of twenty letters left his office daily bound for the Netherlands. In many cases, a Dutch immigrant who had made good in America sent money to the Netherlands for the purpose of bringing his parents or other members of his family. Railroads and steamship companies, as well as state and territorial immigration departments, also distributed literature in the Netherlands extolling the United States as the "land of milk and honey."

Taking into account the above considerations, it is not surprising that the Dutch settlement in southeast Iowa grew rapidly. On the eve of the First World War, there were nearly twenty thousand Hollanders, by birth and descent, living within a radius of about twenty miles of Pella. Long before this, however, the Pella colony had begun to "swarm," as Hollanders left to establish daughter colonies elsewhere—the largest of which was located in northwest Iowa. The actual Dutch settlement of

northwest Iowa did not begin until 1870, but various preparatory steps
were taken during the previous year. In 1869, two committees of land-
seekers were sent from Pella to search out a site for a new colony. On
the basis of their investigation, they took possession of thirty-eight sections (24,320 acres) of land in Sioux County. Early in the following
spring, three wagon trains of Dutch families and single men set out
from Pella with their furniture and farming equipment to begin a new
life for themselves about three hundred miles to the northwest. Upon
arrival, they plotted a town, which they named Orange City—after the
royal family in the Netherlands—and began the arduous task of breaking
the tough prairie soil. The excellent quality of the soil, some of the best
in the United States, together with the Dutch talent for farming caused
the settlement to prosper.

The Hollanders who arrived from Pella were soon joined by others,
some of whom came directly from the Netherlands but many were
immigrants or their descendants who had been living in Dutch communities in Michigan, Illinois, and Wisconsin. With reference to those
who came from other states, their primary reason for relocating was
economic. Especially important was the availability of cheap, fertile
land. Overcrowding in their former settlements and dissatisfaction with
the growing strength of labor unions were also factors. Some also considered the cities poor places for raising children. Clergymen serving
Dutch congregations in various parts of the United States at times encouraged Hollanders to seek a new start elsewhere. Dutch-language
newspapers, as well as personal correspondence, were likewise an important means for informing Dutch-Americans about the new settlement. A weekly paper, *De Volksvriend*, that began publication at
Orange City in 1874, was particularly helpful, but *De Weekblad*, published at Pella, and *De Grondwet*, published at Holland, Michigan, also
frequently carried news about the Dutch in northwest Iowa.

Despite problems and disappointments, the Dutch population of
northwest Iowa increased to more than five thousand by 1880 and was
still growing. As more settlers arrived, additional prairie land was broken for farms and new towns were founded. Several of these towns, too,
bore Dutch names, including East Orange (later called Alton), Maurice
(for Prince Maurice, the son of the renowned William the Silent), Mid-
dleburg, and Newkirk. A few other new communities which did not
have Dutch names, such as Sioux Center, were also settled primarily by
persons of Dutch descent. Soon no more land was available for home-
steading in Sioux County, and land already occupied could be obtained
only at high prices. Many of the Hollanders consequently had no choice
but to look elsewhere for farms. In this way daughter colonies were

founded nearby in the Dakotas and Minnesota. The founding of such settlements later proved important because many young people from these new communities went to Northwestern for their education.

Although the ethnic make-up of the people who supported Northwestern was of significant influence on the development of the school, even more important was their religious background. The immigrants who located at Pella in 1847 were orthodox Reformed in their religious views, as was noted, and it was people with these same characteristics who established the new Dutch colony in northwest Iowa about a quarter century later. Moreover, although dissatisfaction over religious matters declined after about 1850 as a cause for Dutch emigration, most new immigrants who located there during the later nineteenth century continued to be of a conservative religious background. The same was true of new arrivals from Dutch communities established earlier in Wisconsin, Michigan, and elsewhere. This is significant because it meant that as the Dutch settlers increased in number, the colony's original religious foundations were not greatly affected by this growth.

Religion was a very meaningful experience among the Hollanders of northwest Iowa, and in many respects was of a type frequently associated with the simple, rustic life of the prairie. Among these early settlers, family prayers were offered before and after meals. A portion of Scripture was also read at mealtimes and frequently before retiring in the evening. Bible study and catechetical instruction were important in the rearing of children. Because of the absence of a resident pastor during the first two years of the colony, the settlers usually had to rely upon the more literate men of the community to take charge of the worship services on Sunday. Services included reading a few chapters from Scripture, offering prayers, and perhaps reading a discourse from an approved book of sermons. Someone with a good singing voice would lead the group in singing the favorite Dutch psalms. Although these laymen were often plain people with little formal education, they were endowed with leadership qualities that made them highly respected in the community. They were well-versed in the Bible and the Heidelberg Catechism, and were acquainted with the better-known Bible commentaries.

Although the early Dutch settlers of Sioux County practiced their religion daily in their homes and met together for Sunday worship, a formal church organization and a resident minister were urgently needed. Therefore, after careful planning and with help from the Classis of Illinois and the denominational Board of Domestic Missions, a Reformed church was organized at Orange City on May 6, 1871. The initial membership of the new congregation totaled less than twenty families. Most of them were farmers, because the town at this time had only about a dozen houses.

Having a formal church organization solved only part of the problem. Until the Reformed people of northwest Iowa acquired a minister of their own, they were, in the words of one of the early residents, "as sheep without a shepherd." In the fall of 1871, the new congregation therefore extended a call to the Reverend Seine Bolks of Zeeland, Michigan. The choice was an excellent one. Born and educated in the Netherlands, Bolks had led a large group of immigrants to America in 1847, and later served pastorates in Wisconsin, Illinois, and Michigan. He was thus well-acquainted not only with the Dutch language but also with the type of people found in Sioux County and with the difficulties of frontier living. The Hollanders of northwest Iowa were jubilant when news reached them that Bolks had accepted their call. He was fifty-eight years of age when he began his ministry at Orange City in April 1872.

In the same way that the early Dutch settlers were fortunate in having a spiritual leader like Dominie Bolks, they also had an outstanding citizen to help look after the secular needs of the colony. His name was Henry Hospers. Born in the Netherlands in 1830, Hospers had emigrated in 1847 with his parents to Pella, where in time he became a prominent businessman and respected public servant. In 1869, he served on the second committee of "locators" that chose the site for a new settlement in northwest Iowa, and later played a commanding role in its development. His many activities included those of banker, storekeeper, notary, attorney, newspaperman, member of the county board of supervisors, insurance agent, and promoter of education. With reference to the latter, Hospers became one of the principal founders of Northwestern.

When Dominie Bolks arrived in Sioux County in the spring of 1872, religious services were being held in the Orange City schoolhouse, a small, one-room structure. When the congregation became too large for the schoolhouse, a lean-to was built at one end. The addition was constructed so it could be opened on Sundays to accommodate the congregation but closed off on week-days for school. A minister who visited Orange City in November 1873 described this "church" as follows:

Of that church entertain no lofty expectation! It is indeed the most unsightly structure in which I have ever preached. Imagine a small rectangular building of boards, perhaps ten metres long and five metres wide, with a stove in the center and benches around it. That is the school. Perpendicular to this school-room at one end, like the upper part of the capital letter T, there is a shed with a few rough, unplanned boards on supports to serve as pews, and against the back wall opposite the entrance stand a chair and table for the minister. This shed and school-room together form the church.

The primitiveness of the situation during the early period is further indicated by the manner in which the first communion service was celebrated: ordinary cups and an earthen milk pitcher were used.

Within two years after the congregation had been organized, the communicant membership had increased from thirty-four to two hundred sixty-five. Obviously, better accommodations were needed, and steps were therefore taken to build a church. The new building was dedicated on October 4, 1874, although it was little more than an enclosed shell at this time. The congregation sat on rough boards to hear Dominie Bolks' dedicatory sermon. The new church, when finally completed, had a seating capacity of about eight hundred. The settlers were extremely proud of their new house of worship which for many years dwarfed all other buildings in the town, and its tall steeple became a landmark for prairie travelers.

As more Dutch settlers arrived and spread outward from Orange City, new communities arose and in time Reformed churches were organized among them. By 1900, the number of new Reformed churches in Sioux County had reached twelve. The early history of these churches was similar to the one at Orange City. They often had to depend on itinerant pastors at first, and their houses of worship were likewise primitive in their construction. Considering the crude appearance of the church buildings of the early period, the historian cannot help wonder what the settlers of that time would say if they could see the magnificent and commodious structures in which their descendants worship today.

In addition to the Reformed churches, a number of Christian Reformed churches arose among the Dutch settlers of northwest Iowa. A brief description of their appearance must also be noted because Northwestern drew many of its students from among them. The first Christian Reformed congregation in northwest Iowa was established at Orange City in 1871, the same year in which the first Reformed congregation was organized. Thereafter, growth was slow for a few years, but five more were established in Sioux County during the 1890's, and three more were founded soon after 1900.

The Christian Reformed denomination, which was organized in Michigan in 1857, was similar in many respects to the Reformed Church. Both denominations adhered to the Belgic Confession, the Heidelberg Catechism, and the Canons of Dort, and the polity of both was presbyterian, with the usual Reformed trademarks of consistories, classes, and synods. Initially, the differences concerned primarily the greater emphasis that the Christian Reformed Church placed on the Heidelberg Catechism in the Sunday sermons, the degree to which it made use of the psalms in the worship services, and its placing restrictions on open communion and on allowing church members to join secret lodges such as the Freemasons. These differences, however, were more pronounced among congregations in the eastern states than those in the Middle West. In the latter region, the two denomintions drew a large part of their membership from among Dutch immigrants and their descendants, and in many respects have remained to this day about equally conservative in religious matters—two facts that explain why so many young people of Christian Reformed background can be found among Northwestern's alumni.

The strict Calvinism of the settlers helped transform the Dutch communities of northwest Iowa into islands of conservatism. One of the main bulwarks of this conservatism was the *kerkraad*, or consistory, made up of the minister and the elders and deacons of the local church. This body kept a careful check on the behavior of the members of the congregation to see that nothing unorthodox took place and that no sins went unnoticed. Another important means by which the church fathers kept a check on their congregations was *huisbezoek*, or house visitation. In accordance with this practice, the minister and one of his elders paid an annual visit to each church family, at which time questions were raised about such matters as family prayers, Bible reading, study of the Heidelberg Catechism, and church attendance, as well as such un-Calvinist practices as card playing and dancing.

Even community affairs did not escape the scrutiny of the church fathers, and this remained true for many years. As late as 1939, for example, the consistory of the First Reformed Church of Orange City sent a protest to the town's Commercial Club because the latter had scheduled the annual spring Tulip Festival on Ascension Day. Also in 1939, this same group of churchmen requested the Sioux County Fair Association to prohibit public dancing at the fair grounds. Similarly, in 1947, the ministerial association at Sioux Center led the fight in behalf of a local referendum aimed at prohibiting the showing of movies in the town hall.

In summary, the locale in which Northwestern was established a century ago in 1882 and from which it drew much of its support and inspiration for many years was one in which a majority of its early residents were either born in the Netherlands or were second generation Dutch-Americans. In their religious faith, the settlers were staunchly

Reformed, and their strict Calvinist beliefs and customs permeated their daily lives. With reference to education, the Dutch of Sioux County began formulating plans at an early date for a school that would provide young people with an education beyond the normal elementary grades. Given their penchant for religious training, it was to be expected that such a school would have to be both academically sound and well-grounded in Reformed principles. It was in this kind of a setting that Northwestern Classical Academy was founded in 1882.

II

The Formative Years, 1882-1894

It has frequently been said that when a Dutchman of the nineteenth century contemplated moving to a new region, two questions were likely to enter his mind: "Is there a school for my children?" and "Is there a church for my family?" As one of the early arrivals in Sioux County expressed it, "Education and religion had a place in house and heart." In view of this observation, it is significant that the second building to be erected in Orange City was a schoolhouse, constructed in the summer of 1870, which, as has been noted, doubled as a church on Sundays until the settlers were able to afford a formal place of worship.

Orange City's first schoolhouse was typical of those that soon dotted the rural landscape of northwest Iowa. It was small, consisting of only one room, and poorly furnished. Its curriculum, too, left much to be desired. The work consisted of little more than training in the three r's, and classes were initially held for only a few months of the year. In his *History of Sioux County*, Charles Dyke, who had firsthand acquaintance with these schools, has given us the following description of their crude appearance and deficiencies:

The school buildings were about the most bare and cheerless it would be possible to imagine. They were simply four plastered walls with floor and ceiling and windows on the sides and a door on one end, and a blackboard on the other. The furnishings consisted of two rows of home-made seats that were made without any idea of comfort and in the aisle between them and in about the center of the room stood a cast iron cannon stove with a sheet iron drum on the top of it and a long stove pipe leading to a chimney above the blackboard. If it was cold the pupils farthest away almost froze while those near to it almost roasted. A small desk for the teacher was the only other piece of furniture. There were no maps or charts, no dictionary or globe. A few readers, spellers and arithmetics were about the only sources of information.

Aware of the shortcomings that frequently prevailed in public education at the local level, it is not surprising when Orange City was plotted and town lots were sold, that the shareholders of the townsite agreed to set

14

aside one fifth of the proceeds to help establish a school of higher learning.

The type of educational institution that the settlers had in mind was one designed primarily for preparing young people for college. The Reverend Seine Bolks especially did a great deal to keep hopes alive for such a school. Before coming to Orange City in the spring of 1872, he had rendered valuable assistance in establishing an academy at Holland, Michigan in 1851, and in adding a college program there in 1866. Later, in explaining why he accepted the call to the First Reformed Church at Orange City, he reported that "the hope of setting up an Academy there in the near future . . . seemed so desirable, that I was prompted to accept the call right away." In 1875, partly through Bolk's efforts, serious consideration was given to a plan for purchasing a section (640 acres) of Sioux County farm land and to use the rent therefrom for establishing a school. Unfortunately, the invasion of millions of grasshoppers destroyed about two-thirds of the crop that year, causing the proposal to be dropped. As Dominie Bolks expressed it, "the grasshoppers took the hopes for an academy with them when they left." The poor harvest of 1875 was no exception, as grasshopper scourges, together with intermittent floods, hailstorms, and droughts, remained a problem for Sioux County farmers for several years. In 1878, Bolks retired from the ministry because of poor health, but he continued to show an interest in the founding of an academy, as did his successor at the First Reformed Church, the Reverend Ale Buursma.

Although hopes for an academy grew dim at times because of crop failures, interest in the idea continued. Meanwhile, the arrival of more Hollanders from other Dutch communities in the United States and directly from the Netherlands further emphasized the need for an educational institution that could offer more than was available in the elementary schools. This need was soon reinforced by the increase in the number of Reformed churches throughout the region. The extent of this increase is clearly shown in a communication from the denominational Board of Domestic Missions dated June 6, 1872—about a year after the first Reformed congregation was organized at Orange City: "The work in the West has been wonderfully prospered. . . . The Particular Synod of Chicago reports 72 churches, 67 ministers, 6887 communicants, 4710 families, with over 5000 Sabbath-school scholars."

The Church's growth in the West and the responsibilities that went with it did not go unnoticed by General Synod. At its meeting at Schenectady, New York, in June 1882, it adopted the following report submitted by its Committee on Education:

The Reverend Seine Bolks

Hope College, amid many difficulties, has accomplished good results. . . . But the Holland colonies are becoming more and more widely scattered, and the youth find it impossible to take their preparatory course in the Grammar School of Hope College. The Synod, therefore, would direct the attention of the Board of Education to this subject, and suggest that it may be to the best interests of our Church to establish schools under the care of Classes, and under such regulations as the Board of Education may determine, where the youth of our Church may be prepared for college, and where they may be thoroughly indoctrinated in Gospel truths and the standards of our Church.

Better harvests in the early 1880's helped make the dreams and hopes of a dozen years finally become a reality. On July 19, 1882, several local clergymen and businessmen met to finalize plans for a school to be known as Northwestern Classical Academy. Articles of Incorporation were signed on August 1, and a constitution and set of by-laws were drafted. The purpose of the school was clearly stated in Article II of the constitution:

The object of this incorporation shall be to establish an Institution of learning for the promotion of Science and Literature in harmony with, and Religion as expressed in, the Doctrinal Standards of the Reformed Church in America; and to exercise such other and incidental powers as are granted to corporations for Educational and Religious purposes.

The constitution placed the Academy "under the care of and subject to, the supervision of the Classis . . . within whose geographical boundaries it [was] located," but the actual operation was left in the hands of a Board of Trustees. The first Board of Trustees was made up of nine members: Henry Hospers, Finley Burke, and the Reverends Seine Bolks and Ale Buursma of Orange City; Dirk Gleysteen, J. S. Tucker, and the Reverend John W. Warnshuis of Alton; and Teunis Wayenberg and the Reverend James De Pree of Sioux Center. Bolks was chosen as the body's president. Other officers included Warnshuis as secretary and Hospers as treasurer. The constitution provided for later increasing the Board of Trustees to sixteen, including the school's principal as an ex-officio member.

The constitution stipulated that future Board members would be appointed by the classis upon nomination by the Board itself and would serve three years, with five members being appointed each year. The Board was required to hold three stated meetings annually as follows: the first Tuesday in April, the third Wednesday in June, and the third Tuesday in September. To assure that the school would remain distinctly Reformed in its outlook, Article V of the constitution stated that "ten of [the] said Trustees shall always be members in full communion of the Reformed Church in America, and the remaining six Trustees shall be members in good standing of some Reformed Church." In practice, not only were members of the Board drawn from men closely identified with the interests of the Reformed Church but for many years were selected from the surrounding area. In 1927, for example, all of the members were residents of Sioux County—a fact that obviously helped contribute to the insularity of the institution and to its conservatism.

The constitution and by-laws also provided for several standing committees of the Board, the most important of which was the executive committee. It consisted of six members, three of whom were elected annually by the Board; the other three were the president and secretary of the Board and the principal of the Academy. The executive committee met on the first Monday of each month, and had responsibility for such matters as determining the course of studies to be pursued, selecting textbooks for the various courses, deciding on dates for beginning and ending school terms, and overseeing the payment of routine financial obligations.

The year 1882 has been commonly accepted as Northwestern's date of origin. This seems appropriate since the Articles of Incorporation were drawn up in that year, and it is worth noting that the frontispiece of the early catalogues all carried the statement: "Founded in 1882." The confusion that has occasionally arisen over accepting this date apparently stems from the fact that these same early catalogues often also carry a brief chronological memorandum giving September 23, 1883 as the "Formal Opening of the Academy." The key to understanding the relevance of this memorandum revolves around the word "formal." In the dictionary sense of the word, the statement simply means that it was on September 23, 1883 that classes at the Academy took on a more explicit and definite complexion. It does not mean that it was in that year that instruction first began. Confusion over Northwestern's date of origin also stems from some of the early comments made about the school's beginnings, such as a remark in a local paper of early 1884 declaring that, "Last September the first term of study began," and a statement by an instructor who taught there briefly in the 1890's that the institution "opened its first school year on September 23, 1883."

In point of fact, instruction began many months before the so-called "formal opening" of the school. Indeed, already in 1881, a year before the Academy had been organized, the principal of the local public school, Jacob Van Zanten, began privately tutoring a few young people on a part-time basis "in languages and other higher branches." These young people undoubtedly had hopes of someday continuing their education at an institution of higher learning and must have been overjoyed when plans for the Academy finally materialized. In the fall of 1882, shortly after the Academy's Articles of Incorporation had been drawn up, this small band of learners was joined by several more young people, bringing the total to about a dozen. The additional students placed a heavy burden on Van Zanten who was still teaching full-time at the local public school. As a consequence, two members of Northwestern's Board of Trustees, the Reverends Buursma of Orange City and Warnshuis of Alton, began assisting him in the tutoring. Because of the efforts of these men, especially those of Van Zanten, when the *formal* opening of the Academy took place on September 23, 1883, it was possible to enroll three levels of students: the entering, or freshman class, and two advanced classes. On that memorable day, twelve young people assembled for instruction, and by the end of the first week of classes, the number had risen to seventeen and to twenty-five by the close of the second week.

The initial plans called for locating the Academy about midway between Orange City and Alton. This decision was undoubtedly made in order to save on the cost of land and to benefit equally the inhabitants of Orange City and any interested persons who lived to the east and northeast of town. It must be noted in this respect that Alton had a Reformed church since the late 1870's and the communities of Hospers and Newkirk, to the northeast, were soon to have churches of their own. The plans for locating the Academy changed with the acceptance of Henry Hosper's donation of a town block of sixteen lots in the southeast corner of Orange City as a site for the new school. This was one of many donations that this distinguished citizen made to the fledgling institution. These contributions together with his long service as treasurer of the Board of Trustees, merits for Hospers a place of recognition equal to that of Dominie Bolks as a founder of Northwestern Classical Academy.

The donation of a tract of land for a campus helped get Northwestern off to a good start, but it still lacked buildings. Consequently, until better facilities became available, classes were held in the consistory room of the First Reformed Church and in the local public school. Fortunately, the small, one-room schoolhouse had been replaced a few

Mr. Henry Hospers

years earlier by a two-story wooden building. In the meantime, steps were taken to canvass the community for funds which, with the money available from other sources, would enable the Board of Trustees to go ahead with plans for constructing a classroom building. The response was encouraging, and a two-story frame structure was erected. Known as the "Pioneer School," it was ready for occupancy in early 1884. The Reverend James Zwemer, principal of the Academy from 1890 to 1898, described the significance of this step a few years later on the occasion of the school's tenth anniversary:

This building, to whatever uses it may have been put, whether serving as an Academy of learning or as a miniature Castle Garden, has always stood, as it was built to stand, for a testimony to the importance of higher education; a protest against ignorance and materialism; indeed, as a huge ballot box, where the passer-by could cast his vote *yes* or *no* on the important question for these parts, whether we would be a people only for hogs and corn, or also for "dedication" and culture.

Because of lack of funds, only two classrooms were available for use at first. A third room was finished in time for the spring term that opened on April 14, 1884, and a fourth in time for the beginning of the 1884-1885 academic year. At first, students had to find their own lodging, but later a house was acquired where young men could obtain board and room. Called the "refectory," it was placed under the supervision of one of the instructors.

An examination of the "Schedule of Recitations" that was followed during the formative years of the Academy discloses a busy class schedule. All students were required to attend daily chapel exercises for fifteen minutes beginning at eight o'clock. Chapel consisted of the reading of Scripture, prayer, singing one or two hymns, and a brief sermon. The faculty took turns conducting the services, with occasional participation by the students. In addition, an attempt was made to bring in an outside speaker about once every two weeks. Chapel exercises were followed by five recitation periods of forty-five minutes each. Classes were completed by noon each day with the exception of drawing and music, which were taught in the afternoon or evening as elective, non-credit courses. Except for these special courses, afternoons were generally left free for study.

The steady increase in the Academy's enrollment, which had nearly doubled by 1886, soon called for better accommodations than could be provided by the Pioneer School. Accordingly, the Board of Trustees in that year purchased an abandoned skating rink in the downtown area

The Pioneer School

where the present town hall now stands. A large, two-story, plain-looking building measuring forty-five by ninety-five feet, it had been constructed in 1882 in response to the skating craze that was sweeping over the country at that time. The Board purchased it for $3,500 with the intention of converting it into classrooms and a dormitory for men. Initially, only the first floor underwent extensive remodeling, at a cost of $1,200, while the second floor, which had really served as the skating rink, was used as a chapel-auditorium. Increasing enrollment and an expanding curriculum soon placed a strain on classroom space once again, with the result that two classes sometimes had to share the same room simultaneously for their recitations. As a consequence, in 1889, when the enrollment had reached seventy-four, steps were taken to remodel and furnish part of the second floor, including a few sleeping rooms for male students.

The remodeled rink was officially called the "Academy Hall," but the students jokingly referred to it as the "Rink" and as "Noah's Ark." The Reverend Zwemer apparently considered the nicknames appropriate. In 1895, on the twenty-fifth anniversary of the founding of the Dutch colony in northwest Iowa, he remarked "if the cradle of the Academy was the Pioneer School, it was in the Rink that we learned to walk," adding that it

indeed became an ark of salvation. There we were kept; there we grew, and grew from strength to strength; there the students came as doves to their windows; from there systematic efforts to self-reliance began; from there, the blessed Providence led us to a permanent place of living, where we wish to remain with the youth entrusted to us.

The Rink served its purpose for eight years, until 1894, when, upon completion of a new classroom building on the campus, known as Zwemer Hall, the old Academy Hall was sold to the city and converted into a town hall.

The makeshift nature of the classrooms was related, of course, to the

Academy Hall

financial situation, which was always a problem during the Academy's long history and especially so during its formative years. In June 1883, at the meeting of General Synod in Albany, New York, the Reverend Buursma requested that the Board of Education contribute the sum of one thousand dollars for the salary of the principal, and, if possible, sufficient funds to provide for an additional instructor. Buursma also asked that Synod request the churches, especially those in the East, to make donations to the school when possible. In making a plea for financial support, Buursma described the rapid growth of the Dutch community in northwest Iowa and what this growth could mean for the future of the Reformed Church:

> Let me here remind Synod that Orange City, the center of a large and growing settlement in North-Western Iowa, is over six hundred miles west of Hope College, and from seventy-five to a hundred from any kind of institution of higher education. But we have in that settlement alone four growing churches, with the prospect of a fifth in the near future; that of Orange City alone has considerable over two hundred families, and between three and four hundred members in full communion, with many, very many young people. . . . Then in a number of other localities around that center, especially in Dakota, we have the very best prospects for growth of our Church. In some places churches have already been organized, and in others people are waiting for the appointed committees to do so.

Buursma also reminded Synod that the richness of the soil of northwest Iowa would in time make it one of America's wealthiest "garden spots." By properly fostering the Reformed churches there, the region could become "a strong support to our benevolent institutions." With specific reference to the Academy, Buursma pointed out that it could serve not only as a preparatory school for future ministers and as a "feeder" for Hope College, but could play an important role as a teacher-training institution. He noted that there were at the time in Sioux County more than twenty public schools, mostly small, one-room structures, serving children of Dutch background exclusively, but that many of the teachers of these schools were Roman Catholics because no others were available. "Truly," Buursma declared, "here is an opportunity for our Church such as seldom offers itself."

Northwestern's Board of Trustees in its annual reports to General Synod also made regular requests for funds. The amounts asked for varied from $2,000 to $3,000. General Synod, recognized the importance of the Academy, "standing . . . in the midst of a people loyal to our Church, and being the educational centre of a region now newly settled but destined soon to be a power in its religious, intellectual, and material developments." It therefore supported the requests but did so with qualifications, declaring that the amount given should be whatever the Board of Education considered necessary and consistent with other financial demands that had to be met and with the condition of the treasury. Thus, in June 1887, the Synod's committee on education reported:

To what extent [the Board of Education] should involve itself in indebtedness, and directly the Synod, is a matter of grave consideration. If expenses exceed receipts, why the Board should not curtail the reach of its appropriations, your Commettee fails to divine. . . . It is in the power of the Synod to limit the action of the Board, nor should it endorse any action on its part involving troublesome indebtedness.

General Synod also made it clear on several occasions that Northwestern would have to rely heavily on local patrons for financial support.

As a result of General Synod's instructions to the Board of Education to keep expenditures within the bounds of its receipts, the Academy during these early years never received the financial aid it requested. For example, although General Synod had decided in June 1887 to give Northwestern $200 a month if the financial situation permitted it, the *total* received over the next twelve months amounted to $300. Similar results occurred in other years: in 1888, it was $250, and in 1889 it was $310. The delicate financial situation of the Academy is seen in its report of June 1888 to General Synod. At that time, the school had an indebtedness of nearly $1,500, of which $1,200 was due in salaries. By 1890, the indebtedness had reached $2,500 and had increased to $2,900 by 1891 and to $4,000 by 1893.

A look at the Academy's financial statement issued in the spring of 1888, gives a clear indication of where the school's funds came from and how the money was spent.

RECEIPTS

Cash on hand, April 1887	$218.35
Fees	240.00
Rent	22.50
Subscriptions in Sioux County	566.00
Donations from Western Churches	186.45
Appropriations from Board of Education	100.00
Donations from friends in the East	237.38
Temporary Loan	446.31
	$2016.99

DISBURSMENTS

Interest	$245.35
Insurance	52.50
Travel expenses	48.50
Freight	10.00
Sundries	638.14
Salaries	1022.50
	$2016.99

It is interesting to note in the above report that no tuition was charged the students at this time, but there was an annual fee of ten dollars that each student had to pay "for the sake of meeting incidental expenses."

In 1884, the Reverend Lawrence Dykstra was appointed financial agent for Northwestern. Dykstra was pastor of the Reformed church at Newkirk, a position he continued to hold in conjunction with his new post. Soon after receiving this appointment, he addressed a lengthy plea to the readers of the *Christian Intelligencer*, the denominational paper, reminding them of the "grand future" that faced the Reformed Church in the West. Dykstra added, however, that its success would ultimately depend upon the educational facilities available there. "To delay is to suffer loss," he wrote. "We must not only keep what we have, but we must gain ground. Seventy-five cents a member from every communicant in this direction will give us what we absolutely need, and it will do more *ultimate* good than twice or three times that amount for many other Church purposes."

In 1886, General Synod, at the request of the Classis of Iowa, appointed a committee of four ministers to assist Dykstra in achieving Northwestern's newly announced goal of a $50,000 endowment fund. It is interesting to note that all four appointees were from the state of New York—no doubt because that region was considered a primary source of funds. Dykstra left his position as Northwestern's fiscal agent in 1886 when he accepted a call to the Dutch-language church at Albany, New York. Two years later, General Synod appointed the Reverend James Frederick Zwemer, pastor at Alton, as full time financial agent for *all* Reformed educational institutions "in the West." These included Hope College and Western Seminary as well as Northwestern. Along with the financial agents, the principals of the Academy also did their part in collecting funds during this early period, as can be judged from one of the early minutes of the Board of Trustees: "In view of the fact that the principal proposes to canvass the churches in the county in the interest of the Academy, he be allowed to enlarge the barn on the campus so that he can keep a horse."

The appointment of special financial agents together with better harvests in northwest Iowa improved the school's situation, although indebtedness continued to be a problem. Churches gradually increased their contributions so that by 1890, the school's own endowment sum had reached $12,000. Special gifts also began coming in. In 1890, for example, the Academy received $1,000 from the Women's Executive Committee of the Board of Domestic Missions. It was used to move the old Pioneer School to a more favorable location on the campus and to remodel it into a home for the principal, thereby saving $200 annually in rent. In 1891, Northwestern received its first major legacy in the amount of $3,000 from Peter Schoonmaker. In the meantime, Henry Hospers donated an additional town block to the school, thereby doubling the size of the campus.

An examination of the student body for the 1892-1893 academic year reveals some interesting facts about the school after a decade of operation. The total enrollment at that time was sixty-six students, who were distributed by classes as follows: preparatory, seventeen; junior, twenty; middle, sixteen; and senior, thirteen. (Not until the late 1920's were the customary terms freshman, sophomore, junior, and senior used. Until

The Class of 1890

that time, they were also frequently classified respectively as D, C, B, and A levels.) A comparison of the 1892-1893 enrollment with that of the immediately following years indicates there was not much student attrition at this time, that is, the majority of students who enrolled in the Academy preparatory class during the early period completed the four-year program and graduated. It is also interesting to note the geographical origins of the students in 1892. Of the sixty-six students, fifty-one came from Iowa. The remainder were distributed by states as follows: Nebraska, six; South Dakota five; Minnesota, three; and Illinois, one.

III

Finances and Expansion of the Physical Plant, 1894-1928

The primary sources of income during the period 1894 to 1928 remained as they had been previously, namely, student fees, annual appropriations from the denominational Board of Education, interest from the endowment fund, and contributions from churches and individuals. The amount brought in from these sources varied from year to year, making careful budget planning difficult. For example, the income from student fees (they were not referred to as tuition until after 1928) depended on enrollment and the amount being charged the students. When the Academy first opened its doors in 1882, the fees were $10 per year. They were raised to $4 per quarter, or $12 per year, in 1896; to $5 per quarter in 1898; and to $6 in 1901. With the introduction of the semester system in 1906, the fees became $9 per semester. Here they remained until 1920, when they were increased to $12.50.

Although the fees were low, the income derived therefrom was important to the school because the total budget remained small for many years. It is no wonder that the school authorities, pointing out the value of a Christian education to ministers and denominational boards and agencies, added that Northwestern could easily handle more students. Thus, in its report to General Synod in 1913, the Board of Trustees declared:

> What we need most of all is a deeper interest in Christian education, manifested by the sending of students. We have a plant here at which we could educate many more students than we at present have. Shall we not as pastors and consistories urge upon our people the need of young men for the Christian life?

Student enrollment throughout the period before 1928 showed only a modest increase. It generally remained in the seventies during the 1890's, and thereafter hovered in the eighties until after the First World War, reaching its highest figure during the 1922-1923 academic year, when 116 students enrolled. With a few exceptions, girls usually made up slightly more than one-third of the student body before 1928.

28

The increased enrollment after the war was due in part to a larger recruitment of students from Christian Reformed families. They comprised about 25 percent of the total student body during the 1920's, a figure that later was to increase to nearly 50 percent. The increase was also due to a larger enrollment of young people from the Orange City community itself, the annual average being about seventy students during the 1920's. This was nearly twice the number enrolled before 1914. The number of students from other Reformed communities in northwest Iowa, however, remained fairly constant, averaging slightly less than thirty per year. The number of out-of-state students also changed very little, the average being about twelve. Most of them continued to come from states adjoining Iowa, but occasionally a student came from as far west as Montana, Washington, and California.

Despite an overall rise in enrollment, the increase did not occur in a straight, upward line; there were occasional sudden and significant drops. For example, in 1898, the enrollment stood at eighty students, but it declined to sixty-two in the following year, after which it gradually rose again. But in 1908, it took another sudden drop, reaching a low of fifty-three. Significant declines also occurred on other occasions.

Several reasons can be cited for these fluctuations. In a few instances, the decline was caused by an unusual amount of illnesses, including scarlet fever, measles, and influenza. In 1918 and 1919, the school itself had to suspend classes for brief periods on orders from the Board of Health because of epidemics of one kind or another. Poor harvests from time to time also affected enrollments, which was one of the reasons for the decline from 111 students in 1925 to 92 in 1926. A "tightening up" of academic standards also occasionally contributed to a decline in enrollment. In explaining the sudden drop in the number of students in 1908, for example, the principal reported that ten students had failed to return to school that year because they were unable to do the work expected of them. Finally, enrollments varied with recruiting efforts, particularly when those efforts were the responsibility of the principal. He was sometimes so busy with other matters, especially if he were new on the job, that he had only a limited amount of time to solicit new students.

For about the first two decades of its history, the Academy experienced little competition from the public high schools in acquiring students. In 1899, for example, the Orange City high school graduated only eight students, a figure that did not change appreciably during the next several years. Indeed, in 1902, it stood at five, and in 1905 there were only four graduates. During these same years, the Academy averaged fourteen graduates. This situation did not last, however, and in

time the Academy found itself in serious contention with the public
high schools in soliciting new students. In 1908, the principal wrote:

> With regard to increasing the number of students in our Academy
> course, there are also here some obstacles with which we have to con-
> tend. This is the age of high-schools—there are not only many of them,
> but they are popular. To a considerable extent therefore they are our
> rivals. Many send their children to a highschool in preference to the
> academy, because it is less expensive, they can keep their children at
> home and at the same time fulfill their duty of loyalty to their local
> institution as they understand it.

Nor did this problem improve. Almost twenty years after the above
communication, another principal wrote: "In general, it may be said
that increasingly our Reformed Church families are sending their children to the local High Schools instead of sending them away from home
to the Academy." As has been mentioned, this loss was fortunately
balanced by an increase in enrollment of students from Christian Reformed families.

At the time the Academy was founded, it was anticipated that it would
receive significant financial help from the denominational Board of Education. The amounts appropriated by this body, however, were small
and irregularly paid for several years. Indeed, from 1895 to 1897, the
school received no financial aid from this source with the result that
salary payments to the faculty were $2,500 in arrears at the close of the
spring term in 1897. Disaster was averted only by special appeals to
local churches and private individuals. Fortunately, beginning about
1900, the appropriations from the Board of Education were paid on a
more regular basis—usually in the amount of $1,200 annually, with an
occasionally higher increment.

The endowment fund eventually became one of the school's chief
sources of funds. It consisted of money which had been paid in and was
reinvested, usually at five or six percent interest, and of promissory
notes which had not been paid in but which also bore interest. By 1895,
the endowment fund amounted to about $8,000, but for several years
thereafter it increased very slowly. It even declined for a brief period
in 1901 when the unusual step was taken of transferring $3,000 from it
to the contingency fund in order to decrease the school's indebtedness.
Thereafter, the endowment fund was left untouched for several years
until the remaining debt of $4,000 had been erased.

Not until 1907 were serious attempts again made to increase the
endowment fund, but the increase was slow at first. A report of 1910

gives the following information with respect to the sources of the fund and the dates of the contributions:

P. Schoonmaker legacy, 1891	$3000.00
Jessup Fund, 1892	2500.00
Quarles Van Ufort gift, 1900	500.00
A. Hesseling estate, 1901	1500.00
Dr. D'Bois Mulford gift	850.00
Van Osterloo building sold, 1902	315.00
H. Beltman gift, 1904	400.00
H. De Jong legacy, 1908	500.00
Various smaller gifts at different times	2335.00
Total	$11900.00

The endowment fund received a major boost of $1,500 in 1914 from the estate of the Reverend Peter Lepeltak, a former pastor at Alton and a distinguished member for several years of Northwestern's Board of Trustees. This brought the fund to $13,800. It rose rapidly during the following years, reaching the remarkable sum of $50,772.45 by 1920. In that year, the Board reported that the interest from the endowment fund "proves to be our silver mine. It is the largest separate source of money."

The Board obviously did not mean that the interest from the endowment fund was consistently the school's "largest separate source of money." In point of fact, with the exception of a few years, contributions from the churches regularly superseded all other sources of income. In 1925, for example, these contributions topped the list of receipts with a total of $3,355.18, followed by interest from the endowment fund of $2,383.27, tuition of $2,075.50, and appropriations from the denominational Board of Education of $1,418.52. An examination of the budgets of other years indicates a generally similar ratio among the various sources of revenue.

For many years, the raising of funds was included among the duties of the principal. In 1898, however, it was decided that this responsibility should be taken over by someone else in order that the principal could "give his undivided attention to the work of instruction and management." To make this possible, a new position was created—that of Educational and Financial Agent. The Reverend Henry Straks, pastor of the Reformed church at near-by Maurice, was appointed to fill the office. As was true of other positions at Northwestern, his duties were comprehensive: "to solicit funds, interest people in the cause of education, secure students, and aid in the work of teaching, as far as . . . time would permit."

When Reverend Straks left Northwestern in 1901 to accept the Reformed pastorate at Harrison, South Dakota, a new procedure was adopted for securing financial support from churches in the western classes. It was organized under the supervision of the Reverend Anthony Van Duine of Newkirk with the assistance of the Finance Committee of the Board of Trustees. By this arrangement, which became known as the "Syndicate System," each church was assessed a certain amount for the support of the Academy, with responsibility for implementation resting with the respective consistories. The success and advantages of this arrangement can be seen in the following report issued in 1909:

The attention of the Synod is particularly called to the pleasing success which has attended our syndicate system in raising funds annually for this institution among the churches of the Iowa and Dakota Classes, the bulk thereof being contributed by the churches of Sioux County, a few churches of the Pella Classis also making annual contributions. This system has now been in vogue for eight years. During these years almost $19,000 has been contributed for the maintenance of the institution in this way. To secure this, not a dollar has been spent for any financial agency, the syndicates in the various churches being maintained by the several Consistories. Not only do we thus get an annual income of $2,500, but the interests of the school are constantly kept before the people, who thus in a material way learn to take a deep interest in its welfare.

Despite the satisfaction with the Syndicate System as expressed in the above and similar reports, it was by no means a perfect arrangement. Although some churches were quite generous in making contributions, others, especially the smaller ones and those located some distance from the Academy, contributed little or nothing. Moreover, the larger churches and those located near Orange City were not always consistent in the amount of their contributions. For example, in some years the churches of northwest Iowa considered it more important to give financial aid to drought-stricken congregations in the Dakotas than to the Academy. It also happened occasionally that benevolent money intended for the Academy was in the end diverted to meet some special needs of foreign missions. Irregularities such as these obviously made careful budget planning difficult.

The school's contingency budget did not change appreciably before about 1915, with disbursements generally ranging from five to six thousand dollars. In 1913, for example, the principal reported that the necessary expense for maintaining the school generally amounted to slightly more than $5,000 a year. But there were occasional exceptions because of unusual expenses—such as city assessments for paving a street along a part of the campus or the need to make major repairs on the principals' residence. The disbursements shown below for the fiscal year April 30, 1914 to April 30, 1915 were typical of the period before 1915.

Teacher salaries	$3585.00
Janitor's salary	342.00
Furniture and equipment	494.71
Repairs and labor	409.38
Supplies	381.42
Insurance	202.52
Fuel	192.65
Diplomas	90.00
Printing	49.00
Library and reading room	15.85
Repaid loan to endowment fund	175.00
From contingent to endowment fund	25.00
Error somewhere	.10
Balance, April 5, 1915	82.99
Total	$6045.62

After 1915 disbursements increased in a generally steady manner to $10,401.29 in 1925. The increase took place in nearly all areas of operation but particularly in teacher salaries, which rose from $3,585 to $8,344.

The delicate financial situation that faced the Academy from time to time never seriously dampened the optimism of those responsible for the school's operations. It was this belief in Northwestern's future that prompted a movement during the early 1890's to construct a classroom building on the campus to replace the old "Rink" downtown. These efforts were spearheaded by the Reverend Zwemer, the Academy's principal, who in the fall of 1892, two years after he took office, presented plans to this effect to the Board of Trustees. Despite the rather poor state of the school's finances, the Board was impressed with Zwemer's ideas and appointed a committee consisting of Zwemer and Henry Hospers, the Board treasurer, to canvass the community for funds. The results were heartening: by May 1893, more than $10,000 had been subscribed. The financial depression of 1893 caused a slight delay in the plans, but at a special meeting on February 7, 1894, the decision was made to go ahead with plans and advertise for bids. This historic meeting took place in the home of the Reverend Bolks. As recently stated by a former Northwestern professor who has spent considerable time researching the life of the saintly Bolks, "The heart of this old gentleman must have rejoiced to see the steps being taken toward the realization of his hopes and prayers." He was eighty years old at this time and in failing health. Seventeen firms submitted bids ranging as high $21,900. The contract was awarded to the Northern Building Company of Sioux City for the low bid of $12,950. This cost, together with expenses for the heating system and furnishings as well as the architect's fee, brought the total cost to about $16,000, more than half of which was raised locally.

In order to locate the new building in the center of the campus and have it facing directly toward main street, the town council agreed to vacate a street that had formerly divided the campus. The cornerstone for the building, appropriately named Zwemer Hall, was laid on June 21, 1894. The outward appearance of the building has undergone very little change during its nearly ninety-year history. It measures sixty-eight by seventy-two feet and consists of two main floors, an attic, and a basement that extends under the entire building.

In 1975, Zwemer Hall was placed on the National Register of Historic Places. In recognition of this event, Professor Nelson Nieuwenhuis, who taught history at Northwestern for more than a quarter century, wrote the following description of this picturesque building:

Although eight decades have passed, Zwemer Hall today is still beautiful to behold. There is not only strength and beauty, but also balance and proportion in its arrangement of parts. Viewing it from the north, one's attention is drawn to the great Roman arch placed above the steps to the main entrance. An exterior balcony is found just above the arch. Each side of the structure displays a unique character all its own, with a variety of intricate window arrangements and designs. Three sides have strong flat buttresses which are imperceptibly joined with the large gables on the roof. Where wall meets roof, classic cornices add to the delicateness of the ornamentation.

The northwest portion of the building offers a surprise to the viewer. The walls unite to form a large circular extension which gives the appearance of a medieval tower with its circular wall and roof.

Zwemer Hall's graceful tower is hexagonal in design, topped by a hexagonal roof, and rises from the ground level to a height of some 80 feet. The tower is joined subtly with the front entrance archway and part of the north wall, lending beauty to the front and also serving as a buttress. It contains five tiers of windows with varied window patterns for each tier, the upper rank of six windows is open and topped with Roman arches.

The exterior materials consist of quarried rock from Mankato, Minnesota and pressed brick, with cream stone trimming.

The basement was left unfinished at first, except for the furnace room. As originally constructed, the ground floor contained a reading room, a library, and four rather large recitation rooms. The second floor provided for a chapel measuring about forty-four feet square, having a seating capacity of 200, two recitation rooms, an office for the principal, and an "apparatus room." The recitation rooms could be opened up on the chapel to accomodate overflowing audiences. The main floors were decorated with rounded arches, open stairways, beautifully finished wainscoting, and hard maple flooring. There was room for expansion in the attic, and initially it was planned to transform it into a gymnasium. However, it never was finished off completely but served as a storeroom and as a logical setting for freshman initiation activities at the beginning of the fall terms.

The new building was solemnly dedicated on the afternoon of November 27, 1894. The ceremonies began appropriately with a processional by the students (some sixty in number), the four faculty members, and other participants who marched from the downtown Academy Hall to the First Reformed Church. Here the first of the dedicatory exercises (this one in Dutch) took place. The general tone of the speeches was set by the principal, the Reverend Zwemer, in his welcoming remarks: "We are met to dedicate this new building to God for the noble cause of educating our sons and daughters so that they may be equipped to rightly serve the church, the school, and society."

Ministers from throughout the area participated in the exercises, but the honor of delivering the dedicatory sermon fell to the Reverend Peter Lepeltak, pastor of the Reformed congregation at Alton. His remarks stressed the important role that the Academy could play in the development of the community and especially in furthering the causes of God's kingdom. Thanks were expressed to all who had helped make the school a reality, and the accomplishments of the school's graduates were cited as evidence that sacrifices made in behalf of the Academy thus far were bearing fruit. Nevertheless, declared Lepeltak, "lasting and frequent contributions" from churches and individual donors would have to continue because much remained to be done:

There must be an increase in the courses of instruction and in the number of instructors. Our institution must be kept in step with the times in which God permits us to serve. There must therefore be instruction in both the professions and in those social questions which come with each age. . . . We must also have a chemical laboratory that is adequately furnished, as well as instruments for the study of astronomy. And there must be liberal provision made for the acquisition of the latest books for the library. Financial aids must be made available for students who wish to become ministers or teachers but do not have sufficient funds to meet their educational needs.

The services at the First Reformed Church were concluded with the benediction delivered by the Reverend E. Breen, of the Christian Reformed Church. Following this, most of the audience proceeded to the new Zwemer Hall where a few hundred people were already assembled to hear the dedicatory address, this one in English, delivered by the Reverend Dr. John Walter Beardslee of Western Theological Seminary. As described in one of the local papers, the essence of his remarks was as follows:

Perfect education must be three-fold. To be a perfect man, in the first place, our bodies must be cared for. Of greater importance, however, is the cultivation of the mind. Man is an intellectual being, and to use the intellect, he must educate it. But, in the third place, the spiritual and moral nature of man must be educated, for this is the most important. This idea is the foundation of this building. For putting special emphasis on our duties and responsibilities to God and man, institutions like this are founded.

Upon completion of Zwemer Hall, the old Academy Hall was sold to the city for a nominal sum. The city thereupon converted part of the lower floor into a meeting room for the town council and into living quarters for the town marshall and a jail. The upper floor was retained primarily as a meeting place for large gatherings.

The construction of Zwemer Hall was a great boon to the future of the Academy. Not only did its majestic appearance give a sense of pride to the students, but, more importantly, it provided much needed classroom space. Its being located on the school campus rather than downtown also had the desired psychological effect of giving the institution a greater sense of unity and permanence. It also made it easier to devise plans for adding to the school's physical plant in the future. In short, it marked the beginning of a new era in the school's history. Impressed by what Northwestern had accomplished in its first twelve years of operation, General Synod declared in 1894 that the school's latest annual report "deserves to be circulated through every church as an object lesson of the result of faith, courage, and wisdom directed to a noble end."

The construction of Zwemer Hall had hardly been completed when plans were made for additional building programs. High on the priority list were housing and eating facilities for the students, but increasing enrollment and especially the expanding curriculum soon called for more classrooms as well. In 1901, the so-called "refectory" that had been rented downtown as a rooming house for students was purchased and moved to the southeast corner of the campus. Called the Halycon Clubhouse, it was remodeled at a cost of $1,200 to provide rooms for boys at the nominal charge of 70¢ per week. Meals could be obtained on a cooperative basis at cost. Unmarried male teachers also sometimes roomed there. At about this same time, a small dining room was established in the basement of Zwemer Hall for the convenience of other students.

These developments were only stopgap measures; they left unsolved the problem of providing living quarters for girls and supplying more classroom space. As a consequence, in the fall of 1909, the Board of Trustees asked the principal to give as much time as possible to soliciting funds for a dormitory and dining hall. The estimated cost of the proposed building was $20,000. By the spring of 1910, only about $2,000 had been pledged by the residents of Orange City, and the response among neighboring communities was even more unfavorable. The project was therefore dropped.

In view of the increasing interest being shown in athletics, it is not surprising that consideration was also given to the construction of a gymnasium. The town hall auditorium that the school had been using for athletic events left several things to be desired. In addition to the fee that had to be paid for its use, its location several blocks from the Academy campus caused numerous inconveniences. Moreover, it was not always available when needed because of scheduling conflicts with community affairs and with the local high school, which also used it for athletic events.

In 1917, the Classis of Iowa, on the recommendation of the principal and the Board of Trustees, gave tentative approval to the construction of a combination gymnasium and dormitory. During the next two years, various committees and Board members discussed building plans and looked into possible sources of money. In April 1920, the Reverend John De Jongh, pastor of the Reformed church at Edgerton, Minnesota, who had been serving as financial agent for the project, reported that subscriptions had reached $33,307.44, of which $8,827.71 had been actually collected. Unfortunately, when the estimated costs for a gymnasium-dormitory complex were presented a short time later, the figure of $100,000 was considerably higher than had been anticipated. It was therefore agreed to reconsider the plans again at the fall meeting of the Board. When that time arrived, it was decided to hold them in further abeyance.

Building plans were not brought up again until the spring meeting of the Board in 1923, but in a very different form. Although in its report to General Synod in 1921, the school authorities had stated that the greatest need facing the school was "suitable boarding and rooming facilities," it was decided to drop the idea of building a dormitory at this time because of the more pressing need to provide classroom space and a gymnasium. The new plans called for constructing a two-story building, to be located a short distance east of Zwemer Hall, that would have a variety of rooms on the ground floor and a combination auditorium and gymnasium on the second floor. Included on the first floor would be classrooms, a music room, a laboratory, society rooms, and athletic locker rooms. Once again, a committee was appointed to make the final plans. It recommended a building of sixty by ninety feet, with the lower floor partially below ground level to save on costs. As another economy move, it was decided not to give the contract exclusively to one firm but to draw up several contracts and let them out on an individual basis according to the various types of construction work required. The oversight of the entire project was placed in the hands of a local carpenter, Jake Ypma, and a committee of Board members.

The building was completed in time for the opening of the fall term in 1924, and was given the rather plain and unadorned name of Science Hall. Its total cost was $56,241.11, of which nearly $30,000 was still due at the time it was completed. In 1925, the debt was listed as $27,000, on which 6% interest was being paid. In the 1925-1926 school year, a plan was presented to the western churches to wipe out this debt, but in 1927, it still stood at $25,700.

Despite its unpretentious name, the new building quickly served several useful functions. This was well illustrated in the principal's report to the Board in the spring of 1925:

The Science Hall has meant more to us even than we thought it would. We wonder how we ever got along without it. It has been in use every day during the school hours and after school hours most of the time until nine in the evening. The two classrooms and the Laboratory are in use every day. The [literary] society rooms are used every week. And the auditorium is also used every day. Now the students have made a tennis court in it and are using it for that purpose. It is conveniently arranged, heats easily and is changed from a gymnasium into an auditorium and visa versa in about forty-five minutes by the students. The executive [committee] made arrangements for . . . pianos for the society rooms last fall and these provisions have been well appreciated. The hall has been rented for basketball and other things a few times and is always well liked.

IV

The Faculty and Curriculum

Buildings such as Zwemer Hall and Science Hall are, of course, only a part of an educational institution. Of greater consequence are the faculty and the curriculum. As noted, the initial teaching staff was made up entirely of part-time instructors, namely, Jacob Van Zanten, principal of the local elementary school, and the Reverends Ale Buursma and John Warnshuis, pastors at Orange City and Alton respectively. Beginning with the fall term of 1883, Van Zanten gave up his position at the public school in order to devote himself entirely to his duties at the Academy, which included those of acting principal until a regular principal could be found. Meanwhile, the Reverends Buursma and Warnshuis continued to assist Van Zanten until 1884. In filling the position of principal, the Board of Trustees hoped to cut down on salary expenses by employing an ordained minister who could combine his work at the Academy with that of field missionary for the Reformed denomination.

The principalship was first offered to the Reverend Abraham Thompson, a graduate of Rutgers College and New Brunswick Seminary, who at the time was serving as pastor of Knox Memorial Chapel in New York City. Although at first glance it appears surprising that this position was offered to a man whose academic training had taken place in the East and who was living under conditions very different from those found in a predominantly rural area, the choice was understandable. In addition to excellent academic qualifications and some administrative experience as rector at Rutgers College Grammar School for two years from 1874-1876, Thompson was well acquainted with conditions in the Middle West. He had served churches at Pekin, Illinois and at Pella, Iowa at various times between 1862 and 1874, and had become accomplished in handling the Dutch language. It was unfortunate, considering all these qualifications, that Thompson declined the invitation.

The position of principal was next offered to the Reverend John A. De Spelder, pastor of the Reformed churches at Macon and South Macon, Michigan. Born in Michigan in 1851 of Dutch immigrant parents, De Spelder graduated from Hope College in 1870 and from Western Seminary in 1873. Macon and South Macon were his first pastorates. De Spelder accepted the position at Orange City but he had some misgivings about it. In particular, he was fearful that his work as field missionary and part-time preacher might interfere with his responsibilities as Academy principal and instructor. He therefore emphasized that his work would be primarily educational, while his other activities would be kept to a minimum. With De Spelder's arrival on January 15, 1884, the part-time services of Buursma and Warnshuis were no longer required. In the fall of 1885, the full-time staff was increased to three by employing the Reverend William Jones Skillman, but he remained only a few months before accepting a pastorate at Sioux Falls, South Dakota. A local man, Isaac Betten, was then employed to finish out his term, and in 1886, a local physician, Dr. Henry P. Oggel, was added to the staff.

In June 1887, De Spelder resigned as principal, having accepted a call to the pastorate of the local American Reformed Church, which he had been serving as supply minister during the previous two years. Van Zanten also resigned his position in 1887, having decided to enroll at Western Seminary to study for the ministry. Fortunately, until a replacement would be found, De Spelder agreed to serve as acting principal and to teach courses in rhetoric, astronomy, and religion. To replace the others who had left, two women were employed—Emma Kollen and Nellie Zwemer. Both had attended Hope College, although only the former apparently completed work for a degree. Miss Kollen was engaged to teach classical languages and history, while Miss Zwemer's appointment called for instruction in English grammar, mathematics, and bookkeeping. Oggel continued on a part-time basis to give instruction in physiology and modern languages.

De Spelder served as acting principal for only one year, being replaced by the Reverend Buursma of the local First Reformed Church for the 1888-1889 school year. Buursma accepted the appointment with the understanding that he would devote only portions of three days a week to his work at the Academy and would teach only courses in religion. This limited load was considered necessary because of the large congregation he had to serve.

Because of the increasing enrollment and expanding curriculum, the teaching staff obviously had to be enlarged, but lack of funds prevented this. As a consequence, as reported by the Board of Trustees, the existing staff had to give "much extra time to branches outside their regular departments, doing not only what they could, but often more than they ought." Oggel added a course in rhetoric to his responsibilities as well as a new course in chemistry, while Kollen took responsibility for the course in astronomy and a new course in physics. Oggel also assumed responsibility for supervising the refectory. Unfortunately, this kind of rearrangement of instructional responsibilities and increase in teaching loads were to be repeated often during the Academy's history.

The heavy teaching loads and the financial difficulties faced by Northwestern during its early history caused a rapid turnover in the teaching staff. By the close of the 1893-1894 academic year, the school had employed sixteen different faculty members. Although their average stay was about two and one-half years, several left after only one year of service. The instructional and administrative staff during the first dozen years of the school's operation and the dates of their employment were as follows:

Jacob J. Zanten	1883-1887
John William Warnshuis	1883-1884
Ale Buursma	1883-1884, 1888-1889
John A. De Spelder	1884-1890
William J. Skillman	1885-1885
Issac Betten	1885-1886
Henry P. Oggel	1886-1891
Nellie Zwemer	1887-1890
Emma Kollen	1887-1891
James Frederick Zwemer	1890-1898
John B. Nykerk	1890-1891
Herbert G. Keppel	1891-1892
John M. Van der Meulen	1891-1893
E. Christian Oggel	1891-1894
Fannie A. Steffens	1892-1894
Anthony Te Paske	1893-1894

Of these staff members, the Reverend James Frederick Zwemer became one of Northwestern's most capable and best loved principals. Born of immigrant parents in Rochester, New York in 1850, Zwemer graduated from Hope College in 1870 and from Western Seminary in 1873. After serving churches in Michigan and Wisconsin, he served briefly as pastor at Alton, Iowa, from 1886 to 1888 before being appointed financial agent responsible for raising funds for Reformed educational institutions in the Middle West. In 1889, he agreed to become principal at Northwestern as soon as he could be relieved of his responsibilities as financial agent. He began his new duties as Academy principal and instructor in 1890 and served until 1898, when he accepted a call to the Seventh Reformed Church in Grand Rapids, Michigan. After a two year pastorate there, he acted as an agent for Western Seminary until 1907, when he was appointed Professor of Practical Theology at Western Seminary.

Zwemer was one of several ministers who served on Northwestern's

The Reverend James Zwemer

staff during this period and who later had distinguished careers elsewhere. Others included Nicholas Steffens who became the author of
numerous publications and also finished his career as a professor at
Western Seminary, and Thomas Welmers who served on the staff at
Hope College for twenty-five years after leaving Northwestern in 1920.
But it was the Reverend Abraham Muste who perhaps achieved the
most lasting fame. After graduating from Hope College in 1905, Muste
taught briefly at Northwestern before enrolling at New Brunswick Theological Seminary. Later, after serving churches in the East, he became
one of this country's leading pacifists, a role that won for him the title
"America's Gandhi."

During the early history of the Academy, men predominated nu-
merically among the faculty, but beginning about 1910 women usually
outnumbered the men. The teachers were all members in good standing
with the Reformed Church and, with few exceptions, were college graduates. As might be expected, most of them received their degrees from
Hope College, but graduates of other institutions were sometimes represented. Only on rare occasions was a teacher dismissed for incom-
petence. Among the principals, all but three of the eleven who served
during this time were clergymen. Of the latter, five received their theological training at Western Seminary, two at New Brunswick, and one
at Princeton. The persons who held the office of principal before 1928
were as follows:

Jacob Van Zanten (acting principal)	1883-1884
John De Spelder	1884-1888
Ale Buursma (acting principal)	1888-1889
James Zwemer	1890-1898
Matthew Kolyn	1898-1901
Philip Soulen	1901-1906
John Heemstra	1906-1910
Thomas Welmers	1910-1920
Arthur Visser (acting principal)	1920-1921
Gerrit Timmer	1921-1925
John Dykstra	1925-1928

The early practice of using part-time faculty continued. This had the double advantage of keeping costs down and of not having to employ a full-time instructor for courses that had only limited student appeal. Subjects such as music and art lent themselves especially to this approach. The same was true of courses in the Bible and the Heidelberg Catechism, which were frequently taught by a clergyman from the area—usually the pastor of the First Reformed Church of Orange City. Beginning in 1911, a local medical doctor, John De Bey, began offering on Tuesday evenings a special course in biology. He did this gratis for several years and always attracted a sizeable number of students.

Faculty meetings were held on a regular basis, either biweekly or triweekly. An examination of the minutes of these meetings reveals that most of the discussions concerned grades given to students who were doing poorly in their classwork. Other matters that arose for discussion included disciplinary problems, extracurricular activities, the awarding of honors at graduation time, and committee assignments among the faculty. Occasionally there is a hint in the minutes that the faculty discussed the effectiveness of various teaching methods, but no indication is given as to the substance of those discussions.

The matter of faculty turnover that plagued the Academy during the early period continued to be a problem, and on a few occasions, almost complete changes occurred. For example, at the beginning of the 1903-1904 academic year, only the principal, Philip Soulen, was retained among the faculty, the other three instructors being new. Although there was no turnover during the following year, two teachers left in the year after that, and a year later the principal and two teachers departed. The problems that arose from this can be clearly seen in the following report of 1921 from the acting principal, Arthur Visser:

When the school year began in September an unprecedented state of affairs existed. No Principal, and four new teachers, all of them unacquainted with the school and its traditions, and most of them inexperienced teachers. I was the only teacher that remained of last year's Faculty. In addition to that a much larger number of students came than the year before, making it necessary to add four regular classes. To say the least, the outlook was dark and the task seemed unsurmountable.

The frequent turnover was due to several reasons but low salaries was a primary cause. In its annual report of 1907 to General Synod, the Board of Trustees declared that "in the hope of making more permanent the personnel of the Faculty, [it had] increased the monthly salaries of the teachers and opened up for them a large field by expanding the course here." The salary increases were ineffective in retaining faculty members. The 1908-1909 school year opened with three of the five full-time teachers being new, and the same situation was repeated when the 1910-1911 term began. Similarly, two teachers left in 1916, as did two others in 1917.

The failure of the Academy always to meet its salary commitments on time because of lack of funds no doubt further contributed to faculty turnover. In 1914, arrears of this kind totaled slightly more than one thousand dollars. Competition from public schools also presented a special difficulty, as shown in this report of 1920 from the Board of Trustees: "Since public schools pay much higher wages than we can afford, there is danger that we may lose some of our teachers. Some have offers which involve a sacrifice to remain with us." Faculty members also occasionally left to pursue theological studies or, if already ordained, to return to full-time preaching.

The staff complained from time to time about its heavy teaching loads, and the failure to obtain relief no doubt added to the retention difficulty. An excerpt from the principal's report to the Board of Trustees in the spring of 1925 illustrates what the teaching loads meant in terms of actual class hours and also indicates that the teachers had many other duties besides those associated with the classroom.

Miss Wyngarden has five classes a day and one assembly period to take care of supervised study. Miss De Jonge has seven classes every day, two of which are laboratory, except on Fridays, when she has five classes. She has no supervised study. Miss Sikkink has five classes a day and one hour of supervised study. Miss Van Emmerik has four classes a day and two hours supervised study. Prof. Roos has six classes a day and one hour supervised study. I [that is, the principal, Mr. Timmer] have four classes a day and two hours of supervised study. Of the work outside of class Miss Wyngarden has taken care of the affairs of the *Monitor* [the student newspaper] and assisted in girls' athletics. Miss Sikkink has taken the Y. W. and one of the literary societies.

PROGRAM OF DAILY RECITATIONS, 1910–1911

Hours A. M.	Welmers	Pietenpol	Renkes	De Jong	M. ssBrusse
			FIRST SEMESTER		
8:15 to 9:00	Greek A5	Alg. C5	Eng. B5	Eloc. D1 / Econ. A4	Ger. A5
9:00 to 9:45	Greek B5	Phys. A5	Eng. C5	Hist. D5	Ger. B5
9:45 to 10:30	Bible A1 / Bible B1 / Bible C1 / Bible D1	Lab. A4	Eng. D4	Eng. Hist. C4	Physiology A4
10:30 to 11:15	Latin D5	Geom. B5	Psych. B5	Latin A5	School Management A5
11:15 to 12:00	Latin B5	Alg. D5	Eng. A5	Latin C5	Rev. A5

SECOND SEMESTER

Hours A. M.	Welmers	Pietenpol	Renkes	De Jong	M. ssBrusse
8:15 to 9:00	Greek B5	Geom. C5	Eng. A5	Hist. D5	Ger. B5
9:00 to 9:45	Greek A5	Alg. D5	Eng. B5	Hist. C1 / Civics C4	Ger. A5
9:45 to 10:30	Bible A1 / Latin D4	Arith. A4	Latin C5	Latin B5	Eloc. D1
10:30 to 11:15	Bible B1 / Bible D1 / Latin D1	Phys. A5	Dutch B4	Hist. C4	Music D1 / Ped. B4
11:15 to 12:00	Bible C1	Geom. B5	Eng. D5	Latin A5	Rev. A5
P. M.		Lab. A			

Program of Daily Recitations, 1910-1911

Miss De Jonge has assisted Miss Sikkink in Y. W. and has taken care of the other literary society. Miss Van Emmerik has taken girls' athletics and the library. Prof. Roos has taken the boys' athletics. I have taken the Y. M. and now have the boys' baseball.

Because there is no mention of the boys' and girls' glee clubs and the orchestra, a part-time person was apparently employed at this time to take care of those activities. In some years, however, these too became part of the responsibilities of the regular faculty. From time to time, the faculty was also asked to take turns in supervising the dining room in Zwemer Hall during noon hours. Fortunately, teachers could take some comfort from the knowledge that school administrators were also heavily overworked at this time. For example, Thomas Welmers, in his two years as teacher and ten years as principal from 1908 to 1920 taught, as the occasion demanded, courses in Bible, Catechism, Greek, Latin, Dutch, music, psychology, and pedagogy. One can only wonder what else he might have taught if he had been a full-time instructor all twelve years!

With respect to curriculum it was noted that several students were admitted with advanced standing during the school's first year of formal operations. As a consequence, a rather extensive set of courses had to be offered from the very beginning. This is clearly seen in a report submitted by the principal to one of the local papers at the close of the winter term of 1884: "There have been classes in bookkeeping, geography, rhetoric, composition, elocution, arithmetic, algebra, physiology, astronomy, Dutch, English, Latin, and Greek." The report listed the following additional "items of progress:"

An assistant teacher has been appointed; a new lecture-room will be ready for occupancy at the beginning of the next term, April 14th; the number of students has been increased; a principal's desk and a sufficient number of study desks for two rooms have been procured from Andrews & Co., Chicago; the nucleus of a library has been obtained; purchase has been made of a few maps and charts as well as of some apparatus.

In addition to the courses listed in this report, several others were soon added to the curriculum. These included botany, chemistry, physics, penmanship and spelling, philosophy, and German. Many of the course offerings covered three or four years of study.

Minor curriculum changes during this period included the substitution of French for German. This action occurred during the war and was done in response to the anti-German feeling of that time. It was thus in conformity with what other schools were doing and with the official position taken by the governor of Iowa. Although the Academy faculty believed that a knowledge of German was more important than French for students going into theology or science, French continued to be offered in place of German throughout the 1920's.

Another language change that occurred during this period was the disappearance of Dutch from the course offerings. This, however, came about gradually. An excerpt from the 1901-1902 Academy catalogue describing the course in Dutch clearly illustrates the significance that was attached to the language at that time:

The study of the Dutch language is one of the characteristic features of this institution. Considering the fact that most of our students come from Dutch homes, and furthermore, that this language will for a long time be used in the churches which this institution is especially designed to serve, it is altogether fitting that we should give a place in our full curriculum to the study of our mother tongue. . . . The special aim of this work is to give the student a working knowledge of Dutch speech and to create a love for and interest in the language and literature of the Dutch people.

Despite these remarks, which were repeated almost verbatim in the catalogues during the next decade, Dutch was taught only once a week during the early 1900's for each class level. By 1907, it was being taught only one term per year, usually at the sophomore level, and students could even be excused from it if they obtained parental consent. In 1913, the principal wrote: "To give instruction in Dutch is not easy. We can hardly find good textbooks in this country, and most students are indifferent to it. Even many of the parents care not whether their children receive instruction in Dutch or not." No record had been found stating when Dutch was finally dropped from the curriculum, but it apparently occurred soon after 1913. Its fate was in contrast to Latin which continued to be offered daily all four years, and Greek which was taught daily for juniors and seniors. Despite the gradual disappearance of the Dutch language from the course offerings, it is interesting to note that instructors of English composition continued to complain from time to time about the alarming number of Dutch idioms that persistently cropped up in student essays.

Courses in science increased slowly during the early 1900's and were given only as needed. In 1901, no science courses were available for freshmen, but sophomores took a quarter term course in physiology. This was replaced by astronomy for the junior's and physics for the seniors. Despite the limited offerings in science, attention was given at an early date to procuring laboratory equipment, as is evidenced by the following report of 1903:

The scientific work of the school has, by special effort, received an encouraging impetus during the year. A new, modern pneumatic pump, four compound, Columbian microscopes, various models of improved electrical apparatus, and a wireless telegraphy machine were purchased. This was supplemented by the generous gift of a new four-plate, static electrical machine with complete therapeutical and X-ray outfit, valued at $225.00.

Three years later, eighteen individual disecting microscopes were added to the equipment of the department of biology. In time, a course in chemistry was introduced but it was not offered on a regular basis.

Physics during this period remained the most popular science course, and at times was the only science course offered. The science laboratories were at first located in the basement of Zwemer Hall, but chemistry was later moved up one floor.

Students who graduated from the Academy during the early years of the school's operation, received a diploma in what was called "Classical Studies." It was designed primarily for students who were preparing for the ministry. Because not all students intended to enter the ministry, a second program, known as "Modern Classical" was soon introduced. It permitted a few substitutions, including German (later French) for advanced Latin and Greek, and advanced arithmetic for solid geometry. Other modifications were also made in the Modern Classical program from time to time.

In 1894, Principal Zwemer wrote in one of the local papers, "Among the new departures we mention: The addition to our curriculum of practical studies in normal work for the preparation of teachers." Actually, this was not really a "new departure," since courses in education were being offered as early as 1888; rather, what occurred in 1894 was an elaboration of an on-going program. The teacher training courses offered at the Academy included pedagogy, school management, psychology, and "reviews." The latter consisted of a survey of various courses taught at the elementary level, including grammar, spelling, arithmetic, and geography. These were substituted during the junior and senior years for such courses as Dutch and Greek so as to enable a student to complete his or her work in the customary four years. Teacher training eventually became an important means for attracting students and at the same time proved beneficial to the cause of primary education in the region.

Although it appears strange today that a student could take a teacher training program at the secondary level, it must be kept in mind that the standards for teacher certification were low during the early history of the Academy. For many years, the minimum age for a teacher was eighteen, and even this was sometimes falsified. Moreover, although a prospective teacher had to pass a state examination, this was not always observed. Later regulations stated that a candidate having only a secondary school education had to attend a summer course on normal training, but as late as 1916, third-class certificates were sometimes given simply on the basis of having passed the state exams.

Courses in education were offered at the Academy as early as 1888, but it was not until 1908 that the decision was made to award diplomas in that field. This meant that henceforth the Academy offered specific degrees in three subject areas: the Classical, the Modern Classical, and the Normal.

A few years after the formal introduction of the Normal Course, the school authorities faced the question of whether to continue the program. In 1913, the Iowa state legislature passed a law making it mandatory after July 1, 1915 that applicants for teaching certificates have courses in home economics and agriculture. The school thus faced a dilemma. To comply with the state requirement would mean new expenses for adding a teacher and for remodeling classrooms to accomodate these courses; not to do so would mean the loss of students and the opportunity to train teachers. In an attempt to raise the necessary funds, the Board of Trustees, on the recommendation of the Classis of Iowa, sent letters in English and Dutch to all churches among the classes of Iowa, Dakota, Pella, and Cascades asking for special donations. Convinced that the money would be forthcoming, the decision was made to go ahead and offer the courses beginning in the fall of 1915. Unfortunately, a new problem soon arose: to obtain certification, the courses had to have enrollments of ten students and this proved difficult for several years. The Normal program, however, continued to be offered and Academy graduates received either temporary teaching certificates or enrolled in a summer extension course offered by Iowa State Teachers College. By 1925, a little more than a third of the juniors and seniors were enrolled in the Normal Course. About another third were taking the Classical Course, while slightly less than a third were following the Modern Classical program.

All students, no matter what program they were enrolled in, had to take the same subjects during their freshman and sophomore years. Choices were not allowed until the junior year, and even these substitutions were carefully circumscribed. As reported in 1911:

During the "D" and "C" years, the programs are alike. This gives the student an opportunity to give evidence of his ability to find himself; and the teacher time to study the student, so as to advise impartially what course during "B" and "A" years could be pursued with most profit. We try to induce such as are able to do the work to take the Classical Course. But many find this too difficult; and even the Modern Classical Course is beyond the power of some. The Normal Course is made somewhat more elastic, so as to meet the various needs of different students.

A look at the courses required for graduation during this period reveals several differences between the secondary programs of that day and those of today. Required courses included, among others, four years of English and of mathematics, three years of history, and two years of Latin. For those who desired them, two additional years of Latin and two years of Greek were available. The amount of class work demanded of the students was also different from that of today. For example, according to the school catalogue of 1920, a student who had completed the four years of required English would not only have written numerous compositions and made a careful study of English grammar, but would have read many of the great classics in literature. These would have included Scott's *Ivanhoe* and *Lady of the Lake,* Eliot's *Silas Marner,* Hawthorne's *House of Seven Gables,* Tennyson's *Idylls of the King,* and Shakespeare's *Merchant of Venice, Julius Caesar, Macbeth,* and *Hamlet,* as well as a variety of poems and essays by such writers as Emerson, Goldsmith, Irving, Longfellow, Lowell, Macauley, Ruskin, and Shelley.

All students received instruction of one period per week in the Bible. The rationale for this was carefully explained in the school's 1902-1903 catalogue as part of a statement entitled "Character of the School:"

The systematic study of the Bible finds a proper place in the curriculum. Christianity should be made an element of all general education; the Bible should become a text-book from the infant school to the university, not only because it is the fountain of duty and usefulness, but because it contains (a) history the most authentic and valuable; (b) biography the most instructive and interesting; (c) philosophy the most profound, theoretical and moral; (d) wisdom the most enlarged and practical; (e) eloquence and poetry the most sublime, pathetic and beautiful.

Generally, the Old Testament was covered during the freshman and sophomore years and the New Testament during the last two years. Weekly instruction in the Heidelberg Catechism was also required of all students at each grade level. According to descriptions of the course, students were expected to commit to memory the questions and answers contained in that memorable document as well as take careful notes on the supplementary information supplied in class by the instructor. Although there was discussion from time to time about dropping the Catechism course and having Bible meet twice instead of once a week, the old procedure was still being adhered to in 1928.

Beginning in the early 1900's, questions were being raised in academic circles throughout the United States about the value of many of the traditional liberal arts courses being taught in the secondary schools of the nation. As reported by Northwestern's overseers in 1913: "Perhaps no subject is being discussed in educational circles these days more than that of the curriculum. The conception of what constitutes an education is undergoing a change. The present age is a practical one and everything that does not contribute directly to practical use receives cold treatment." Northwestern, however, according to the report, intended to keep the old curriculum intact: "Our aim as before is still to develop the possibilities of the student and to leave specialities to technical schools. No change has been made in any of the courses. This institution is primarily a preparatory school and herein we believe it is fulfilling its purpose." This position was reiterated from time to time during the years that followed. In 1926, for example, the Board declared:

In carrying on the work certain principles which we consider of fundamental importance have been kept in mind. We aim to train the whole student, body, mind, and heart, always remembering "that the fear of the Lord is the beginning of wisdom." We also constantly try to maintain a high standard of scholarship, so that our students may be able to pursue with profit the various courses offered at other institutions. We further impress upon the students the necessity of a well-developed Christian character, revealing itself in every walk and duty of life.

Despite high-sounding statements about "leaving specialties to technical schools," the Board of Trustees began approving at an early date the introduction of courses that trained the "hand" as well as the "mind." In a sense, the approval of the Normal Program was a departure from early principles, especially when courses in domestic science and agriculture were added as part of the teacher training program. Even more significant was the introduction of a course in bookkeeping. According to the faculty minutes, such a course was being offered as early as 1896, and a local paper in 1906 reported that "steps [had] been taken to enlarge the commercial work of the school to include typewriting, stenography and such other branches as will, with the strong English course now offered, give those who desire it a thorough business education." In the following year, the school's commercial classroom was fitted out with several used counters and desks which had been donated by one of the local banks. A course in manual training was also offered from time to time—further proof that the school offered at least a few courses aimed at training more than the student's mind and heart.

The Academy at first operated on the so-called quarter system of three terms of three months each, but in 1906 this procedure was replaced by the semester system. The change was made in order to place the school's program more in line with those of other schools, both secondary and collegiate, and at the same time make it more convenient to offer certain branches of study which were not carried on throughout the entire year. The school day was also gradually extended in order to accomodate the expanding curriculum. By 1923, class hours had been extended to 2:45 P.M., with an hour and a quarter intermission for noon lunch. Two years earlier, the practice of a faculty-supervised study hall was introduced, and students were expected to be there when not attending classes. To facilitate matters, each student was given an assigned desk in the study hall.

During the morning of the first day of classes, examinations were given to freshmen to determine if any of them should take remedial work or carry a light academic load because of deficiences. A normal load at this time in the school's history was four regular subjects; to carry more than that, a student had to have an exceptionally high grade point average. The grading system used during most of the period before 1928 would appear confusing when compared to what is used today. For many years, students were given four possible grades: E for excellent, G for good, F for fair, and P for poor—each with the usual +'s and −'s when appropriate. In 1915, the letter grade of C, for conditional, was added to indicate work that was below P. A student was usually allowed six weeks to remove a condition, after which if, in the judgment of the teacher, the student showed "entire inability to proceed with the work," it was changed to failure. The old system was not replaced until the fall of 1921 when the following letter grades and numerical equivalents were introduced: A (90-100), B (80-90), C (70-80), D (conditional), and E (failure). It was decided later that numerical grades between 65 and 70 would be considered conditional, while work below 65 would be justification for failure. Grades were usually sent home to the parents every six weeks with the hope that this would have a salutary effect on students who were doing poorly.

One of the weakest aspects of academic life at Northwestern during this period was the library. For many years, disbursements for it were usually under twenty-five dollars annually. Although by 1920 this was supplemented by the interest from a $2,000 endowment, the amount derived from this was small and part of it was often used to purchase library equipment rather than books. As a consequence, the increase in library holdings was dependent to a large degree on donations in kind. Unfortunately, many of the donated books were from private libraries of retired ministers, with the result that although the library contained about 2,000 books in 1894, these were heavily weighted on the side of theology and philosophy. There were also many duplicates.

The only bright side to this part of the Academy's history was the activity of a few donors, most of them in the East, who made it a point to purchase special sets of works for the library or to give money and let the faculty make its own selections. Among these donors, Mrs. Cornelius Rapelye of Astoria, New York stands out preeminently among all others. Almost from the time that the school was first organized and continuing for about three decades, scarcely a year passed by in which she did not enrich the library shelves with a valuable set of literary or historical works or with a significant sum of money. It was thus very fitting that Northwestern's library was named the Rapelye Library in 1895.

Another erstwhile donor who showed a special interest in the library was the Reverend Alfred De Witt Mason, who at various times served pastorates in New York and New Jersey and was the author of numerous books and articles on religious subjects. He took a special interest in furnishing the library with periodical literature. A report of 1906 states that thanks to such support, "the Reading Room now contains among others the following: *Harper's Monthly, Scribner's, McClure's Cosmopolitan, World's Work, The Outlook, Scientific American, Christian Herald, Intelligencer, Public Opinion, Chicago Daily Record-Herald,* and the local English and Dutch weeklies."

Rapelye Library, 1898

Despite these donations, the library holdings continued to be weak in several academic subjects because the school's own contributions remained small. According to the annual financial statements from 1913 to 1923, the library portion of the budget varied from a low of $12 in 1914 to a high of $196 in 1916, with the average for the ten year period being about $80. In 1926, the holdings numbered about 4,000 volumes, a not insignificant number, but by the school's own admission this was deceiving:

When we mention that the library contains 3,850 volumes, friends may think it is sufficient to meet all our needs. However, many of these books would be of greater value to the theological student than to the teen-age student of a secondary school. By actual count we find that only about fifteen hundred of these works might be of practical value to the Academy students.

A report of 1903 states that the Academy was placed, following careful examination, on the list of accredited schools by the Iowa Federation of Colleges and Universities. This meant that Academy graduates were given unconditional admission into Iowa's colleges and universities. According to the Federation's standards, unconditional admission to college required thirty semester units of work. These had to be distributed as follows: algebra, 3; geometry, 2; English, 6; history, 2; science, 2; Latin or Greek, 8; and electives, 7. In point of fact, the Academy's requirements for graduation not only met these standards, but exceeded them.

In 1918, the Academy made an effort to secure accreditation from the North Central Association of Colleges and Secondary Schools. It failed to achieve this on the first attempt, one of the reasons being lack of adequate water and sewer facilities at the school. Soon after these facilities were extended to that part of the town in 1920, the principal petitioned the Board of Trustees that "toilets be placed in the building as soon as possible for the following reasons: (a) Present toilets [are] insufficient and unsatisfactory; (b) Too much time is wasted by the students going outside during school sessions." Indoor toilet facilities were provided in 1922, but the matter of seeking accreditation from North Central was not taken up again until 1927. Unfortunately, the application was turned down once more, this time on the grounds that the faculty lacked certain qualifications. The Academy did not finally achieve North Central accreditation until 1930.

V

Extracurricular and Other Activities

The Academy from the beginning showed an interest in extracurricular activities, although these were somewhat limited at first because of the small enrollment and the lack of adequate facilities. In 1887, a literary organization known as the Philomathean Society was founded. It met one afternoon per week and was devoted to intramural debates and "recitations in elocution." That it was popular is demonstrated by the fact that in 1892, it boasted a membership of fifty-nine out of a student body of seventy-seven. In addition to its regular weekly meetings, it sponsored annual oratorical contests as well as occasional entertainment programs that were open to the general public. The following is a description of one of the programs as carried in a local newspaper:

Singing by the Society
Debate—Resolved that parents exercise a greater influence over children than teachers.
  Affirmative—Miss Rouwenhorst, Mr. Aelts
  Negative—Mr. Will Hospers, Miss Beyer
Ladies Quartette—In charge of Miss Evelyn Hospers
Current Events—Miss Slob
Recitation—Miss Staplekamp
Practical Jokes—Mr. Cupido
Business
Adjournment

Because of growing interest, the Philomathean Society was divided in 1912 into two separate bodies, called the Alethean and Chrestomathean. In 1926, a third literary society, known as Delphi, was organized.

Intramural debates were particularly popular among the students, perhaps because debate topics were frequently selected on the basis of their providing entertainment rather than serious information. Note, for example, the topics chosen in 1901 and 1906 respectively: "Resolved, That civilization is progress," and "Resolved, That a spendthrift is more injurious than a miser." A significant step forward was taken in 1919, when juniors and seniors having a grade point average of 90 or better were given permission to form an intermural Debating Society, which soon began fielding teams for debate with other schools. Western Christian High School at Hull became its archrival, but debates were held on a regular schedule with St. Mary's Academy at Alton and Western Union Academy at Le Mars as well.

In 1891, a student paper, called *The Classic*, began publication. It was issued monthly during the time that school was in session, but it ceased publication about 1907. Beginning in 1922, a new student paper, called *The Monitor*, made its appearance, but it too was soon discontinued. In 1925, *The Classic* was revived for a brief period through the efforts of the junior class. Following this, no student paper appeared again until 1928, when the present *Beacon* began publication on a triweekly basis. Lack of funding was the major cause for the failure of the earlier student papers. They were dependent primarily on advertising and when this proved insufficient, they began appearing irregularly and finally ceased publication altogether.

The Academy also showed an interest in the fine arts at an early date. According to the catalogue of 1896-1897, instruction in vocal music was offered on Fridays from 1:00 to 3:00 p.m., and in drawing from 3:00 to 4:30 p.m. A few years later, instrumental music was available at special rates. In 1906, in accordance with the expressed desire of the Board of Trustees, steps were taken to establish a department of music. A music room was fitted out and Mrs. Cornelius Rapelye of Astoria, New York, who had already contributed considerably to the school's library, sent a check so that the school could acquire a fine, new piano. By 1908, the Academy had a small orchestra and soon a mixed chorus was organized, followed later by boys' and girls' glee clubs.

As has been noted, daily chapel attendance was required of all students, and they occasionally were asked to take part in these devotions. In 1901, a chapter of the Young Men's Christian Association was organized on the campus, followed soon after by a similar organization for young women. These organizations were run by the students themselves, and were designed to minister to their spiritual life and growth in a special way.

Athletics also quickly became an important part of the school's extracurricular activities. According to faculty minutes and newspaper accounts, students engaged in sports among themselves for purposes of relaxation and recreation from the time that the school first opened its doors. However, the first official mention of this occurring under faculty supervision is found in a report of 1894: "Both indoor and outdoor athletics under the supervision of the Faculty, have contributed toward the maintenance of a fine school spirit." The primary sports were football in the fall, basketball in the winter, and baseball and tennis in the spring. The lack of satisfactory facilities at first created a problem for indoor sports, but in 1916 the Board of Trustees agreed to rent, at a seasonal cost of $75 (later raised to $100), the auditorium of the local town hall for boys' and girls' basketball. The athletic field for outdoor sports was located on the west side of Zwemer Hall.

It might be argued by some critics that the introduction of athletics was a departure from the principles upon which the Academy had been founded, but this is not correct. The founders of the school and the various members of the Board of Trustees often expressed the view that athletics were important for building healthy bodies and for student morale. Sports therefore were not only permitted, they were encouraged. This attitude, however, was always taken with the proviso that athletic participation never be considered an end in itself but only as a means to an end. Hence, restrictions were laid down regarding when games could be played and which students would be eligible to participate.

The teachers were made responsible for seeing to it that athletics were not abused, and, judging from an examination of the faculty min-

Baseball Team of 1913

utes, they carried out this mandate assiduously. In 1900, the faculty decided that only those students who maintained an average class standing of 85 percent or better would be allowed to engage in sports with other schools. Moreover, the scheduling of athletic events was limited to Friday evenings and Saturdays. A petition from a group of students in the spring of 1913 requesting that the requirement be lowered to 80 percent was at first turned down, but approved a few days later when it was pointed out that the regulations of the Amateur Athletic Association regarding eligibility had been placed at the lower figure. In 1922, the faculty changed the eligibility requirements slightly to read that in addition to the 80 percent demanded in all subjects, a student could not have any grade lower than 70 and had to be carrying four subjects, in addition to Bible and Catechism.

In 1923, the faculty took what today would be considered a revolutionary step by requiring teachers to turn in the grades of athletes every two weeks and by decreeing that henceforth eligibility would be determined on the basis of two-week intervals. The new ruling placed a burden on the coaches because they frequently did not know from game to game which students would be eligible to play. Despite this handicap, the ruling remained in force for several years.

Rules were strict regarding certain kinds of student behavior and were published in the school catalogues for everyone to read. In so far as possible, the rules were made to apply to off-campus activities too. For example, the 1892-1893 catalogue stated that "on the Sabbath every student is expected to worship regularly with one of the churches in the city or vicinity." From an early date, the catalogue also carried the stipulation that "dancing, card-playing, and the use of tobacco on the campus [was] forbidden," which was later amended to make the restrictions apply to "public places" as well as "on campus."

That the school intended to enforce these "blue laws," is shown in the action taken by the faculty in February 1919 when it learned that fifteen students, nine boys and six girls, had attended a dance at the local town hall. In addition to severely reprimanding the students for "transgressing" the school rules, letters were sent to the parents asking them to do the following:

First, that you send to the [secretary of the faculty] by return mail, a signed statement to the effect that you will cooperate with the teachers of the Academy and do what lies in your power with your son [or daughter] to prevent the recurrence of a transgression of this and all other rules of this institution.

Secondly, that you inform your son [or daughter] that the teachers will meet on Friday, February 28, 1919, at 2 p.m., to hear an apology for this offense and a promise faithfully to abide, while a student at this institution, by all its rules.

The letter concluded with a statement declaring that "if these requirements are not complied with or if a second offense of this nature is committed, the relation of your son [or daughter] as a student at this institution is thereby automatically severed."

In view of the student body's being made up mostly of young people in their teens, it was to be expected that some of the rules laid down by the Calvinist fathers of the school would be broken from time to time. Most disciplinary problems, however, were minor and a warning or word in private from the principal or a teacher was often sufficient to deter a student from continuing his or her misbehavior. When deemed necessary, a variety of punishments were meted out, including the requirement that a student be confined to his or her room during the evening hours, retention in the study hall for an hour after regular classes had ended for the day, dismissal from a class, suspension from school for a period of time varying from a day to a week, or making a public apology before the faculty and student body at chapel time.

Only on rare occasions was a student's misbehavior considered serious enough to warrant expulsion from school. Except in cases of cheating on an examination or persistently ignoring the rules against smoking on campus, the faculty minutes are rather vague in explaining why a student was expelled. Generally they cite such reasons as "insubordination and defiance of authority," "detrimental influence among the students," and "neglect of duty and contempt for discipline." Expulsion from school occurred less than a dozen times during the period before 1928, and in most instances the student was reinstated on trial after making a plea for readmission.

Fortunately, there were a number of "legitimate" ways in which students could escape the humdrum of academia. In addition to the various extracurricular activities already described, these included such events as ice cream socials, class plays, and class banquets. Also to mollify the tediousness of daily booklearning, there was the traditional rivalry among the several classes, highlighted by such annual affairs as freshman initiation and the "fox and goose chase." Needless to say, there also was some occasional "horseplay" between one class and another. Note, for example, the following account of an incident that took place in 1906 as described in one of the local newspapers:

There has been considerable excitement at the N.W.C.A. the latter part of last week, in the fight for the different classes to get their respective flags on the flagstaff, especially between the '06 and '07 classes. Friday afternoon '07 perched their flag on the staff, but it had no more than got there when three members of the "A" class got it down and tore it to pieces. This was the beginning of the strife. Saturday morning saw the '07 flag up again and remained there until noon, when one of the "A" members took it down. If any one would have taken the trouble to look towards the Academy tower at 5 o'clock Monday morning, they would have seen about 7 members of the '06 class on top of the Academy. They succeeded in putting their flag, which was considerably larger than the former flags, below old glory and tying the rope on the flag staff. Now the persons who wished to take the '06 flag down must take the flag pole down, and this some of the '07 boys did early Tuesday morning. At about 8 o'clock the climax of the whole affair came. The '06 class had hurriedly mustered some of their patriots and came down. They found that their flag had been taken down, the '07 put up and the "B" boys guarding it. Then followed a scrap between the '06 and '07 classes. The "A" boys broke through the doors and succeeded in pushing the "B" class boys out. No one was seriously injured, although some bruises were received. The '06 class came out victors. They pulled down the '07 flag, put the '06 up, and on looking toward the tower the '06 flag can still be seen waving. Good for you '06, don't let the '07 class get ahead of you.

Of the various school activities, commencement was undoubtedly the major event of the school year—not only for the students but for the community as well. For several years, graduation exercises were held in the "opera house," as the auditorium on the second floor of the town hall (the former Academic Hall) was called. Beginning in 1900, these were held instead in the First Reformed Church. On the occasion that this change of location took place, one of the local newspapers hailed it as a welcome practice, stating that in addition to providing more extensive accommodations, it encouraged more orderly conduct among the guests. The paper attributed this happy development to two things, "firstly, because there were no noisy boys in the gallery, and secondly, because everyone has some respect for a church and will refrain from creating a disturbance."

In contrast to the commencement exercises of later years, graduation programs of the early period were primarily in the hands of the students themselves, with participation by the faculty and outsiders limited largely to an opening prayer, the awarding of the diplomas, and the benediction. Serious addresses were presented by the class valedictorian and salutatorian—students who graduated with the highest and second highest academic honors respectively. In addition, a humorous report entitled "Class History and Prophecy," was delivered by the student having

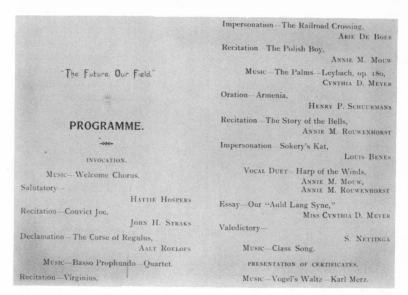

"The Future. Our Field."

PROGRAMME.

INVOCATION.

MUSIC— Welcome Chorus.

Salutatory—
HATTIE HOSPERS

Recitation—Convict Joe,
JOHN H. STRAKS

Declamation—The Curse of Regulus,
AALT ROELOFS

MUSIC—Basso Prophundo—Quartet.

Recitation—Virginius,

Impersonation—The Railroad Crossing,
ARIE DE BOER

Recitation—The Polish Boy,
ANNIE M. MOUW

MUSIC—The Palms—Leybach, op. 180,
CYNTHIA D. MEYER

Oration—Armenia,
HENRY P. SCHUURMANS

Recitation—The Story of the Bells,
ANNIE M. ROUWENHORST

Impersonation—Sokery's Kat,
LOUIS BENES

VOCAL DUET—Harp of the Winds,
ANNIE M. MOUW,
ANNIE M. ROUWENHORST

Essay—Our "Auld Lang Syne,"
MISS CYNTHIA D. MEYER

Valedictory—
S. NETTINGA

MUSIC—Class Song.

PRESENTATION OF CERTIFICATES.

MUSIC—Vogel's Waltz—Karl Merz.

Commencement Program, 1896

the third highest graduation honors. In this instance, the speaker usually resorted to some fictitious plan for lifting the curtain of the future in order to forecast what each member of the graduating class would be doing with his or her life. Graduation exercises also included several musical numbers as well as an assortment of orations—sometimes in Dutch or even in Latin—by other members of the student body. In this respect, it is interesting to note how prevailing events and conditions were often reflected in the choice of subject matter for the speeches. Thus at the commencement of 1898 when the Spanish-American War was raging, the program included orations on the following topics: "Cuba Libre," "Spain's Record," and "The American Volunteer." Similarly, some of the special music included patriotic songs, and the prize for the best composition was awarded for a 600 word essay, in Latin, on the Spanish-American War.

A primary purpose in founding Northwestern Classical Academy had been to prepare young people for college. Judged in that light, the school must be given high marks for fulfilling its function, especially during the early period. In 1896, the principal reported that of its eighty-eight graduates, four were serving in the ministry, two were college professors, and two were medical doctors. Moreover, twenty-four were currently enrolled in colleges, and eleven were studying in theological seminaries. Sixteen others were serving as teachers in elementary schools. During the following years, the Academy continued to fulfill its primary function of preparing young people for college. Thus, at the time of the school's twenty-fifth anniversary in 1907, it could be announced that of its approximately 250 graduates, 75 percent had pursued a college course in whole or in part. The fact that 35 percent of these graduates went into the Christian ministry indicates that another of the school's primary functions was also being fulfilled.

The first graduation occurred in June 1885 and involved three young men: Isaac Betten, Henry Hospers Jr., and Teunis Muilenburg. Because formal classes had begun only two years earlier in September 1883, it is obvious that these graduates had been admitted with advanced standing. Very probably they were among those that Van Zanten had started tutoring in the fall of 1881. Of these graduates, Hospers and Muilenburg later became clergymen in the Reformed Church, and Betten entered the teaching profession. In the following year (1886), there was only one graduate, Dirk L. Betten, and he too went into the ministry. A look at the list of forty-nine Academy alumni in 1892, on the occasion of the school's tenth anniversary, reveals that the ministry continued to have the greatest appeal but other professions were also proving attractive. These included teaching, medicine, law, and business. Nine of the alumni were women, of whom eight were listed simply as "At Home," while one was classified as a teacher, indicating that the teaching profession at this time appealed more to men than women.

The persons responsible for founding the Academy in 1882 had hoped it would become a kind of "feeder" for Hope College. This generally proved to be true, but Academy graduates also attended other schools, especially at first. For example, of the five male graduates of 1887, two went to Hope College while three enrolled at Iowa State College at Ames. Other schools in which Academy graduates enrolled during the first decade included the University of Iowa, Grinnell College, Yankton College, Harvard University, and the University of Michigan. Later, Hope College for a time began attracting a larger number of students. In 1891, for example, of the nine graduates who continued their education, five enrolled at Hope, and in 1892, eight of eleven did the same. Similarly, of the twelve students in the graduating class of 1901 who went on to college, ten entered Hope, and of the class of 1914, seven out of eleven did so. Beginning in the 1920's, however, a trend toward attending schools nearer home is discernible. Thus, of the nine students of the class of 1922 who went on to college, four enrolled at Hope; three at Central in Pella, Iowa; one at Grundy in Grundy Center, Iowa; and one at Morningside in Sioux City, Iowa. Other Iowa colleges that began attracting more of Northwestern's graduates included Western Union at Le Mars and Iowa State at Ames.

The number of Northwestern graduates who went on to college began declining soon after the First World War. For example, of the twenty-six graduates of the class of 1924 (the school's largest graduating class to date), ten remained home after graduation, as did twelve of the twenty-four graduates of the class of 1926. This development was part of a nation-wide trend as secondary schooling became more popular and was viewed as an end in itself. To the credit of Northwestern, it can be noted that in comparison to the public high schools, the percentage of Academy graduates who went on to college continued to be high. Moreover, an interest in Church work also remained popular among the students. A report of 1925, states that "about one-third of the total attendance of 104 are tending towards the service of the Christian ministry." The founders of the school would have been pleased with such reports.

The attitude of the students toward their classwork during the early period was highly commendable. There appeared to be a genuine thirst for knowledge and a high respect for scholarship. Beginning in the early 1900's, however, serious questions were being raised about the abilities and attitudes of the students. Although the Academy continued to have a significant number of highly-motivated young people each year, the percentage seemed to be declining. The Reverend Jerry Winter, who occasionally taught part-time at the school while serving as pastor of Orange City's American Reformed Church from 1899 to 1909, explained the change in this way: "Some students have self-starters, some are easily cranked, and others are quite balky." In part, the problem resulted from poor preparation at the primary level, as can be seen in the principal's report of 1907 to the Board of Trustees:

We find that there are some students, coming from our rural families, who are not sufficiently advanced to enter our present "D" class. Entrance into this class requires preparatory training thru the eighth grade, unless the student is particularly bright. We find that our rural schools, as a rule, do not advance their students to this grade, or that the pupils have not availed themselves of this elementary training when they had the opportunity, and hence are not ready to take up the first year's work at the Academy.

The Academy staff refused to lower its standards to accomodate the ability of the students who did poor work. In explaining that ten students had failed to return for the fall term in 1908 because they were unable to do the work, the principal declared: "This shows that we are getting a more uniformly substantial body of students; the idea is being exploded that anybody can become and continue as a student with us, and we believe that this is a good thing." Principal Zwemer expressed a similar view a few years earlier when he wrote: "Diamonds are not made but they are sought, and found, and polished. We do not want anybody and everybody for the sake of getting somebody." In 1907, it was decided to introduce "sub-D" courses for beginning students who were deficient in English and arithmetic, but the experiment was given up after a brief trial because of staff shortages. Students had the greatest difficulty with Latin—generally about one-half of all poor grades were given in that course. Low grades were also common in history and algebra.

The problem of immaturity and unpreparedness among new students did not improve during the years that followed. Various explanations for this could be heard, including the "increasing independence that was characteristic of the age" and the war for having created "an uncontrollable desire for play." The fact that the average age of the students was younger than in the past and the growing acceptance of the view that all young people should have a secondary school education were also cited as causes for the existing situation, as is evident in the following report of 1917:

The students of today are on the whole younger than they were a few years ago. The cause for their being here is not so much a desire for an education, a hunger and thirst for knowledge; but many come here because they are sent. The almost immeasurable increase in wealth among all classes has decreased the estimate put upon the value of an education, and incredibly increased the number of those who continue their studies beyond the grades. This fact has had an incredible influence on both the scholarship and behavior of students. This is true everywhere, and to some degree this condition must be contended with here.

Despite the sending of grades home to the parents and warnings being given to the students, as well as opportunities for removing conditional grades, academic problems continued to arise. The six-week grade reports of early 1920, for example, which were not unique, show that forty students were doing conditional work in one or more courses and sixteen were receiving failures in at least one course. Nor did this situation show much improvement at the end of the term. A few weeks before graduation in 1920, the principal reported:

The quantity and quality of the work done are not in every respect encouraging. Six of the D class have been dropped from Latin, two from Algebra, and two from History. Two of the B class have left largely because of their troubles in Greek. There has been a large number of conditions in all classes. Four of the A class cannot graduate, and eight others still have back work to make up. Two of the B class cannot graduate next year.

To deal with the problem, the faculty began making it a practice to go over the student roll every three weeks in order to advise those who were doing marginal work. What effect this had on young minds can be gathered from a remark by Principal Dykstra in 1927: "On many, this has had a good effect, while on some it has had no other result than to create a smile."

Freshman Class, 1911

PART TWO
THE ACADEMY AND
JUNIOR COLLEGE:
1928-1961

VI

A Junior College is Added

Northwestern entered upon a new day in the fall of 1928 with the introduction of a junior college program. For the next several decades, the institution was known as Northwestern Junior College and Academy. The idea of adding college work was not new. As early as 1894, on the dedication of the new academic building known as Zwemer Hall, the principal, the Reverend James Zwemer, included the following in his closing remarks: "It is our prayer that soon, if it be the will of the Lord, that He in His own good time will inspire among our people a readiness to raise this spacious building to become the home of an institution of college level."

Zwemer's remarks were no idle words, and in 1907, another principal, the Reverend John Frank Heemstra, recommended to the Board of Trustees that the freshman year of the college be introduced. "To take this step," he declared, "would meet with the approval of a large body of our constituents, and would hasten the realization of the ultimate purpose of our Institution." His recommendation was approved, and college work began in the fall of that year with courses in Latin, Greek, French, chemistry, trigonometry, and surveying. Interest in the college program was badly misjudged; only three students enrolled, and one of these soon dropped out. Optimism nevertheless still prevailed, and in the spring of 1908, the principal reported: "The work . . . has been full and thorough, which ought to recommend this movement and ensure larger success in numbers for next year." Unfortunately, the number of college enrollees remained virtually unchanged, and the college program had to be dropped after only one year.

Despite these reverses, views favoring a junior college continued to be expressed from time to time. Thus, in 1911, the principal, Thomas E. Welmers, reported to General Synod that although it did not seem wise at the present time to add a fifth year, "the idea of expanding into a college" should not be dismissed "entirely and permanently from our minds. If I should see my way clear, I would advocate it." A few years later, Welmers did see his "way clear" and, following his suggestion, the Board of Trustees on April 5, 1917, adopted the following resolution:

Whereas, parents earnestly request it, students approve of it, the time seems to be ripe for it, prospects of continuing it are good and the institution will thereby be furthered in its growth, therefore be it resolved that we, the Board of Trustees, N. W. C. A., authorize the proper authorities to provide for the instruction in those subjects as far as is feasible which are commonly given in the Classical and Modern Classical courses during the first year of the College course, and that this instruction begin with the opening of school in September.

Nothing came from the proposal at this time—perhaps because of the uncertainty of conditions due to America's entry into World War I the day after the above resolution was adopted. But in his annual report of 1920, Welmers informed the Board:

Undoubedly the purpose of the founders was that some day [this institution] would become a college; and throughout these years many have looked forward to the realization of this fond hope. There are particular reasons why at this time this matter should be energetically pushed. In a measure the life of the institution is threatened. Competition is strong and with the consolidation of rural schools, which is certainly coming, competition will be still keener. Sympathy for denominational schools is decreasing, but this fact applies more to schools of secondary grade than to colleges, and the dawn of a new day seems to be approaching for the Christian College. We believe there is room in this community for a college. The college might not become large but the large college is not desirable. The ideal is a small college with good instructors to give individual attention to the students. There are enough students in this community to make a good sized college.

The Board of Trustees accepted the principal's views. In its report to General Synod in June 1920, it declared that although the Academy was "in a flourishing condition . . . we are not blind [to the fact] that it is facing a critical period in its history." The report added that it was the Board's "profound conviction" that the only solution was an "extension of the courses . . . so as to include collegiate work." Support for junior college programs as adjuncts of secondary schools was gaining ground at this time, and there was growing fear that if Northwestern did not also soon move in that direction, the Academy would be at a decided disadvantage in competing for students. Several junior colleges had been founded in Iowa towns by this time or were soon to be founded. These included Sheldon, Fort Dodge, Estherville, Mason City, Boone, Britt, Emmetsburg, Forest City, and Eagle Grove. Most of these institutions were associated with the local public high schools.

Principal Welmers' resignation in 1920 to accept a position at Hope

College did not diminish interest in the junior college idea. Under his successor, the Reverend Gerrit Timmer, who served as principal from 1921-1925, the Board of Trustees took some preparatory steps to realize these hopes. On December 11, 1923, a committee was formed to study the feasibility of a junior college program, and in the following spring the Board asked the three classes that would be most affected by the proposed institution—West Sioux, East Sioux, and Dakota—to determine the sentiment of their constituents regarding "the matter of a Junior College."

The classes discovered that general sentiment was favorably disposed toward establishing a junior college, but a few persons expressed alarm at the effect it might have on the enrollment at Central and Hope. Rather than create a third Reformed Church college, they suggested strengthening the two already in existence. Serious questions were also raised about financial costs, and whether a small denomination like the Reformed Church could support that many schools.

In answer to these and other objections, the supporters of the junior college idea had several ready answers. The possibility of an initial loss of students at Central and Hope was acknowledged, but it was argued this would quickly be offset by a resultant gain in the upper classes of those schools. Some of the more outspoken defenders of the proposal declared that the sixty-plus Reformed churches in northwest Iowa and nearby in South Dakota and Minnesota had for too long been "hewers of wood and drawers of water" for Central and Hope, and that the time was overdue for the western churches to begin supporting a college for their immediate area. It was also pointed out that this could cut down the cost of an education for many students who would be able to commute daily to Orange City and thereby realize a savings in the matter of board and room. Indeed, according to some studies that were made, such expenses currently made it impossible for many young people in the mid-West to attend college at all. It was also noted that travel expenses in the past caused some students to attend a state institution, such as Iowa State college at Ames, the University of South Dakota at Vermillion, or a college sponsored by another denomination. This could mean that ultimately these students might leave the Reformed Church altogether.

In answering questions about finances, supporters of the proposal also pointed out that much of what was needed for a junior college program was necessary for a secondary school as well. Therefore, very little had to be added to what was already available at Northwestern in the way of a physical plant. Similarly, by confining the college program to a few courses, only a limited additional teaching staff was needed. As to the necessary teacher qualifications, it was argued—rather speciously—that the first two years of college were textbook oriented, and the same texts used at "Yale or Princeton or Hope or Central" would be available at the new school. "The last two college years," it was further stated, "are early enough to dole out to the students the predigested knowledge in the form of lectures." Moreover, the money saved by attending a school nearer home could be used by the students to purchase reference books.

In further support of the junior college idea, it was argued that such an institution would enable some parents to keep their children home or near home a few years longer and thus keep an eye on them. Principal Welmers expressed the views of many parents in 1920 when he declared to the Board of Trustees: "I am still of the persuasion that most of our [secondary school] graduates are too young to go far from home and that a secluded spot such as [Orange City] affords less temptation than the larger places for our young people." When critics of such views declared that it was good for young people to attend school away from home and to make contacts with the outside world, supporters of the junior college proposal pointed out that the radio and automobile were already succeeding in breaking down the clannishness of the past. Moreover, because the proposal called for only a junior college, there would still remain two years of college work elsewhere which would provide young people with opportunities to "shake off" some of the old provincial shackles.

In view of arguments like the above and a favorable report from the special committee appointed to investigate the feasibility of adding a junior college program, it is not surprising that the Board of Trustees decided to go ahead with its plans. On June 30, 1926, at a special meeting of the Board and after full discussion, it was resolved that the first year of junior college work be added, "providing we can get an enrollment large enough and necessary funds to warrant this step." The tuition was set at "not less than $70," and it was suggested that the alumni of the Academy be asked to help "raise the necessary funds for the additional [professorial] chairs for the college work." The canvassing of students was placed in the hands of the principal, and if everything looked good, the executive committee of the Board was empowered to make the necessary arrangements for beginning the college program in the fall of 1926. Because of the difficulty of completing preparations in time, a later meeting of the Board changed the date to 1927 for the freshman class, and to the following year for the sophomore class.

Meanwhile, it was decided to seek a definite endorsement from the Classes of West Sioux, East Sioux, and Dakota. Resolutions of support from the first two classes came soon, but the Classis of Dakota remained silent on the matter for a time—either through its having mixed views about the matter or simply because it neglected to bring it up for discussion. Support was also sought from General Synod. This is interesting because in previous discussions about adding a junior college, there seemed to be little concern about getting such approval. That it was seriously pursued at this time was perhaps from a belief that approval would be accompanied by a promise of denominational financial support for the junior college—just as the Academy had been receiving such support for many years. The overture in behalf of the junior college program was formally presented to General Synod by the West Sioux Classis at Synod's annual meeting in June 1927. After some discussion, the matter was referred to the Board of Education for investigation. This arrangement naturally caused further delay so that once again the opening date for the junior college had to be postponed—this time, to the fall of 1928.

To help win the support of the denominational Board of Education, its secretary, the Reverend Willard Dayton Brown, was invited to meet with the Board of Trustees on October 25, 1927. The visit was not entirely rewarding, as Brown expressed some reservations about the proposed school. He feared it would hurt the other two Reformed colleges and was worried that money spent on the new institution would divert funds normally given to other benevolent causes. Fortunately, another report was more favorable. This one was by Dr. Robert L. Kelly, whose services were secured in 1927 by the Board of Education to make an independent investigation of the matter. Dr. Kelly was eminently qualified for making such a study. A long-time educator who had at various times been associated with Christian education, he was currently a professor of education at Columbia University in New York. He also held executive positions in the Association of American Colleges and in the Council of Church Boards of Education. His report made a favorable impression on General Synod, but so, too, did the efforts of several other individuals and groups.

As might be expected, the Academy principal and the Board of Trustees directed several appeals to General Synod. Letters of support also were sent in from the Classes of West Sioux, East Sioux, and Dakota, as well as from the Particular Synod of Iowa. Appeals also came from the three Reformed ministers of Orange City. At nearby Sioux Center, following a public meeting in the First Reformed Church in the spring of 1928, a resolution was passed asking General Synod "to act favorably upon the matter of the Junior College." Pledges of financial support were made at this meeting, with one person promising $900, another $300, and a third $100. Others pledged smaller amounts.

The Alumni Association of the Academy likewise contacted General Synod. At its annual meeting in May 1928, it dispatched a letter outlining various reasons why Synod should act favorably on the request. A few days later, the Association went a step further by choosing one of its members to attend the meeting of Synod to plead its cause. The man selected, Anthony Te Paske, was an excellent choice. He was a graduate of the class of 1889, a prominent public-minded citizen well-known in business circles, and a long-time member of the Board of Trustees. For a brief period in the 1890's, he had also taught at the Academy.

From the beginning, Orange City businessmen worked closely with the Board of Trustees on the matter of the junior college. Shortly before General Synod met in June 1928, the town's Commercial Club sent two communications to that body. In particular, they stressed the increase in the number of public high schools and the threat this posed to the Academy's existence unless a junior college were added to the program. The Orange City business group mentioned that $7,000 had already been raised in Orange City alone to support the school, and added that a recent study indicated that upwards of thirty-five students would enroll in the first year's class. The virtues of Orange City as a site for the school were also extolled. In addition to having five churches (three Reformed and two Christian Reformed), it was pointed out that there were "no Sunday baseball games or movies" and that "everything [was] closed on Sunday." In short, declared one of the letters, Orange City was "a town where no one should hesitate to send their boy or girl."

In the end, General Synod supported the request of the Board of Trustees to establish a junior college. This was done, however, with the understanding that it would be for a trial period of three years and that "all responsibility, financial and otherwise, [would] be assumed by the local constituency." It urged the school's Board of Trustees to "study carefully the requirements for a Junior College as outlined by the North Central Association of Colleges and Secondary Schools and seek to conform to these standards from the beginning."

When Principal Welmers set forth his arguments in 1920 for adding a junior college, he informed the Board of Trustees that leadership would be the key to establishing a successful school. "What we need to accomplish this ideal," he declared, "is a man who is enthusiastic and can give all his time in canvassing the churches in the interests of this institution." Such a leader was found in the Reverend Dr. Jacob Heemstra, who came to Northwestern in June 1928 to assume the principalship of the Academy and the presidency of the newly-established Junior College.

Dr. Heemstra was born January 2, 1888, on a farm three miles south of Orange City. He spent his boyhood days there and near Boyden, a small town located about fifteen miles northeast of Orange City. In 1903, he enrolled at Northwestern Academy, from which he graduated in 1906; four years later, he graduated from Hope College. Uncertain about whether to pursue a career in education or to go into the Christian ministry, he decided to try the former first. However, after one year as school superintendant at Sioux Center, Iowa, he enrolled in 1911 for a year at Princeton where he took classes in both the university and seminary. This he followed by two years at Western Theological Seminary in Holland, Michigan, from which he graduated in 1914.

Following his ordination into the ministry, Dr. Heemstra accepted a call from the Trinity Reformed Church in Chicago, where he remained four years, 1914-1918. Ever interested in scholarly pursuits, he combined his parish work with further graduate study at the University of Chicago. In 1918, he accepted a position at Central College as professor of education, but exchanged this four years later for that of professor of religion and psychology. He was also appointed college registrar, thereby acquiring some administrative experience. It was with considerable regret on the part of the people at Central that Dr. Heemstra decided to accept the position offered him at Northwestern in the spring of 1928.

Dr. Heemstra's guiding hand and cordial spirit were quickly recognized and appreciated, as is evident in the following editorial published in *The Beacon* at the close of Northwestern's first semester as a Junior College and Academy:

The Beacon Staff knows that most of the credit for Northwestern's present high standing is due in great part to the untiring zeal of our President. He it is who is our inspiration, counselor, and good friend. In chapel, his talks are always timely and bristling with good suggestions for all students. He is heart and soul behind the two Christian organizations [the Y. M. and Y. W.], the literary societies, the music clubs, and the athletic teams. His sage advice and up-to-date ideas have benefited the school in countless ways, both as to educational standards, curricula and equipment.

Dr. Heemstra held the position of Junior College president for twenty-three years (1928-1951) and served as Academy principal for fourteen years (1928-1934 and 1943-1951). Even after 1951, until his retirement in 1957, he continued to be closely associated with Northwestern as president emeritus and as an instructor in religion.

In June 1939, Dr. Heemstra was awarded a doctor of divinity degree by Hope College. In this present day when honorary degrees are given out so readily, it must be said of Jacob Heemstra that his was richly deserved. There has been no single individual more closely connected with Northwestern's history and more responsible for its success than Dr. Heemstra. It is very probable that without his determination and faith in the future of the school, it would have closed its doors during the gloomy depression of the 1930's. It is therefore with good reason that this history of Northwestern has been dedicated to him.

In addition to Dr. Heemstra, Northwestern began the fall term in 1928 with eight other instructors. Two more were soon added, bringing the total to eleven when the sophomore year was introduced in the Junior College department in 1929. Their names, together with their degrees and responsibilities, were as follows:

Jacob Heemstra, M. A., President; Academy and College Bible

Hiram Gillespie, M. A., Registrar; Academy and College Latin and Greek

Ethel Adcock, M. A., Librarian; College English and Speech

Charles Van Zanten, M. A., Athletic Coach; College History and Social Science

B. Elwood Fahl, M. S., Academy Physics and College Chemistry

Houston T. Karnes, M. A., Academy Science and College Mathematics and Biology

Lydia Jepson, M. A., Academy and College courses in Education and College Psychology

Fern Smith, B. Mus., Academy and College Music

Mathilda Korver, B. A., Academy English and French

Theodore Mansen, B. A., Academy English, Latin, and Science

Wilemina Eppink, B. A., Girls Physical Training; Academy History and Mathematics.

VII

Academic and Other Adjustments

The efforts that won approval from General Synod for establishing a Junior College were considerable, but even more pressing tasks lay ahead. The school authorities were now faced with the greater burden of working out specific details regarding new courses, additional staff, classroom and equipment needs, and extracurricular activities. The role of the Junior College vis-a-vis the Academy also had to be worked out. While dealing with these matters, Northwestern also had to cope with problems arising from the severe economic depression of the 1930's. In the end, finances became the greatest challenge of all and, as will be discussed in the next chapter, nearly brought about the closing of the school.

Plans for the new Junior College called for introducing only freshman level courses in the fall of 1928, to be succeeded by sophomore work the following year. On June 21, the Board of Trustees approved courses for eleven departments: Bible, English, French, Greek, German, speech, history, music, mathematics, chemistry, and education. Two programs were available, namely Liberal Arts and Teacher Education, each involving sixty hours of course work. Graduation from the Liberal Arts program initially required four hours of Bible and six of English, but eight hours of laboratory science were added later. Students enrolled in the Teacher Education program also had to complete these basic requirements plus courses specified by the State Department of Education.

Much of the final planning was left to the faculty, with the result that some decisions were not made until after the fall term had already started. During the first week of classes, for example, the faculty decided to give three hours credit to college students enrolled in certain Academy courses meeting five times a week, thereby increasing slightly the number of college courses available. On October 25, the following system of grading was adopted for both the Academy and Junior College departments:

$$A = 94\text{-}100 \text{ (3 grade points)}$$
$$B = 86\text{-}93 \text{ (2 grade points)}$$
$$C = 78\text{-}85 \text{ (1 grade point)}$$
$$D = 70\text{-}77$$
$$F = \text{anything below } 70$$

Later, the "F" grade was changed to anything below 60, and an "E" grade, signifying incomplete, was introduced with the numerical equivalent of 60-69. Students were given one semester to remove conditions, after which time they were changed to "F." In order to "foster as much as possible the desire on the part of the students to do their best academic work," the faculty adopted the plan of publishing an honor roll every six weeks to include the names of students doing "B" work. The faculty also agreed that a college student had to have 24 credit hours and 20 grade points to be classified a sophomore and had to have 60 credit hours and 60 grade points (that is a "C" average) to graduate.

With the introduction of the sophomore year in the fall of 1929, the offerings of the Junior College were broadened. The catalogue for that year listed fourteen departments with the following number of credit hours available in each:

Bible 4	History 14
Biology 8	Latin 12
Chemistry 19	Mathematics 20
Education 20	Music 12
English 20	Psychology 6
German 8	Social Science 12
Greek 4	Speech 4

Not all courses listed were offered on a regular basis, but depended on student demand and on the availability of instructors. New departments and additional courses were added from time to time. By 1935, these included art, 6 hours; business and secretarial science, 30 hours; and physics, 12 hours.

The Junior College made satisfactory academic progress during its initial years. The Intercollegiate Standing Committee, which represented Iowa's three state institutions of higher learning, accredited the first year of college work as early as May 1929, and did the same for the sophomore year in February 1930. This meant that credits earned at Northwestern would be accepted by other colleges throughout the state. Accreditation was not given, of course, in perpetuity; it could be taken away about as easily as it had been granted. As President Heemstra stated in his annual report of March 1932: "The close check constantly

First Junior College Graduating Class, 1930

made by the Intercollegiate Standing Committee shows that we will have to abide very strictly by the rules which they have laid down."

The regulations of the Intercollegiate Standing Committee stipulated that college teachers shall teach only those subjects in which they have a graduate major or minor and shall not carry teaching loads of more than sixteen or eighteen college hours and not more than twenty hours of college and secondary school hours combined. Several examples can be cited to illustrate steps Northwestern had to take from time to time to comply with these regulations. In 1934, the Committee directed the school to cut the load of an instructor who was teaching ten hours of Academy French, five hours of Academy Latin, and seven hours of college French, as well as supervising the Academy study hall several periods per week. In 1936, a faculty member who had been employed to teach history at the college level was obliged to limit himself to Academy subjects when it was discovered he had not quite completed the requirements for his master's degree. Similarly, in the spring of 1939, the administration was informed that the instructor of typing and shorthand would have to be replaced because she lacked the necessary requirements for teaching those courses.

The teacher training program was also carefully scrutinized by the State Board of Educational Examiners. This body was obviously pleased with the school's initial progress, as can be judged from part of its report of 1932:

Considerable improvement is noted in the teacher training work at Northwestern Junior College. . . . The teacher training program is conscientiously administered and the administration appears to be willing to make the work as strong as possible.

As state requirements changed, additions had to be made to the education program from time to time. Thus, in 1935, courses in art and health had to be added to the curriculum. Because no one was qualified to teach art, an instructor from Western Union (now called Westmar) College at nearby Le Mars was employed to visit the school twice a week.

Two kinds of teaching certificates were offered at Northwestern: the First Grade County Certificate and the Standard Elementary Certificate. The former was awarded after two years of college and involved only about ten hours of education and psychology. It was essentially a liberal arts curriculum with a minimum of courses in the field of education and entitled the holder to teach in rural schools. For teaching in town schools, the Standard Elementary Certificate was required. This program was rigidly prescribed, leaving the student few electives. Moreover, the required thirty hours of education and psychology courses included a course in practice teaching for which a special fee of twenty-five dollars was charged—no mean sum during the depression years. Because of the more rigid program and the additional fee, most students interested in teaching took the easier of the two programs. Indeed, the curriculum for the Standard Elementary Certificate was not offered on a regular basis until 1938 because of insufficient demand.

Teacher training became Northwestern's most popular program, with nearly one-half of the students enrolled in it. In 1939, President Heemstra reported that of the twenty-nine Junior Colleges in the state doing teacher training, only Waldorf Junior College prepared more teachers than Northwestern. By 1941, Northwestern was furnishing about one-fourth of the teachers for the area's rural schools.

Along with the growth of the Teacher Education program, considerable expansion took place in the Department of Business and Secretarial Science. The 1935 catalogue describes the following courses:

Economics 6 hours	Accounting 6 hours
Money and Banking 2 hours	Business Law 6 hours
Marketing 2 hours	Typing 2-4 hours
Economic Resources 2 hours	Shorthand 4 hours

Since the catalogue listed only one instructor for these courses, they obviously were not offered on an annual basis—especially since the instructor also served as athletic coach for the Junior College. Business courses were popular, and the school authorities made it a point to capitalize on this as a means of attracting students, as can be judged from this announcement in the *Beacon* for April 15, 1935:

Within the last few weeks, the professor of commerce, Prof. J. Hootman, has been formulating plans for extensions in the department and so another step toward perfection is taken—business students may get a full course right in Orange City without the extra cost of large city commercial colleges and with the additional advantage of a good Christian training.

The transition from what was simply an Academy to an institution that included two years of college work created some unique problems, as might be expected. For example, should there be one graduation for both groups, or should each have its own? If just one, to what extent should each department be involved in order to keep the program to a reasonable length? And what about the alumni—should there be one or two associations? Similarly, should there be separate social activities for the two departments? Questions also arose over whether certain introductory courses, such as beginning Greek, should be offered separately in each department, combined into single courses offered to both groups, or taught only as college level courses. Although initially there was some rivalry over student leadership, the adjustment went more smoothly than anticipated, as seen in the annual report of the president to the Board of Trustees on March 15, 1930:

Last year there was some competition as to leadership in the institution between the senior class in the Academy, where it had previously centered, and the junior college that had just been introduced. However, this year it is taken for granted that the main leadership among the student body centers in the junior college, mainly because of the age of the students and the fact that this department has considerably grown, but it is also fully recognized by the college students of the share which the Academy should have in the activity of the school. There has been, therefore, unanimity of spirit and full cooperation between both departments in the various student activities.

Several changes were made in the Academy curriculum at the time the Junior College program took form. The final result was that two new diplomas—General Studies and Scientific—became available for graduation in addition to the Classical and Modern Classical. Requirements for General Studies consisted of the following:

> Bible 1 unit
> Composition and Rhetoric 2 units
> Literature 1 unit
> Algebra 1 unit
> Plane Geometry 1 unit
> History 1.5 units
> Civics 0.5 unit
> Science 1 unit
> Foreign Language 2 units
> Electives 5 units
> Total 16 units

Students enrolled in one of the other programs also had to complete the above courses plus others depending on the diploma desired. For the Scientific diploma, these included two additional units of science plus a course in advanced algebra and another in solid geometry; for the Classical, three units of Latin and two of Greek, or four of Latin and one of Greek; for the Modern Classical, two units of Latin and two of French.

There can be little doubt that the quality of teaching improved in the Academy during this period because many of the instructors also taught college courses and therefore had graduate degrees. As evidence of the Academy's improved status, it became accredited in 1930 by the North Central Association, thereby giving the school a national rating. It had from an early date been fully accredited by the Iowa Department of Education, but the additional achievement was noteworthy because its credits would now be recognized by any college or university in the United States.

Although both the Academy and Junior College curriculums expanded during the 1930's, the staff never numbered above fourteen instructors, and a few of these were on a part-time basis. Consequently, teaching loads were heavy. For example, in 1938, Hiram Gillespie taught college Latin, Greek, and German, and served as registrar. Similarly, George Russman taught Academy and college physics, Academy mathematics, and served as director of athletics and Academy athletic coach. But the "jack-of-all-trades" was B. Elwood Fahl, who was at Northwestern from 1929 to 1943. His primary teaching responsibility was chemistry, but at various times he also taught physics, mathematics, and German. In addition, he had primary responsibility for keeping the furnace fired up in Zwemer Hall, was advisor to the *Beacon* staff, and

Northwestern's Faculty, early 1930's

served as Academy principal from 1936 to 1943. He also showed off his fine tenor voice by leading the student body and faculty in sacred music at daily chapel and even served as director of the Junior College Glee Club for a brief period. Despite heavy workloads, faculty turnover was light; replacements were seldom more than one or two per year. Turnover would perhaps have been higher if economic conditions had been better, but teaching vacancies were not easy to find during the depression years.

Unfortunately, the addition of the Junior College did not result in a corresponding increase in the holdings of the library. These were described in the 1941 school catalogue as follows:

Our library now contains more than three thousand volumes. A careful list of the books of the library shows that fully half of these are on the subject of morals and religion; and of the remaining works, dealing with the various branches of instruction, many are old and, though still useful, do not serve the same purpose as more recent publications would. A large number of books are added to the library each year, and further and continuous expansion of the library is needed.

The fact that half the books were concerned primarily with one discipline and many others were out of date points to serious weaknesses. Moreover, its statement that a "large number of books" is added each year is inaccurate. In 1929, when the second year of college work was added, the library was described as having "more than three thousand books"—the same description given twelve years later. Because of the library's limited facilities on the main floor of Zwemer Hall, more than half of the holdings were stored in the attic, further adding to the library's weakness. In 1940, the library was moved to the north half of the large room on Zwemer's second floor that had been serving as a combination chapel and Academy assembly. The latter continued to occupy the south half of that room, but the chapel was transferred to the gymnasium in Science Hall.

College enrollment fluctuated widely during this period. The number of freshmen vacillated between 30 and 35 during the first few years, but rose to 55 by 1935 and then dropped to 43 the following year. By 1939, it had risen to 84, but took a significant drop to 58 in 1940. Sophomore enrollment also varied. The retention rate was very high initially, as most freshmen returned for a second year of college work. This began changing, however, during the mid-1930's. For example, the sophomore class in the fall of 1935 was less than two-thirds the size of the previous year's freshman class, and in 1940, it was less than one-half the 1939 freshman class.

Academy enrollment at first showed an increase, reaching 82 in 1930, but declined steadily thereafter, raising questions about its continuance. When the three local classes were asked to express themselves frankly on this matter, the West Sioux Classis at its regular fall session in September 1933 passed the following resolution:

Resolved, that it is the conviction of this Classis that we need our Academy Department now as much as ever, if not more, with a view to the Christian training of our children and that the Board [of Trustees] be encouraged in its struggle to maintain the Academy. Further that we pledge ourselves and those whom we represent, to do all we can through prayer and cooperation, to secure students and financial support, and that we as ministers and elders will instruct our people in the matter of Christian secondary education.

The resolution passed without any dissenting votes, as did a similar resolution by the East Sioux Classis.

On May 26, 1934, a faculty committee was appointed to study ways in which Academy enrollment could be increased. Acting on the recommendation of this committee, the Board of Trustees agreed to offer six scholarships to students from local grade schools and another five to those from schools in other parts of Sioux County. These were to be awarded on the basis of scholarship and character. As another means of increasing enrollment, the Board resolved to offer a reduction in tuition when there were two or more students from the same family.

The efforts to increase Academy enrollment met with little success.

By 1941, enrollment was down to 37—less than one-half what it had been a decade earlier. In part, the decline can be attributed to the poor economic conditions of the 1930's, but it was also due to the growing popularity of public high schools and the changing attitude of Reformed Church parents toward the need for Christian schools at the secondary level. In fact, if it had not been for students from Christian Reformed families, Academy enrollment during the 1930's would have been considerably less. Throughout the 1930's, students of Christian Reformed background constituted one-third or more of the Academy's student body. This was less true in the Junior College, where they constituted about one-fifth of the students.

Both the Academy and the Junior College drew most of their students during the 1930's from the immediate area. For example, of the forty-three students enrolled in the Academy during the 1939-1940 school year, all but nine came from Orange City. Similarly, of the 127 students in the Junior College, all but twenty-nine were from Sioux County. Of those who were not, only ten came from out of state. They were distributed as follows: Minnesota, six; South Dakota, three; and Michigan, one.

Because of the large number of commuting students, the Board of Trustees soon resolved to purchase a bus. It was pointed out that this would be useful for the college choir when it went on tour and for transporting students to athletic events away from Orange City. Financial problems, however, delayed matters until April 1934, when a used eighteen-passenger Diamond-T bus was acquired for $850. It was immediately put to use transporting students from the area west of Orange City, including Sioux Center and Maurice. Students were charged a fee of $30 a year for this service. The enterprise worked so well that shortly before the beginning of the 1934 fall term, the school brought a thirty-passenger bus for a route north of town to the Hull area. Still later, a third bus was acquired, this one to serve Boyden and the area northeast of Orange City. The buses transported about fifty students daily, with a few more on weekends.

In view of the fact that students of Reformed and Christian Reformed backgrounds continued to make up the vast majority of the student body, the religious temperament of the school underwent little change. Chapel attendance was required as before, and students were penalized for excessive unexcused absences. For example, at a faculty meeting in the spring of 1935, it was decided that any college student having more than five unexcused absences in one semester would lose one hour of credit in a course to be decided on by the faculty. It was also agreed at this time that three tardinesses during a semester would count as one

Northwestern's First Buses, ca. 1936

unexcused absence. A poll taken in December 1939 by the staff of the *Beacon* indicates that the majority of students favored the practice of compulsory chapel attendance. To the question of whether Northwestern should continue the practice, thirty-five students replied in the affirmative and only seven in the negative. Typical explanations of those favoring the old policy included the following: "We put little enough stress upon spiritual education as it is;" "By making chapel a matter of personal choice, I feel that the school would be relinquishing one of its Christian strongholds;" "If they wouldn't continue the practice, the students would lose sight of the fact that this is a Christian institution and stands for a high purpose;" and "What would it look like to have Northwestern, as a Christian institution, discontinue this practice?" It is interesting to note that before the poll was taken, the administration made it clear that the results would in no way affect the school's policy on required chapel attendance.

The requirement that students take religious courses as a prerequisite for graduation also remained intact. For Academy students, this meant two courses in Bible—"Old Testament" and "Bible History." In 1929, the course on the Heidelberg Catechism was dropped from the regular Academy curriculum because "the program was too heavy." Henceforth, Academy students were expected to take such a course in their own churches. College students, too, were required to take two courses in Bible, namely, "Life of Christ" and "Apostolic Age," each offering two hours credit.

Certain regulations regarding student conduct also remained in force, including rules against smoking and the use of tobacco. These rules were regularly published in the school catalogue, as was also the taboo against dancing. With respect to the latter, the Board of Trustees reasserted its position in 1935 by passing the following resolutions:

Be it resolved that the Board of NWA and JC again hereby go on record that we are strictly opposed to dancing in any form. Be it [further] resolved that the Board hereby prohibit all dancing on the school campus and all dancing as a school function either on or off the school campus. Be it also resolved that all students and parents be urged to cooperate with the school in observing the foregoing rules and aim especially that no student learn to dance while attending this school.

In other ways, too, the Board of Trustees took actions from time to time during the 1930's indicating that its conservative religious views had changed very little over the decades. For example, on March 17, 1930, it approved a report from one of its members asking the faculty "to be very careful in regard to the thoughts expressed on religious subjects in order that nothing may be said that would be out of harmony with the accepted teachings of the Churches of the Reformed faith." Similarly, at a meeting of the Board on September 3, 1934, one of its members was delegated to meet with Houston Karnes, Professor of Biology and Mathematics, who had earlier expressed an unwillingness to submit to the Board's request to have his church membership transferred from the Church of the Disciples to a church in Orange City. In meeting with Karnes, the Board member was instructed "to assure himself that said brother will not urge his views against infant Baptism upon any of his students." A few years later, on April 19, 1939, the Board of Trustees, by a vote of 15 to 4, agreed not to re-hire Miss Sinnia Billups, Professor of English and Speech in the Junior College. This action was taken because of dissatisfaction with the type of dramatic productions she had been putting on. A few weeks later, however, this decision was reversed following visits with the instructor in question and further discussions among the members of the Board.

As has been noted, Northwestern's founding fathers believed there should be more to education than booklearning and classroom lectures, a view that continued to be observed. Indeed, extracurricular activities took on added significance with the establishment of the Junior College. In 1939, the Board of Trustees, eager to attract college students who would excel in extracurricular activities, authorized the administration to offer Special Achievement Scholarships "to such students and in such amounts as the administration deemed advisable, such enrollments recognizing any and all lines of special attainment."

Students who were musically inclined found increasing opportunities to develop their talents. The arrival of a new instructor, Miss Fern Smith, in 1928 was one of the best things that ever happened to the school. A fine musician and dedicated teacher, she gave unselfishly of her time and talent for thirty-three years, until she retired in 1961. Under her capable direction, the Glee Clubs and orchestra steadily expanded. Along with a variety of local programs, the Academy and Junior College choirs began showing off their talents in neighboring communities. The college group also soon began making an annual tour each spring to Reformed churches in states as far away as Kansas and Michigan. By 1930, the combined Academy and Junior College orchestra had expanded to twenty pieces, including six violins. Under Miss Smith's direction, Northwestern also acquired its first band. Unfortu-

College Choir, 1936

nately, as interest in the band increased, membership in the orchestra declined and it eventually had to be disbanded.

A literary society was organized among the college students almost immediately after the Junior College was established, and it soon divided into two bodies known as Pi Epsilon Pi and Alpha Beta. Both were dissolved in 1932, however, because of the greater interest being shown in dramatics and debate. In 1933, a Forensic Club was organized, which during the years that followed put on a number of plays as well as an occasional opperetta. The Forensic Club also fielded teams in debate, original oratory, and extemporaneous speaking, and soon won high honors in all these divisions. Its best year was 1938, when, at the State Junior College Tournament at Iowa City, one of Northwestern's students took first place in oratory, another won a superior in artistic reading, and a third shared first place in extemporaneous speaking. The Academy too became more interested in forensics, having replaced its three literary societies with two dramatic clubs. Like their Junior College counterpart, they too put on frequent plays. In the early 1930's, the Academy also became more active in debate when it was admitted to membership in the State High School Debating League. In order to accommodate better the needs of the forensic and dramatic organizations, a stage was constructed in one of the ground floor rooms of Science Hall. It soon became known as "The Little Theater."

Journalism too proved attractive as an extracurricular activity. Soon after the Junior College got underway, another attempt was made to start a student newspaper. (Past efforts had failed, usually after one or two years of operation.) The new paper, called the *Beacon*, was published tri-weekly, but sometimes appeared bi-weekly and even weekly. In 1930, a second school paper, the *Classic*, began publication as a quarterly. It was intended more for alumni and friends of the school than for current students. Both the *Beacon* and the *Classic* are still published today.

Throughout this period, Northwestern continued to stress the idea that healthy bodies must go hand in hand with sound minds. Therefore, students in the Junior College, like those in the Academy, were required to take non-credit physical training for one period a week. Activities consisted of calisthenics and various indoor and outdoor games.

Intermural sports took on new significance with the founding of the Junior College. Basketball games began almost immediately by competing with local independent teams and with those of other two-year colleges. Scores were low—sometimes amazingly so—in the initial contests; in its first three games, Northwestern defeated an independent Sioux Center team 23 to 13 and Trinity Junior College of Sioux City 20 to 5, and lost to Esterville Junior College 34 to 22. By the mid-1930's, Northwestern was playing a full slate of junior colleges in Iowa, including Waldorf, Marshalltown, Fort Dodge, Esterville, Boone, Mason City, Webster City, Emmetsburg, Ellsworth, Eagle Grove, and Sheldon. At first, Northwestern broke about even in these contests, with as many wins as losses, but it did much better in the later 1930's. For example, in the Esterville Junior College Invitational Basketball Tournament, which started in 1937, Northwestern won the championship trophy the first year, the sportsmanship trophy the following year, and both trophies in the third year. In 1939, Northwestern also advanced to the semi-final round in the state tournament for junior colleges. The Academy basketball team for its part, continued to include such old rivals in its schedule as Western Christian at Hull and St. Mary's at Alton, but gradually also began competing with more public high schools.

Football was also included in the Junior College intermural program from the very beginning. The initial encounters, however, were a disaster. In its first game, it lost to Sheldon Junior College by a score of 122 to 6. The *Beacon* of December 7, 1928 did not exaggerate when it reported that "Northwestern fought a valiant battle but was outclassed, outcharged, and outnumbered from the first kickoff." The addition of the sophomore class did little to help the situation. In a return match with Sheldon in the fall of 1929, Northwestern lost 63 to 0. Such lop-

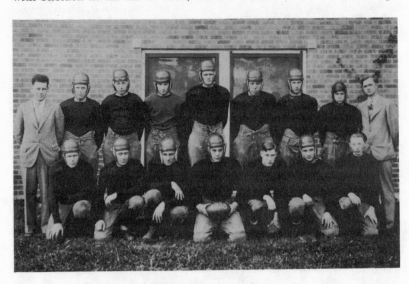

The First Football Team

sided scores were not confined to games with Sheldon. During the 1931 football season, Northwestern lost to Norfolk Junior College 69 to 0 and to Emmetsburg Junior College 101 to 0. In reporting these games, the *Beacon* could always be depended on to report that the Orange City school had put up a "game fight." In view of the poor showings in the football field, it perhaps was a blessing in disguise when the Board of Trustees resolved in 1932 to discontinue football for financial reasons. Six-man football was introduced in 1938 but was suspended in 1941 because of scheduling and other problems, including the lack of a good practice field. The *Beacon* of October 6, 1941, reported that the latter was overgrown with "carloads" of sand burs, with the result that members of the team "were pulling thorns from their hands and other parts of their anatomy for weeks after the close of each season."

In 1933, the Junior College introduced a track and field program, which was considered far less costly than football. Efforts at this time to allow the college girls to organize a basketball team to play against other junior colleges, however, failed because of opposition from the Board of Trustees. A similar plea in 1938 was also rejected. The explanation was that it did not seem "wise from the stand-point of health especially, to introduce competitive basketball for girls at our school."

As evidence of the growing maturity of the student body, discussions arose during the late 1930's over the need for a student senate or council. In late 1938 and early 1939, several letters appeared in the *Beacon* citing advantages to be derived from this kind of an organization—such as providing a means for making student wishes known to the faculty and Board, helping arrange entertainment for the student body, giving students practical experience in self-government, and building up school spirit. Academy students generally opposed the idea at first out of fear that, because of their smaller numbers, they would be "out-voted and bossed" by the college department. When permission to form a student senate was given in 1939, this problem was solved by giving the two departments each seven representatives. These were divided as follows: for the college, the sophomores were given four delegates and the freshmen, three; for the Academy, the seniors were given three delegates; the juniors, two; and the sophomores and freshmen, one each. The officers consisted of a president, vice-president, and secretary. Terms of office were for one school year, and it was stipulated that the president should be chosen from among the representatives of the college sophomore class. Meetings were scheduled every other Wednesday, with special sessions when necessary. A faculty member, chosen by the faculty, was present at all meetings but without voting privileges. The faculty member was responsible for reporting developments to the faculty as a whole, and no decision reached by the student senate could take effect until it had received faculty approval.

For many years, the members of Northwestern's Board of Trustees were elected by the local classes and by the Board itself. In 1935, for example, when the number of delegates increased from fifteen to twenty-one, it was left to the Board to choose four, while the remaining seventeen were elected by only two classes—those of West and East Sioux. In an attempt to make the Board more representative of the denomination as a whole, by 1941 the Board had been increased to twenty-eight (eighteen ministers and ten laymen) and included Trustees from several bodies formerly not represented. These, and the number of Trustees elected by each, were as follows: West Sioux Classis, six; East Sioux Classis, six; Dakota Classis, three; Germania Classis, three; Particular Synod of Iowa, two; General Synod, one; and the Board of Trustees, seven. Despite this wider group representation, the Board's structure remained much the same in terms of geographic distribution: of the twenty-eight Trustees in 1941, twenty-one came from northwest Iowa, and of these, nineteen were from Sioux County.

VIII

Coping with the Depression

From the time of its founding in 1882, Northwestern frequently faced financial problems, and as would be expected, the addition of a Junior College program added to these difficulties. Although arguments had been made occasionally that the expanded program would not add significantly to the school's financial needs, it is not likely that many thoughtful persons took these remarks seriously. Salaries had always been a major part of Northwestern's budget, and this was certain to increase in the future. Not only would the staff need to be enlarged, but it would have to be paid more because of the graduate training required of those teaching at the college level. Similarly, as college courses were added, additional classrooms would have to be found— either through partitioning existing rooms or finishing unused space in Zwemer Hall and Science Hall. The expanded program would likewise require several thousand dollars of additional equipment, especially for science courses. In view of the above, it is not surprising that Northwestern's budget increased from $13,000 in 1927-1928, to $24,000 in 1928-1929, and to $34,000 in 1929-1930. It thus almost tripled in two years.

Unfortunately, about a year after the Junior College opened, the great economic depression occurred—a development that greatly multiplied the financial problems and nearly brought about the closing of the school. Within a brief period, the school's income dropped from a high of $34,148 in 1929-1930 to a low of $14,966 in 1931-1932, or only about two-fifths what it had been two years previously. The greatest initial drop occurred in gifts from individual donors, down from about $15,000 in 1929-1930 to less than $2,000 in 1931-1932. In time contributions from churches also declined sharply. Even with strict economizing, it was impossible to avoid deficits under such conditions. The seriousness of the situation can be readily seen from the following excerpt from President Heemstra's annual report to the Board of Trustees, dated March 28, 1932:

With the first part of next month there will be two months' salary due the teachers, with practically no funds to pay. The salary then due will

93

be practically $3,500. This together with the previous debt in the contingent fund will make our indebtedness $10,000. In addition to this, it will take $4,000 more to finish the school year. There is $1,500 tuition still due, of which probably not more than $1,000 can be collected before the close of school. Probably some $700 may be received from the Board of Education. So that if we are to keep our indebtedness from mounting up to $12,000 something drastic must be done.

On September 7, 1931, faculty members at the first meeting of the new school year voted "to make a voluntary relinquishment" of 10 percent of their present salary. This was done because of "the financial stringency of the time" and in the hope "that this sacrifice on the part of the members of the Teaching Staff will also lead others to be willing to do what they can for the needs of the school." The faculty was commended for its sacrifice and loyalty to the institution, which meant a savings of about $2,000 for the school, but it should be noted that salary cuts were certain to come, and actually occurred several times throughout the 1930's. For example, the salary of Hiram Gillespie, professor of Greek, Latin, and German, was cut from $2,000 in 1928, to $1,800 in 1931, to $1,400 in 1935, and $1,200 in 1939.

Faculty salaries usually made up about two-thirds of the annual budget. In view of the frequent deficits facing the school, it is therefore not surprising that money sometimes had to be borrowed to meet the payroll at the end of a school year. Thus, in May 1931, $2,500 had to be borrowed for that purpose, as did $1,200 in May 1939. Even by borrowing money, the faculty did not always receive the full amount due them. For example, on May 29, 1934, the Board of Trustees instructed the school treasurer to pay the teachers 80 percent of their summer checks. Similarly, in re-hiring faculty in May 1936 for the coming school year, the Board "guaranteed" the same salary figure as the previous year but added the following condition: "In view of the fact that 7 months' salary had been paid so far, the Board and faculty compromise to the extent that 8 months salary be guaranteed for the coming year and that every effort shall be made as in the past to raise the full contracted salary, *but if unable to do so we expect the faculty to share our difficulty with us.*"

The faculty on the whole accepted the salary cuts along with uncertainties about being paid in full and on the due dates. They realized their experiences were not unique, but were shared by Americans in all occupations—professional, skilled, and unskilled alike. Indeed, most people at this time were grateful for merely having work, no matter how little it paid. This must not be interpreted to mean, however, that the faculty did not complain occasionally about certain matters related to their salaries. For example, in a letter of December 1931 to the Board of Trustees, the faculty, although declaring itself "anxious to cooperate fully in the present financial difficulty," complained that they had

not been taken into the confidence of the Board with respect to the financial situation and outlook; and we have not received even our reduced salaries for the past one and one-half months; and we are absolutely dependent upon our salaries for our living; some of us are now in serious financial difficulties; we cannot afford to teach without wages; some may be unable to complete the year without financial assistance; the fear that the school will not be kept open all year has been expressed; it is of the greatest importance to the faculty to know the exact situation and prospects within a few days.

In view of the above, the faculty asked the Board of Trustees to delegate a committee "or some other agency, to communicate to us your plans for taking care of teachers' salaries for this year, before we depart on our Christmas vacations, so that we may make our plans for the future."

The faculty also made suggestions to the Board from time to time on the matter of improving the school's finances. Thus, realizing that student tuition payments were more than a thousand dollars in arrears, the faculty in March 1933 recommended that students having unpaid tuition be charged six percent interest on the unpaid balance and that such students appear before a committee of the Board or faculty or both. Similarly, in April 1936, a letter signed by the entire faculty was presented to the Board's Executive Committee asking that every effort be made to acquaint the churches and friends of the school with the needs of the faculty. The Board was urged to act with "all haste" to get as many contributions and pledges paid as possible before the close of the school term.

Tuition was the largest single source of income during the depression, generally constituting about one-half of the school's total receipts. In normal times, a school that is hard pressed for funds usually resorts to raising tuition as a remedy. But the 1930's were abnormal times, and Northwestern felt obliged to lower rather than raise the cost of attending the school. Even with lower tuition, hardly a year went by during the 1930's when students were not from $1,000 to $2,000 behind in meeting their tuition payments. Various means were pursued to collect these arrears, including letters and personal visits by President Heemstra and members of the Board of Trustees. Sometimes promissory notes were taken for back tuition and occasionally when these became long overdue, they were turned over to a local attorney for settlement. Employment of the Private Schools Collection Agency and the Midland Finance Company was also resorted to on occasion. Everything considered, however, the school authorities showed great leniency in the matter, and some of the debts never were paid.

Unable to increase tuition, the school authorities followed various other procedures to raise money. Attempts were made from time to time to collect pledges that had been made when economic conditions were better, but these efforts had meager results, as did appeals to the classes of the area. The same was true with letters written by President Heemstra to consistories and various church societies. On April 18, 1932 the Executive Committee of the Board appointed a three-man committee to supervise borrowing $5,000 from private individuals. The plan called for one hundred subscribers to be responsible for giving $50 each. Two weeks later, the committee reported back that there was no possibility of borrowing such an amount under those conditions.

Occasionally, local solicitors were employed to canvass the area for funds. In the fall of 1933, Cornelius Landhuis, a 1931 graduate of the Junior College, was hired to canvass "all the churches and all the families" of the classes "contingent" to Northwestern. For this, he was paid $50 a month and 3¢ a mile for traveling expenses. The nature of his work and its early results can be seen in the following report made to the Executive Committee in March 1934 concerning visits to families in some of the nearby towns:

At Hull: 129 calls made; 74 refused; 55 gave $65.50. In Middleburg church: 70 families visited; 34 gave nothing; 36 gave $48.50. At Sheldon: 155 families visited; 128 nothing; 27 gave $24.55. On the whole canvass, Mr. Landhuis reported the following: 1,730 families visited; 89½ days work; 2,700 miles traveled; 407 families gave $430.00.

Mr. Landhuis' initial efforts in Orange City were particularly demoralizing. After calling on about seventy-five families for two and one-half days, he had netted only $12.35. This meager amount and the fact that the gate receipts at a recent football game in Orange City had totaled $60 prompted President Heemstra to remark: "Have we lost our sense of values?"

Special consideration was likewise given to getting financial support from local businessmen. In early December 1933, about twenty businessmen were invited to President Heemstra's home for an evening discussion of Northwestern's financial troubles. The businessmen were reminded that the school was a great financial asset to the town. Not only were about $10,000 being spent in the community each year by students from other towns, but local students were also spending money in Orange City—money that would not be spent there if they went to college elsewhere. The businessmen were asked to raise $500 among themselves for the campaign currently being directed by Mr. Landhuis. The school authorities promised they would use pledges from the businessmen as credit for purchases from local merchants whenever such merchandise could be used in the school's operations.

The meeting in Heemstra's home proved to be a good idea. Although Landhuis' early efforts in Orange City had been very disappointing, several late contributions by some generous merchants brought the total to slightly more than $500. This was more than the total amount Landhuis had collected from other communities. The success of the meeting with the businessmen prompted several similar gatherings in the following years. In 1936, as a gesture of goodwill toward the business community, three local businessmen were elected to the Executive Committee of the Board of Trustees.

Federal assistance was also obtained. This was in the form of financial aid for students unable to pay for their education. The money was made available through a program known as SRE (Student Relief Employment) and administered as a department of the Federal Emergency Relief Administration. The program provided $15.00 a month to qualified students, in return for which the recipients did clerical or manual labor on their school campus. The number accepted could not total more than 10 percent of the total enrollment—a percentage that frequently amounted to less than ten students for Northwestern. The recipients were selected by a faculty committee, and the president was charged with primary responsibility for administering it at the local level.

In addition to the work-study program funded by the federal government, Northwestern always had a number of needy students (eighteen in 1934 from both the Academy and Junior College) on its payroll who performed various tasks throughout the year to help meet their educational expenses. These tasks included caring for the furnace and heating systems, keeping the campus buildings clean, mowing grass and shoveling snow, repairing equipment, surpervising the library, and doing clerical work. As was true of the federally funded program, students receiving these "service scholarships" had to use the money for tuition and other necessary school expenses. In 1935, the amount of SRE money available for college students was $1,080 and the service scholarships totaled $1,500.

As might be expected, Northwestern also sought aid from General Synod. These efforts met with some success but only after warding off an attempt to close the school. The events surrounding this story are rather complicated but noteworthy as clear illustrations of the faith that the Board and President Heemstra had in Northwestern's future and of their determination to persevere no matter what the odds.

Although the Academy had been receiving some denominational aid quite regularly since it was founded, it will be recalled that when General Synod in June 1928 approved the request to establish the Junior College, it did so for a trial period of three years, during which time Synod would not assume any financial responsibility for its operation. As the end of the three years approached, President Heemstra and members of the Board as well as the Classes of West and East Sioux worked diligently to obtain Synod's unqualified approval when that body met in June 1931. Their efforts were successful, but in granting approval, General Synod declared that the Junior College should receive no aid from the Board of Education funds "for the present school year." It was to be expected, therefore, that Northwestern's leaders would make a determined effort to obtain General Synod's support for financial aid when that body next met in June 1932.

A significant step in obtaining denominational aid was taken when, through the efforts of Dr. Heemstra, the presidents of the various educational institutions of the Reformed Church adopted the following resolution at a meeting convened at Chicago on March 9, 1932:

Resolved, that this body request the Board of Education to revise the percentages on the basis of which appropriations from the various funds of the Board are made to the Educational Institutions so that Northwestern Junior College may receive its adequate share of support from the funds of the Board. This revision to be on the basis of the differentials between fixed receipts and fixed expenses.

The school presidents at this time also resolved to ask General Synod to increase the percentage of benevolences allotted to the Board of Education from 10.3 percent to 15 percent.

As a follow-up to these actions, Northwestern's Board of Trustees, at its meeting on March 28, 1932, resolved to ask the Classes of West Sioux, East Sioux and Dakota to endorse the above resolutions and overture General Synod to approve them. A few months later, the Board adopted the following resolution:

Resolved, That we, as a Board, overture General Synod of the Reformed Church in America to place Northwestern Junior College on the same footing with our other Colleges, Hope and Central, so that the

Junior College may receive its proportionate share of the financial aid given by the Board of Education to our Colleges.

Once again, the "lobbying" efforts were successful. At its annual meeting in June 1932, General Synod declared that the Junior College was deserving of "some financial aid." The exact amount of aid was not specified, but was left to the discretion of the denominational Board of Education.

In early July 1932, the Board of Trustees received a lengthy letter from the Reverend Willard Brown, secretary of the Board of Education, that took the Trustees by complete surprise. The letter also sent shock waves throughout the community when it was published in the local *Orange City Journal.* The letter began by reviewing the recent General Synod resolution favoring financial aid for the Junior College but leaving the amount of aid "squarely up to the decision" of the Board of Education. The letter then went on to explain in great detail that there were only two funds from which aid could be derived: the "Educational Institutions Funds" and the "Board of Education Appropriations Funds." Money from these funds was distributed to the various schools according to a schedule of percentages that had been adopted by the heads of the institutions in conference with the secretary of the Board of Education. For example, with reference to the Educational Institutions Funds, the three academies (Northwestern; Pleasant Prairie at German Valley, Illinois; and Wisconsin Memorial at Cedar Grove, Wisconsin) received 15 percent of the total; the two theological seminaries (New Brunswick and Western), 10 percent; and the two colleges (Hope and Central), 75 percent. These amounts were then divided among the institutions on the basis of their budgets, except in the case of the seminaries which shared equally in the 10 percent allotment.

The Board of Education declared that the academies and seminaries "were receiving the irreducible minimum now," and it would be unjust "to reduce their appropriation by even a dollar." Any appropriation for the Junior College would therefore have to come from the 75 percent allotted to Hope and Central. Unfortunately, the allotments for these two schools were already far from sufficient to meet their needs and to cut their funds would "certainly reduce their efficiency." After three pages of text describing the limited funds available to the Board of Education and the small amounts allotted to each school from these funds, the Board came out with a startling proposition. It suggested that "Northwestern Junior College close temporarily (for a year or two) or until our country and our Reformed Church begin to see their way out of this depression and until the receipts of the Board of Education begin to show an increase."

To soften the blow to Northwestern's students, the Board of Education explained that during the interim while the school was closed, Central College had signified its willingness to accommodate any college students currently enrolled at Northwestern. In doing this, Central agreed to pay the round-trip travel expenses of such students from Orange City to Pella twice during each academic year, and also promised that tuition and board and room would not "in general" exceed those prevailing at Orange City. In addition, for a trial period of from two to five years, Central agreed to do the same for young people living within a seven mile radius of Orange City who were planning to enter college later. Although Central seemed to be very liberal in agreeing to these terms, a condition was attached to the proposal. In order to meet Central's expenses, the churches of the Classes of Dakota, West Sioux, and East Sioux would be asked to contribute to Central College one-half the amount they had given to the Junior College during the 1931-1932 fiscal year. This would, of course, be in addition to what those churches normally gave to Central College. To assure Northwestern's Trustees that the Board of Education bore no ill will, Brown's letter concluded with the following remark:

In our presentation of this proposition please be assured of the high esteem in which the Board of Education holds all those who are in any way responsible for the welfare of the Northwestern Junior College, as well as all the friends of the Institution whom we also wish to consider our friends. We are trying to feel our way toward a solution of what has become a problem of some dimensions in the educational work of our beloved denomination. We wish to express the hope that we can all work together toward an end that will bring the greatest good to the greatest number.

The reaction of Northwestern's Board of Trustees to the proposal was immediate and direct. After a "full, free and frank discussion of every item contained in the letter," the Trustees adopted the following resolution at a special meeting on July 18, 1932:

Resolved that the Board of Trustees feel that it cannot and may not close the doors of our Institution at Orange City, and that it has no intention of doing so. Further, that in accordance with the resolution of General Synod, we expect the Board of Education, as "servants of the Church," to do nothing less than to give this Institution its proportionate share of the Board's funds.

A seven-page reply was sent to the Board of Education along with a copy of the resolution. The letter expressed surprise that the Board of Education would even "entertain any such idea" as was presented in their proposition:

Does it appear clear that the Board of Education is the servant of the Church when immediately after Synod has voted that aid should be granted to the Junior College, the Board wishes to close the doors of this institution and has discussed the conditions upon which this is to be done with Central College? It has been very pertinently asked by some—If the Board is the servant of the Church, where did they get the right to discuss such a proposition with another institution without the consent either of Synod or of Northwestern Junior College?

The Board of Education was reminded that General Synod had approved the initial founding of the Junior College in 1928, had given its final approval in 1931, and had voted aid for it in 1932. The Board was also informed of the resolution of March 9, 1932 by the heads of the denomination's educational institutions announcing their support of aid for the Junior College from the funds of the Board. It was pointed out that if the Junior College were closed, the Academy would likewise have to be closed because it could not survive by itself. "Is the history of this institution for the past fifty years," asked the Trustees, "such that any fair-minded person would recommend its closing at this time?" The Board was asked to bear in mind that among the Academy's graduates were 118 who entered the ministry and 30 who became foreign missionaries. Finally, as to Northwestern's operating at a financial loss, it was mentioned that even Hope College in her history had acquired a deficit of considerable size during a period of years and "this at a time when she was receiving Board aid."

The letter further stated that adoption of the proposal would create considerable bitterness among Reformed communities served by Northwestern and would result in a drastic reduction of their contributions to Central College. In reference to helping future students attend Central, strong criticism was directed at the Board of Education's reasoning in limiting this help to an area within a seven mile radius of Orange City. The territory served by Northwestern was much larger than that. Moreover, the amount asked from the Classes of Dakota, West Sioux, and East Sioux to pay for the traveling expenses of these students was considerably more than what the expenses would be.

A copy of the reply to the Board of Education was sent to all ministers of the Particular Synods of Iowa and Chicago, along with a letter from

President Heemstra explaining that the proposal had been made without Northwestern's knowledge and with no one present to defend its interests. "Is this a fair way," asked Heemstra, "of dealing with this institution after Synod had decided that it should receive aid?" Although the reply to the Board of Education contained no counter-proposal, one had been suggested by ministers and others in the area, and Northwestern's president cleverly took this opportunity to call attention to it. The counter-proposal, in brief, suggested that instead of closing Northwestern, which was geographically located "just where a Reformed Church school should be," it would be better to reduce Central to junior college status and have its juniors and seniors complete their work at Hope College. In that way, the appropriations currently granted to Central could be equally divided between the two junior colleges in Iowa—Central and Northwestern. Such an arrangement would "reduce Central's operating cost by a large amount, relieve the church, unify our educational program, strengthen Hope College, and solve the problem now existing."

The Reverend Willard Brown, as secretary of the Board of Education, responded quickly to the remarks made by the Trustees of Northwestern. In a letter of July 26, 1932, he addressed the question of his organization's "right" to propose closing the school and to discuss this with Central without the consent of either General Synod or Northwestern. The mandate to do so, he declared, was "inherent in the action of the General Synod which put upon the Board of Education the responsibility to determine what aid the Junior College should have." In the minds of the members of the Board of Education, the instructions from Synod carried with it the injunction to consider *all* phases of the matter before determining how the Board's money should be spent. Brown's remarks, however, did not shed any new light on the questions that had been raised by the Trustees. He did, however, indicate that Hope College had recently also declared its willingness to do the same as Central for students wishing to attend that institution.

By early 1933, the Board of Education began backing away from its proposal. In a letter of January 23 of that year, Secretary Brown informed the Board of Trustees: "There is a great deal of sympathy for the Junior College in the minds of some of our members, and some sympathy in the minds of all. The Board will, without doubt, make appropriation to the Junior College." Brown also implied that the amount would be retroactive to the beginning of the current fiscal year. In determining exactly how much the appropriation should be as compared to the other two colleges, Brown asked the Trustees to furnish him with information on such matters as budget, size and training of the staff, average number of students during the previous three years, number

of college hours taught during that same period, and so forth. About
two months later, in late March 1933, Northwestern received a check
for $566.65 for the Junior College. This amount, together with what
had earlier been received for the Academy, brought Northwestern's
total share to 12 percent, which compared to 32 percent for Central and
37 percent for Hope. The remainder went to the other two academies
and the seminaries.

To understand why some members of the Board of Education felt as
they did about Northwestern, it can prove helpful to quote from a letter
received by President Heemstra from the Reverend John Powell several
months after the controversy died down. Powell, a pastor of the Reformed church at Bronxville, New York, was an influential member of
the Board, having served as chairman of the committee entrusted with
the task of working out the percentages allotted to each school. The
letter, dated November 16, 1933, was prompted by an appeal for financial assistance Northwestern was making to the consistories of various
churches in the East, including the one at Bronxville. The consistory
there decided not to give any aid, and asked its pastor to write a reply
to the appeal. Powell's letter pointed out two reasons for the consistory's
decision. In the first place, the Bronxville church was having budgetary
problems of its own, and in the second place, declared Powell,

our people are neither directly interested in church colleges in the
Middle West, nor do they believe very strongly in the whole project.
Practically all our young people here go to Eastern colleges, and the
people of our local church would feel much more like contributing to
some religious instruction in these institutions, the main support of
which is borne by some agencies.

We do not discount the work that your institution has done and is
doing, but we are inclined to feel that a more effective service of the
Kingdom of God might be rendered in this day and generation through
educational agencies. I think it is only fair to tell you of our attitude in
order that you might know definitely that however much we may admire
your devotion to this cause, we do not agree with you as to its necessity
and worth.

The annual amount received from the Board of Education remained
small for several years. Northwestern therefore continued trying to raise
money by other means as well. Most of these efforts took the same form
as those of the early 1930's, but there were two special endeavors. In
April 1935, the school took steps to refinance its standing indebtedness
through the issue of 120 bonds of $100 each, for a total amount of
$12,000. The bonds bore 4½ percent interest and were serially arranged
to mature at the rate of $1,000 a year beginning on April 15, 1937.

Paying off the bonds was not easy during the first few years, as is seen in this excerpt from the annual report of the president to the Board of Trustees dated April 22, 1937:

Of the thousand dollars now due, thus far only $300 has been paid off. This means that funds are needed to pay off the remaining $700 of these bonds. Furthermore, the interest due on these bonds amounts to approximately $500. Of this amount, interest on Endowment Funds provides only about $400. Hence an additional $100 must be provided to meet the interest. Therefore some $800 needs to be raised in order to retire the bonds now due, and make up the deficit needed for interest.

Nor did the situation with respect to retiring the bonds improve very soon, as is evident in the president's annual report of April 20, 1938:

The bonds which matured April 15 of last year were paid, but in order to pay the same we were necessitated to borrow $700 at the bank. Of this amount, $600 still stands as a loan at the bank. The second series of bonds in the amount of $1,000 were due April 15 of this year. Although interest on the bonds has been paid, the $1,000 of principal of these bonds due on the 15th of this month has not been paid, and at present there are no available funds to pay the same.

The need for funds to retire the bonds was, in a sense, only the tip of the iceberg. Additional receipts were sorely required for other projects as well. To quote again from the president's report of April 22, 1937:

Northwestern Junior College and Academy are . . . in need of building space at the present time. This has been repeatedly announced during the past years. Several teachers are without classrooms of their own, laboratory facilities are inadequate, library facilities are inadequate, [Academy] assembly and chapel must be crowded into the same room, there is no adequate parlor for the girls and none at all for the boys, there are no lunch-rooms, there is a lack of equipment in many departments, and need for repairs and renovation of buildings is constantly being faced. Furthermore a need for a girl's dormitory is felt at the beginning of every school year when efforts are made to increase the enrollment at Northwestern.

The second major endeavor aimed at solving the financial crisis was more ambitious. It originated with the Board of Trustees at their spring meeting in 1937, and called for a campaign to raise $125,000 from throughout the denomination as a whole. In adopting this approach, the

Board was undoubtedly motivated in part by similar campaigns being conducted or planned by two other educational institutions of the Reformed Church: Hope College was seeking to raise $300,000 and Central $500,000. At the time Northwestern's campaign was being discussed, President Heemstra informed the Trustees:

It has been repeatedly emphasized in other sections of the church that the northern part of the Reformed Church is responsible for the growth and development of Northwestern Junior College and Academy. If this is the case, then our responsibility to this institution supercedes our responsibility to all other institutions. We cannot afford to permit other campaigns to set the needs of this institution in the background at this time when a program of expansion and increased facilities for this institution is, and has been, an outstanding necessity.

The purpose of the campaign was to clear the school of its debts, to rebuild the endowment fund that had been diverted to the payment of debts, and to expand the school's physical plant. More specifically, the money was to be used as follows: $10,000 for debt retirement, $83,000 for the endowment fund, $20,000 for a dormitory, and $12,000 for a library. There was at this time, $17,000 in the endowment fund, which would then be raised to $100,000 if the campaign were completely successful. The plan called for raising $50,000 from private individuals and $75,000 from the churches. After General Synod approved the campaign, Dr. Walter A. Stevenson of Milwaukee, Wisconsin, was engaged to manage it under the direction and control of Northwestern's Board of Trustees. Stevenson's duties began on June 1, 1938. His salary was set at $300 per month, but he was to pay his own traveling expenses and the contract could be terminated by either party upon thirty days written notice. Stevenson's services were dispensed with on November 1, 1938, apparently because the results of the campaign thus far had not, in the minds of the Trustees, justified his salary.

After the dismissal of Stevenson, the Reverend Hubert Muilenburg was engaged to carry on the campaign among the churches of the Particular Synods of Albany, New Brunswick, and New York. He had already achieved a measure of success as Northwestern's field representative and solicitor among the churches in the Particular Synod of Chicago. For his services, Muilenburg was paid $100 monthly salary and 3¢ a mile for expenses. President Heemstra himself also spent considerable time contracting churches and influential persons in the East, primarily in New York.

Although the depression was by no means over, the financial situation gradually improved during the late 1930's. Total receipts rose from $18,363 during the 1936-1937 fiscal year to $22,369 in the following year and to $25,594 for 1938-1939. The improved financial situation, however, could hardly be attributed to the fund-raising campaign that got underway in the spring of 1938, since the increase in contributions had begun during the previous year. Moreover, income from the churches remained virtually unchanged—in fact, it actually declined by about $500 between 1938 and 1939. The additional income at this time came primarily from tuition, which increased by almost $2,500 due to a larger enrollment, and from private donors, who contributed almost $4,000. It should be noted, however, that although the results of the financial campaign among the churches were rather meager at first, the campaign must be judged a success. Important contacts were made and interest awakened in a region where not much had been known about Northwestern before, all of which would result in more financial support when economic conditions improved.

IX

World War II and the Postwar Years

The history of Northwestern from 1941 to 1951 was in many respects a repeat of previous decades. Problems over finances remained as did the need to increase the size of the physical plant. There were also the usual concerns over faculty qualifications, student enrollment, and accreditation. Questions about curriculum and extracurricular activities also continued to arise. Some of these problems were compounded by America's entry into World War II. Enrollment in the Junior College, for example, dropped by almost 75 percent by the close of the war. Fortunately the situation gradually improved in the late 1940's. Enrollment began reaching record highs, and the physical plant grew in terms of both new construction and the acquiring of additional land.

With respect to Northwestern and the war, it is interesting to note that the isolationist view of the world politics that generally prevailed in the upper mid-West during the 1930's was shared by a significant segment of Northwestern's student body. Thus, on April 12, 1935, the students of both the Academy and Junior College joined in the nationwide "strike" against war by gathering in front of Zwemer Hall and hearing an address by one of the Board members, the Reverend Bert Brower, a veteran of World War I and a strong advocate of peace. Following the address, one of the student leaders, Benjamin Ver Steeg, proposed adoption of four resolutions: refusal of students to take up arms in an aggressive war, government ownership and operation of munition plants, abolition of ROTC programs at state universities, and cancellation of naval maneuvers scheduled to take place in the Pacific Ocean the following month. When given an opportunity to vote on these resolutions, the students voted overwhelmingly in their favor. The vote against the planned naval maneuvers, for example, was 112 to 12.

Articles having a pro-isolationist bias also appeared from time to time in the *Beacon*. An editorial of April 29, 1935, for example, urged readers to be careful about being hoodwinked again, as in the recent World War, when "our silk-hatted politicians in their ermine robes and with their toy water guns" told us that our intervention in that war was necessary for the protection of our citizens. Even more to the point was an article of February 27, 1939, written by Professor Cecil McLaughlin of the Department of Education and Psychology. It was a classic defense of isolationism, containing all the standard arguments: George Washington's warning in his farewell address urging Americans to stay out of Europe's affairs; the failure of the last war to make the world safe for democracy; the huge debt still remaining from that war; the propaganda being put out by the armament manufacturers; and the natural barriers surrounding the North American continent which would protect her from German, Italian, and Japanese bombs. As late as November 13, 1939, after war had broken out in Europe, the *Beacon* carried an article declaring that democracy would have a better chance of surviving this "new war" if the United States stayed home. "If we really value our American institutions," it stated, "we will not endanger them a second time by leaving them unprotected while we sail off to fight in a foreign war."

The fact that many of the students shared the isolationist views of the area is not surprising considering they also tended to identify with the conservative political views of the area's voters. For example, in the presidential elections of 1932, a straw poll taken among the students gave 80 votes to Hoover, 28 to Roosevelt, and 1 to Norman Thomas. The results were similar in 1936, with 90 for Landon, 48 for Roosevelt, and 2 for Lemke, and again in 1940, when Wilkie polled 77, Roosevelt 30, and Thomas 6. The faculty participated in only one of these polls— that of 1932—and it cast all eleven votes for Hoover.

As the region's mood regarding isolation changed and growing concern was shown about the threat of fascism, a change of thinking could also be found among Northwestern's student body. No longer did the *Beacon* carry articles supporting isolation and denouncing war as an instrument of policy. Instead, occasional articles of a super-patriotic nature began appearing. Thus, an editorial of April 8, 1940, expressed strong criticism over the use of a worn-out American flag as a "stopper" for a leaky pipe in the attic of Zwemer Hall. Readers were reminded that instead of treating a tattered flag as if it were "a monarch in exile," it should be disposed of in the customary way of burning it and scattering the ashes. "Zwemer Hall," declared the article, "must be a hall of patriotism, as well as a hall of intellect. The future of America depends upon the patriotism of the younger generation. True patriotism includes respect for the American flag. . . . In these days of Communist and Fascist ideas let us insure our freedom and equality by remaining true to the American flag." It is also interesting to note that the *Beacon* raised no questions when discussions were going on among the politicians concerning peacetime conscription—not even when, on October

16, 1940, four faculty members and six students had to register with their local draft boards in accordance with the Selective Service Act.

The Selective Service Act and America's entry into the war cut deeply into student enrollment as young men went into military service. Although Academy enrollment remained quite stationary at about fifty students, the number of Junior College students dropped from a high of 128 in 1939-1940 to a low of 33 in 1943-1944. As might be expected, there was a significant numerical dispartiy between the two sexes—only 5 of the 22 freshmen enrolled in the fall of 1943 were males. Although the Junior College was approved for reserve officer training for both the Army and Navy, very few young men took advantage of this program. By it, freshmen and sophomores could enlist immediately in the reserves but remain in college until the end of the second year. Following this, after passing certain qualifying examinations, the participants could go on active duty as commissioned officers.

Because tuition was one of Northwestern's major sources of revenue, the decline in enrollment hurt its financial standing. For example, tuition income during the 1943-1944 academic year was $9,000 less than the previous year. Northwestern's decline in enrollment was higher than that of most schools. President Heemstra reported in March 1944 that whereas the average loss in college enrollment throughout the United States was somewhat less than 50 percent, Northwestern's enrollment in the Junior College was down almost 70 percent as compared with the previous year—having dropped from 114 to 33. Fortunately, Northwestern demonstrated, as it had during the depression years, an ability to carry on in difficult times—although twenty of Iowa's junior colleges closed down during the war. Northwestern was able to remain open primarily because of very careful budgeting and because Academy enrollment was not greatly affected by the war. It also received assistance from the War Emergency Fund established by the Reformed Church to help its educational institutions during the emergency.

As was to be expected, the faculty, too, was adversely affected by the war. In terms of size, the instructional staff was reduced from fourteen in 1941 to ten in 1945. In part, this was due to declining enrollment, but it was also the result of a shortage of teachers because of conscription and high wages being paid in defense plants. Faculty turnover was also great—for example, in 1943, there were six new instructors (all women), and in 1945, five of the ten instructors were new. Because of difficulty in obtaining qualified replacements during the war years, accrediting bodies occasionally had to make allowances to permit instructors to teach courses for which they did not have the necessary background.

The academic program also had to be adjusted, and this became increasingly necessary with each passing year. Adjustments were necessary in part because of the limited staff, but at the college level they also resulted from declining enrollments. In the 1943-1944 school year, sixty-six semester hours of Junior College courses were dropped from the 221 semester hours offered the previous year—a cut of about 30 percent. The distribution of the number of hours dropped from each department was as follows:

Chemistry	11	Greek	16
Economics	3	History	6
French	14	Mathematics	10
German	6		

In the spring of 1945, the last year of the war, Dr. Heemstra reported:

Our curriculum in both departments has been cut down to an absolute minimum. Outside of the Normal Course, it will be difficult for students in the second year of college to find courses to complete the two years of college; and in the Academy, electives have more and more been eliminated, so that students now coming with advanced standing have difficulty in being able to register for full schedules.

The end of the war in August 1945 saw Northwestern quickly "pick up" where it had left off when the conflict began. One of the most pressing problems concerned enlarging the physical plant. In 1941, the campus comprised about ten acres, on which were three buildings: Zwemer Hall, Science Hall, and the president's manse, all located on the eastern half of the campus. The western half, where Heemstra Hall and Ramaker Library are located today, was open land used primarily as an athletic field. Zwemer Hall, constructed in 1894, housed the biology, chemistry, and physics laboratories, several classrooms (which also served as offices for the instructors), the library, the Academy assembly, and the administrative offices. Science Hall, constructed in 1923, served various purposes. On the first floor were three classrooms, a music studio, a room specially fitted with a stage and curtains for small dramatic productions, and locker rooms for men and women. The second story consisted of an auditorium with a balcony on three sides. It was used primarily for chapel and athletic events but it also had a stage equipped with scenic backdrops and a curtain for large dramatic and musical productions. As an auditorium, Science Hall could seat approximately one thousand people.

A long-standing problem at Northwestern was that of obtaining housing for women students. Although this question had been brought to the attention of the Board of Trustees several times, it was not until 1940 that a special committee was created to investigate the matter more closely. It met several times throughout 1940 consulting architectural engineers from Sioux City regarding specific plans and materials and corresponding with various lending agencies. The committee also made an inspection tour of dormitories at Trinity and Briar Cliff Colleges in Sioux City and sought the advice of the Department of Engineering at Iowa State College at Ames. On the basis of these findings, the Board passed the following resolution on April 16, 1941:

Resolved, That the Board approve the plans for the building of a Girls Dormitory as thus far formulated and authorize the President to proceed with efforts to secure funds for the construction of this building through the solicitation of individuals, churches, or organizations. Further, that when one-half of the funds necessary . . . shall have been secured or satisfactorily pledged or promised, the Executive Committee be authorized to issue bonds for the remainder of the cost of the building, and to proceed with the construction of the same.

The need for a girls' dormitory was also presented to General Synod at its annual meeting in June 1941.

America's entry into World War II delayed the implementation of plans for the dormitory. Although an architectural firm in Sioux City assured the institution early in 1942 that there would be little difficulty in getting the necessary material and that costs had not gone up significantly, the Executive Committee decided to postpone construction "until finances were more certain and government restrictions and priorities became less severe." A decline in college enrollment during the war also made the need for student housing somewhat less pressing. It was agreed, however, that the solicitation of funds for a girls' dormitory should continue. By the close of the war, the dormitory fund totaled approximately $60,000.

In anticipation of increased enrollment after the war, the school purchased a house located about one half block north of the campus. It was remodeled and opened in the fall of 1945 with accommodations for thirteen women and a housemother. Its dining room was of sufficient size to seat forty people for meals. The building was named Dykstra Hall in honor of Miss Anna Dykstra of Firth, Nebraska, who had bequeathed a significant sum of money to Northwestern a short time earlier. In the summer of 1947, Dykstra Hall was enlarged at a cost of $11,000, by constructing a 26 by 28 foot three-story addition to the west end. The added space provided rooms for sixteen more girls, plus dining facilities to accomodate sixty persons. The rates for Dykstra Hall for the 1947-1948 school year were as follows:

Board and room, per semester $145.00
Room only, per semester 45.00
Board only, 7 days per week 7.20
Board only, 5 days per week 6.00

All students (both men and women) as well as faculty members were permitted to avail themselves of the dining facilities at Dykstra Hall.

The need for dormitory accommodations having been alleviated somewhat by Dykstra Hall, the Board of Trustees began giving attention to another pressing problem, namely, the need for more classroom and laboratory space. Already in 1941, President Heemstra called the attention of General Synod to this problem:

These two buildings [that is, Zwemer Hall and Science Hall] afford inadequate classroom space and insufficient laboratory space for the science work. Many of the classrooms are too small. The music department, housed beneath the gymnasium, without sound-proof ceiling is greatly hampered in its work, and is also too small for work with the College Mixed Chorus, Academy Choir, Band, Orchestra, etc. There are no recreational rooms, and the only Ladies Parlor is located in a basement room in Zwemer Hall. One of the outstanding needs in this line, therefore, is more adequate classroom space, and rooms for auxiliary purposes, and more adequate laboratory space and facilities.

College enrollment increased after the war from 49 students in the fall of 1945 to 125 in the fall of 1946, and the likelihood that this increase would continue, further magnified the need for more classroom space. Initial discussions favored the construction of a unit joining the southern extremities of Zwemer Hall and Science Hall into a single U-shaped building, at an estimated cost of $25,000 to $30,000. This solution was soon discarded, however, in favor of a three-story structure attached to the south end of Science Hall. The general contract was awarded to Holtz Construction Company of Sioux City, but local Orange City firms were given the plumbing, heating, and electrical contracts. Construction got underway in the spring of 1947 and was completed in time for the 1948-1949 fall term. The addition measured approximately thirty-two by seventy-two feet, adding about 6,500 square feet of floor space. It was designed primarily to serve three departments, with physics on the first floor, music on the second, and biology occupying the third. The cost, including fixtures and furniture, was slightly more than $55,000.

In June 1949, the Executive Committee authorized the purchase of approximately thirteen acres directly east of campus. This tract, including a house and some other buildings, belonged to the William Reickhoff estate. The price was $19,000, one-half of which was paid on the date of purchase and the remainder on March 1, 1950, when the school took possession of the property. A "corn-gleaning" bee that fall was participated in by students and faculty as well as townspeople in order to raise funds to help pay for the landscaping. The corn was stored on the campus until it was ready to be shelled and sold at public auction for approximately $3,000. Plans were to use the newly acquired property to accommodate outdoor athletic activities.

Dykstra Hall was considered from the beginning as only a temporary dormitory for women. Even with its enlargement in the summer of 1947, it was unable to accommodate all the women who wanted to be housed there. Moreover, the enrollment of an increasing number of veterans caused growing demand for male student housing. For a brief period, the vacated Doornink hospital downtown was rented to meet this problem, but it was only a matter of time before other provisions had to be made. In his annual report to the Board of Trustees in March

Homecoming, 1948-1949

1949, President Heemstra declared that the situation in this respect was becoming acute. The logical solution was to construct the long-planned-for residence hall for women, and then convert Dykstra Hall into men's housing.

As early as June 27, 1946, the Executive Committee authorized the drawing up of specifications for a women's residence hall, but stop-gap measures and the need for more classrooms and laboratories delayed implementation until the late summer of 1949. The date for submission of bids was set for September 27, and it was agreed that the building should be completed by August 1, 1950, with a $50 penalty for each day beyond that date. The general contract was let to N.W. Wiltgen and Sons of Le Mars.

The four-story brick building, located on the northwest corner of the campus, cost approximately $195,000 and had accommodations for eighty girls. The lower floor contained a dining hall and snack bar, open to both sexes. Appropriately, the Board of Trustees decided unanimously to name the new addition Heemstra Hall, in honor of the man who had worked so hard for its realization and who had served the institution so ably as president since 1928. After the completion of Heemstra Hall, Dykstra Hall served for a brief period as a residence for married students, but was soon converted into men's housing. Because the dining facilities were no longer required there, they were turned into rooms, thereby increasing the building's capacity to forty students.

Ground-breaking for Heemstra Hall

The general budget for the 1941-1942 school year was approximately $30,000. This seems very small when compared with those of later years, nevertheless even this amount put a severe strain on the school because of the lingering effects of the depression. For example, as of June 1, 1942, about $6,000 were still needed to meet current operating expenses before the close of the fiscal year on August 1. In addition, $1,000 in unpaid salaries and $500 in other unpaid bills were still being carried over from the previous year. Thus, with only two months remaining in the fiscal year, $7,500 were needed to avoid a deficit. By the close of the decade the general operating budget had more than tripled. This was due primarily to the growth in the instructional staff and higher salaries as well as higher maintenance costs resulting from the enlarged physical plant.

To help meet the steady increase in the budget during the postwar years, tuition was raised from time to time. For the Junior College, it was raised from $70 in 1945 to $85 in 1947, to $110 in the following year, and to $125 in 1951. Academy tuition was also raised—from $25 in 1947, to $37.50 in 1948, and to $45 in 1949. Although Academy enrollment remained quite constant during these years at about fifty students, the increase in the number of college students from 49 in 1945 to 161 in 1951 was significant and made the increase in college tuition doubly important. Despite these favorable developments, considerably more revenue was required to meet Northwestern's needs.

In seeking funds from sources farther afield, Northwestern experienced stiff competition from its two sister institutions, Hope and Central, which together with the denominational Board of Education, seemed at times to view the Orange City school as an inferior "stepchild." Several developments during the 1940's did nothing to allay this view. On these occasions, Dr. Heemstra worked energetically to establish Northwestern's rightful position vis-a-vis the other schools. Thus, on May 19, 1944, following discussion about employing a public relations man to solicit funds for all three schools, he made it clear that Northwestern would no longer be satisfied with the ratio by which common denominational funds had been distributed among the three institutions in the past—45 percent for Hope, 40 percent for Central, and 15 percent for Northwestern.

Similarly, in March 1945 the Board of Trustees, under Heemstra's leadership, strongly objected when the Board of Education asked Northwestern to wait with its planned expansion program to raise $150,000 until Hope and Central had completed their united program to raise $500,000 for new dormitories. Through its secretary, Willard Brown, the Board of Education declared that because Northwestern had completed its campaign for a new dormitory (which was not entirely true) and because Hope and Central had postponed action involving new dormitories, "the Junior College should now be willing to give the two senior colleges the right of way." Secretary Brown concluded his remarks by stating: "I think this is sufficiently clear so that I do not need to make any further comments."

If Brown thought this would end the matter, he was very much mistaken. Dr. Heemstra, in his report of March 19, 1945 to the Board of Trustees, was quick to point out the error in this reasoning:

Since the Junior College was organized [seventeen years ago], Central and Hope have each added two very substantial buildings to their campuses, while no additions have been made to the Academy plant where the Junior College is housed. The total cost of the two new buildings at Hope was probably nearly $600,000 and at Central nearly $500,000. Surely the raising of $50,000 for a Girls' Dormitory at Northwestern should not now be considered sufficient reason to deny the Junior College the privilege of raising funds for its imperative needs, until after these senior colleges have raised another $500,000.

Northwestern's Board of Trustees emphatically supported Dr. Heemstra in his appraisal of the situation and agreed to bring the matter to the attention of General Synod if necessary. The controversy was finally resolved by developing a unified expansion program among the three institutions to raise $650,000, of which $150,000 would be allocated to Northwestern.

One of Northwestern's problems in resisting the efforts to close the school during the 1930's had been the fact that its existence and importance were not well known. This continued to be the case during the 1940's, as was clearly brought out in a letter of early 1945 to Dr. Heemstra from the Reverend Albert Mansen, a Reformed pastor at Martin, Michigan and member of the Board of Trustees from the Classis of Kalamazoo.

In regard to the interest of the churches of the Kalamazoo Classis in the church-related schools—the churches all feel keenly that our schools are necessary to the maintaining and propagating of the Christian Faith, and to the maintaining of the Reformed Church as a distinctive denomination. The feeling of some toward Northwestern Jr. College and Academy, however, is somewhat different. Some of the men of this area know very little of the Reformed Church west of Chicago, and their feeling is that the Jr. College is a local institution. Such an attitude, of course, is not right, for the Jr. College does have General Synod's approval, but such an attitude does carry weight with consistories and churches, so that they are rather unresponsive to the needs of Northwestern.

Two important steps were taken during the 1940's to make Northwestern better known throughout the denomination, namely, increasing the geographical representation of the Board of Trustees and adding a public relations person to the staff. In pursuing the first course of conduct, the membership of the Board was increased to fifty-two by 1951. Although delegates from local classes were still dominant, with West Sioux and East Sioux each having six, Germania and Dakota each having three, and Minnesota having two, eleven other classes had one each. These included Chicago, Erie, Grand Rapids, Holland, Illiana, Illinois, Kalamazoo, Muskegon, Pella, Pleasant Prairie, and Wisconsin. In addition, there were eighteen delegates from the Board of Trustees at large and three from General Synod. Of the latter, two were from New York and one was from New Jersey.

With reference to a public relations person, it had been suggested several times that Northwestern should add someone to the administrative staff who could devote himself to canvassing churches and private individuals for funds. As early as April 22, 1942, the Board adopted the following report from a special committee appointed to "wrestle with the problem of [finding] ways and means to raise funds" for the school:

It is detrimental to the school that its president and faculty must be constantly under the shadow of the financial burden. The financial burden does not need to be there in view of the prosperity of the surround-

The Board of Trustees, 1945-1946

ing territory. There is money, but the problem is how to get it for the school. There seems to be lacking the feeling of loyalty and responsibility toward our own faithful servant—the Northwestern Junior College and Academy. . . . If the churches are to really give for Northwestern . . . they must appreciate what she means to them and the Kingdom of Christ. It must be shown that [she] really fills a needed place in the life of the church. We need a man who is gifted along the line of discovering from graduates, as to what Northwestern Junior College and Academy has meant and means to them; from the community, as to what she has meant to the community; from the church, what she has meant and means to the church for world evangelism. . . . We feel that if this is done in an era of good will, optimism and more liberal contributions will follow.

At first, part-time people were hired to carry out the intent of the above report, but in 1944 the Reverend Henry Vande Brake was employed as full-time director of church relations, a title later changed to director of public relations. His primary duties involved seeking funds for the institution through personal contacts with individuals and churches and, "at intervals as the president may direct, . . . the solicitation of students and promoting the enrollment of the school." When the Reverend Vande Brake left in 1947 to return to fulltime preaching, the position was left vacant until the appointment of the Reverend Everett Van Engelenhoven, who began work on September 1, 1949. A short time later, the primary responsibility for recruiting students was turned over to others, at which time Van Engelenhoven's title became director of development. Reverend Van, as he was popularly known, served ably in this capacity until his retirement in 1971.

Increasing the membership of the Board of Trustees and the appointment of a director of public relations, along with other developments, helped awaken enthusiasm for Northwestern and its expansion program. During the fiscal year of 1949-1950, for example, a number of gifts ranging from $500 to $5,000 were received from private individuals. In addition, the Reformed churches of Orange City agreed to raise $55,000 for the Dormitory Fund, and the First Reformed Church of Sioux Center adopted a plan to raise $50,000 during the next five years. The United Advance campaign which got underway in 1946 among the three Reformed Church colleges was pressed with renewed vigor. Northwestern's share of this program amounted to $143,456 by 1951. In that year, a new unified campaign, known as the Dollar Drive, was initiated among the three schools to raise funds for emergencies. It is interesting to note that of the undesignated funds raised in this campaign, 22 percent of the total was designated for Northwestern. Although it had hoped the percentage would be higher, this nevertheless represented a gain of 7 percent over what had frequently been past practice.

The endowment fund also showed considerable improvement during the late 1940's. For many years it had not been uncommon to borrow money from this fund to meet various institutional needs, and sometimes these loans were slow in being repaid. For example, as late as 1945, more than $17,000 was still due on sums that had been borrowed in the mid-1920's for the construction of Science Hall. There had also been occasional borrowing from the endowment fund to meet current expenses during the depression years, and as late as 1944, $3,100 was borrowed to assist in the purchase of what became Dykstra Hall. Beginning in the late 1940's, however, the endowment fund was placed on a more secure footing as more of these "inactive" loans were repaid and the money was invested in interest-bearing enterprises. By 1951, the amount of these investments totaled $57,902.23.

Financial problems and the growth of the physical plant were, of course, only a part of what transpired during the period 1941-1951. Of equal—one might even say, of greater—importance was the role played by the faculty. As was noted, the faculty was adversely affected by the war, but this situation gradually improved in the postwar period. By 1951, the staff consisted of eighteen full-time teachers and administrators. The latter included (besides the president) a dean, a dean of women, a registrar, a director of public relations, and a business manager. There also were a part-time admissions counsellor and a part-time campus pastor. The president and dean of women taught only part-time, but the dean, the registrar, and the librarian taught almost full-time. A normal load at this time was the equivalent of fifteen college credit hours, but it was not unusual for instructors to teach more than that.

Although none of the instructors or administrators had an earned doctorate in 1951, several of them had taken graduate work beyond the masters degree. In 1948, for example, five of the eleven staff members who renewed their contracts earned additional credit attending summer school. Such professional advancement was encouraged by the administration. Beginning in 1949, the institution began giving staff members $100 to help cover their summer school expenses, a figure that was raised to $150 in 1951. Also in 1951, a leave of absence policy to do graduate work was instituted by which a faculty member was granted a loan of $100 per month at 2 percent interest for a period not to exceed fifteen months. The loan could be repaid by what was termed "teaching service," in which case the amount of the loan was reduced by one-sixth for each year of service following the leave of absence.

Instructional salaries in 1941 ranged from $900 to $1,500 on a nine-month basis. They rose steadily after the war, ranging from $1,800 to $2,600 by 1946, and $2,200 to $3,200 by 1949. From time to time during the late 1940's the Faculty Committee of the Board of Trustees discussed the possibility of drafting a salary schedule based on the degrees held and the length of service to the institution. After careful study and examining the salary schedules of other Iowa schools, the following was adopted by the Board at its regular metting in March 1951:

	1st year	6th year	11th year	16th year
A.B. Degree	$2,600	$3,100	$3,600	Same
A.M. Degree	2,800	3,550	4,000	$4,200
Ph.D. Degree	3,400	4,100	4,600	4,800

As can be seen, the step-up in salaries varied from year to year. For persons with master degrees, for example, the annual raise was $150 for the first five years, but only $90 during the next five, and $40 after that. The salary schedule made no mention of increases for those who had taken graduate work beyond the degree currently held, but the Faculty Committee of the Board was permitted to make exceptions to the schedule when it was thought necessary. In late 1950, the federal government made Social Security available to employees of non-profit institutions. Members of Northwestern's staff immediately expressed interest in this program and requested it be made available, to which the Board of Trustees agreed in March 1951.

As was noted, Academy enrollment fluctuated little during the war, remaining quite constant at about fifty students, but enrollment in the Junior College, as has also been noted, was not that fortunate. After the war, however, college enrollment increased as returning servicemen took advantage of the G.I. Bill, although the continuation of the draft offset some of the gain. Junior College enrollment rose from 49 in the 1945-1946 school year to 125 in the following year, and continued to increase after that. In the fall of 1946, about one-third of the student body consisted of veterans.

The religious make-up of the students changed very little during the period 1941-1951. Thus, of the 158 students enrolled in the Junior College in 1950-1951, 111 were Reformed and 23 were Christian Reformed. Of the remaining 24 students, 9 were Presbyterian, and 4 were Methodist. Other denominations were represented by only 1 or 2 students. Of the 51 students enrolled in the Academy, 22 were Reformed and 29 were Christian Reformed. With respect to geographical origins of the student body, the great majority continued to have their roots in the immediate area.

Y. M. Cabinet, 1948

As was true of so many facets of Northwestern's history after the war, the academic program of the Junior College underwent considerable adjustment. In particular, losses in the curriculum had to be replaced. On March 19, 1947, President Heemstra announced that seventy more semester hours were being offered than in the previous year, and that approximately forty-five more would be added in the following year. Teacher training and courses in business remained the most popular programs. During the war, teaching certificates were even easier to obtain than before. In fact, students who had taken the right courses were awarded "war-time emergency certificates" for secondary teaching with only sixty hours of college work, and it was possible for a person to teach in a rural elementary school with less than one year of college work. Teaching requirements were tightened up, however, soon after the war. In 1948, the Iowa Commission on Teacher Education and Professional Standards announced that by 1952, two years of college work would be required of *all* elementary teachers, and that ultimately this would be increased to four years.

Because the Academy's enrollment did not change significantly during the war and because it was easier to obtain secondary school teachers, it was not affected quite as adversely as was the case with the Junior College. Moreover, the Academy program of study never had been very broad, as is clearly seen in this statement of 1941: "It will be observed . . . that the subjects offered in [the Academy] are not many, and are such as have received the approval of time. The object is not to touch upon many things, but to acquire a thorough grasp of a few." Virtually the same statement was still being made a decade later. Although the

Classical Course for Academy students was still listed in the school catalogue in 1941, it was no longer being offered and even its description disappeared from the catalogue in 1943. In 1949, the Modern Classical Course was also dropped, leaving only two remaining—the Scientific and the General.

X

Change and Continuity: the 1950's

The decade of the fifties was one of transformation but also one of continuity. The Junior College became fully accredited and soon expanded into a four-year school, even as plans were made to phase the Academy out of existence. With the development of a senior college program came an increase in the staff and an enlarged curriculum, as well as an expanded building program—all of which caused the school's budget to triple in size. Despite these alterations, several characteristics of the institution remained unchanged. Except for a few additions in the late 1950's, staff members were virtually of the same background and training as in past decades. The ethnic and geographical roots of the student body also underwent little change. The factor that especially gave continuity to the school, however, was the conviction that the Christian faith could not be separated from any meaningful education.

A memorable era in the history of Northwestern came to an end in 1951 when Dr. Jacob Heemstra officially stepped down as president after having served in that capacity for twenty-three years. He tendered his resignation in March 1950, to take effect on August 1 of the following year, asking to be appointed to serve in some other position after that date. With the arrival of a successor, Dr. Heemstra remained on the staff as a full-time instructor and head of the Department of Religion until the summer of 1957, when his duties were reduced to part-time. He enjoyed his new role only briefly. On October 23, 1958, he suffered a fatal heart attack and passed on to his reward at the age of seventy.

Upon receiving word in the spring of 1950 of Heemstra's impending resignation, the Board of Trustees elected a special committee of five members with power to make nominations for a successor. On the basis of its recommendations, the position was offered in March, 1951, to Dr. Frederick H. Wezeman of Chicago. The new president was eminently qualified for the position, having not only a broad educational background—which included degrees in science, law, and theology—but considerable experience in school administration as well. The latter included twenty-four years as principal of Chicago Christian High School (1927-1951) and six years as president of Chicago Christian College

(1931-1937). During the immediate years before coming to Northwestern, he also served as associate pastor of the Oak Park Christian Reformed Church and as guest preacher at the Evangelical and Reformed Peace Memorial Church, both of which were in Chicago. Despite a heavy schedule, he found time to serve on several charitable organizations, and was a member of the Illinois Bar and the Chicago Bar Association.

President Wezeman came to Northwestern in the fall of 1951 determined to carry to fruition the work begun by Dr. Heemstra and others. In particular, he was anxious to raise the intellectual standing of the institution, as is clearly shown in the opening remarks of his first annual report to the Board of Trustees in March 1952:

The main business of a college is to produce trained minds. . . . It is often forgotten, however, that getting a trained mind is hard work. Many want learning to be painless. It must be made "interesting." In many colleges, as a noted educator recently observed, "the whole apparatus of football, fraternities and fun is a means by which education is made palatable to those who have no business in it." Things trivial and frivolous are the preoccupation of many in our day. Good Christian education requires that adequate emphasis be placed unceasingly on scholarship, on intellectual attainment, on the essentials for which a school exists, and that the incidentals be kept in their proper secondary place.

The new president was quick to add, however, that intellectual enlargement by itself was not enough.

We want a trained mind to be counter-balanced by a sanctified heart. These two belong together. Such a unified conception of life calls for and justifies Christian education. . . . Principles are indispensable to Christian education. Only principles can bring unity and timeless purpose into the whole program. For us, for our institution, these are the principles of our Christian faith, our Reformed doctrine, our Calvinistic world- and life-view.

With a president who held views such as the above, Northwestern could not help but continue to make forward strides. His tenure in office, however, was brief—especially when compared with that of his immediate predecessor. On September 30, 1954, Dr. Wezeman informed the Executive Committee that he was resigning at the end of the fall semester. A committee of five was thereupon appointed to make recommendations for a new president. Meanwhile, until a replacement could be found, primary responsibility for running the school was placed in the hands of an administrative committee consisting of the dean, the director of public relations, and the registrar and director of admissions.

The choice for a new president fell on a young man only thirty-one years of age—Dr. Preston J. Stegenga, a professor of history and political science at Berea College in Kentucky. A graduate of Hope College (class of 1947) and holding a master's degree from Columbia University and a doctorate from the University of Michigan, Dr. Stegenga's interest in the Reformed Church was well-established long before coming to Northwestern. He was the son of a Reformed minister, the Reverend Miner Stegenga, and the author of several articles pertaining to the denomination and of *Anchor of Hope*, a history of Hope College. His long-time contacts with various friends from throughout the Reformed Church in America proved to be extremely helpful in broadening the denominational relationships of Northwestern.

The new president began his duties in the fall of 1955 and remained for eleven years until 1966. As explained in his first report to the Board of Trustees, he was determined to carry on in the tradition of those who held the office before him: "Northwestern of today must continue to progress as a tribute to the devotion of all those connected with our institution in the past. Surely, the achievements of the past will serve as a challenge for greater Christian service in the future."

Of the many challenges facing Northwestern during the decade of the fifties, two of the most significant were the acquisition of regional accreditation for the Junior College program and expansion into a four-year college. With respect to accreditation, the Academy had been accredited by the North Central Association of Colleges and Secondary Schools since 1930, but the Junior College refrained for many years from seeking such membership. It was accredited, however, at an early date by the Iowa Committee on Secondary Schools and College Relations and by the State Board of Educational Examiners. The former was concerned with general accreditation and the latter with teacher certification.

In early 1948, the question of whether to seek accreditation was taken out of Northwestern's hands. On February 13 of that year, the Iowa State Board of Educational Examiners set a definite date—September 1, 1950—by which teacher training institutions were expected to be accredited by North Central. Because it was essential that Northwestern fulfill this requirement if the school were to continue its work of training teachers, steps were immediately taken to meet the deadline. Faculty committees were appointed to study various aspects of the problem and consultants were brought to the campus to make recommendations. A committee of faculty and Board members also visited Waldorf College at Forest City, Iowa in the fall of 1949. This was considered advisable because Waldorf had recently been admitted to North Central membership.

A lengthy report was filed with North Central in late 1950, and on January 8 and 9 of the following year, two of its representatives visited the campus. As reported in the *Beacon*, the two men "inspected the buildings, attended chapel exercises, held conferences with the Administrative Committee, Faculty, and students. They ate at the College Dining Hall and in general looked at almost everything on the college campus." Upon completing their visit, the representatives reported their findings to North Central's Board of Review. The next step occurred in April 1951 when President Heemstra and Dean Edwin Aalberts met with the Review Board during its annual meeting in Chicago. To everyone's dismay, Northwestern's application was turned down.

The reasons for refusing accreditation were many and varied. The overall qualifications of the faculty were criticized as were the heavy teaching loads of several staff members. The low salaries and marginal fringe benefits enjoyed by the faculty were also noted. Library facilities were likewise declared inadequate. Finally, although the school was described as having excellent community support, it was not, in the view of the examiners, capitalizing sufficiently on this fact. The curriculum concentrated too much on teacher training and on pre-professional courses, while giving only limited attention to liberal arts courses for students in the community who simply wanted two years of college.

With the resignation of Dr. Heemstra, the problem of achieving accreditation fell on the shoulders of Dr. Wezeman, who gave the matter high priority. As he expressed it, academic credits from the Junior College must be "as negotiable as a U.S. dollar bill anywhere in the nation." His announced aim was to achieve full accreditation by the spring of 1953. To achieve this goal, he enlisted the help of the entire faculty in drafting a "self-survey." Committees were assigned to study the weaknesses and strengths of the school, including the faculty, curriculum, library, student services, finances, and physical plant. March 15, 1952, was set as the deadline when all committee reports had to be completed. The significance of this date elicited the following interesting observation from the editor of the *Beacon*: "March 15 has had an ominous sound since the days of Julius Caesar. If it isn't the soothsayer with his 'Beware the Ides of March,' its the income tax. Now a new deadline has been added to the woe of faculty members." Based on the committee findings, an elaborate report totaling 264 pages was submitted to North Central on July 1, 1952.

Once again, a delegation from North Central visited the campus for a personal inspection. Fortunately, steps had been taken to correct weaknesses that had been pointed out during the first North Central examination or had been uncovered in the self-survey. This time the report of the examiners was favorable, and in March 1953 the North Central Executive Committee approved the Junior College for full membership.

If final honors for acquiring Junior College accreditation can be attributed to the efforts of President Wezeman, final credit for expanding the institution into a four-year college must go to his successor, Dr. Stegenga. It must be noted, however, that discussions on this matter had been going on for many years. Already in March 1945, the Board of Trustees expressed the "hope that in due time this institution may grow to the proportions of a Senior College," and in the late fall of 1947, a special delegation from the Executive Committee met with the denominational Board of Education to explain that the "due time" was fast approaching.

Steps were also taken to obtain General Synod's approval for the change. This approval was necessary because in allowing the Academy to add a college program in 1928, Synod stipulated that permission was being granted with the understanding that "the institution should remain a Junior College unless authorized by General Synod to expand." In March 1948, the Board of Trustees therefore overtured Synod to remove the limitation. The overture stated that the Board had no intention of establishing a four-year program *immediately*, but simply wished to obtain the necessary approval and then work toward expansion at its own discretion. General Synod referred the request to a special five-member commission for study and a report.

The commission did not visit Northwestern until March 31, 1949. Its report, which was discussed at Synod's annual meeting a few months later, was not particularly favorable. It declared that "the founding of colleges in these days is financially hazardous and should be taken only when the Synod is convinced that such an expansion program will not harm existing institutions, and that it will contribute to the whole denominational program." The commission therefore recommended that a careful plan be submitted by the Board of Trustees regarding the steps it proposed to follow and that Synod take no action until after sufficient consideration had been given to this plan.

Having received prior notice of the commission's recommendations, President Heemstra once again took up the gauntlet—as he had when efforts were made to close the school during the 1930's. In a lengthy letter, he explained to Synod that all the information requested by the commission had already been furnished, and added the following pertinent observation: "The Commission's recommendation is evidently intended to cause Synod to delay action" by asking that "some Commission again be appointed to once more study this matter." Dr. Heemstra also pointed out that the commission had spent only a brief time on Northwestern's campus and that some of its members had never before been in that part of the United States and knew little about the denomination's strengths and needs in that region. On the other hand, Northwestern's Board of Trustees was a *representative* body composed of twenty members elected by the six classes of the Particular Synod of Iowa, as well as one member from each classis of the Particular Synod of Chicago and three members from General Synod. "Surely," Heemstra declared, "the Synod can place its confidence in a Board of Trustees [that] knows the mind of the western section of the Church." As to whether the region served by Northwestern could support a four-year college, it was noted that the four classes of East and West Sioux, Dakota, and Germania in the past year had contributed approximately one-sixth of the entire denominational benevolent budget and nearly one-seventh of the funds taken in by the United Advance Campaign.

In a second overture to General Synod, the Board of Trustees pointed out the size of Northwestern's constituency, and noted that the future development of the Reformed Church in the area was closely related to adding two years to the Junior College program. The new overture also reminded Synod that a movement was under way in Iowa and throughout the nation to raise the minimum requirement for teacher certification to four years of college training, a move that would leave the school no choice except to expand. Similar overtures came from several classes and from the Particular Synods of Iowa and Chicago.

The debate that finally ensued on the Synod floor over the various overtures was reported as follows in the *Beacon:*

Numerous delegates, particularly from the Northwestern Iowa area as well as from Chicago and Michigan made pleas on behalf of lifting the two year restriction. The discussion was upon a very high plane, and before the vote was taken prayer was offered by the Rev. Gerrit Rozeboom of Coopersville, Michigan, and the Rev. Edward Fikse of Oak Harbor, Washington.

When a vote was finally taken, the resolution passed by the narrow margin of two votes: ninety-six favored lifting the restriction, while ninety-four opposed such action.

With the restriction on expansion removed, the next step involved setting up a timetable. Already in May 1949—one month before General Synod voted its approval—the Executive Committee stated it hoped "to add the Junior year in September 1952 and the Senior year in the year following." These target dates were missed by several years. In fact, the annual presidential *Reports* and the *Minutes* of the Executive Committee and of the Board of Trustees of the early 1950's contain few references to expansion. The delay was due primarily to the decision to secure North Central accreditation for the Junior College before expanding to a four-year institution.

Junior College accreditation was finally acquired in 1953, as has been noted, but a change in the presidency caused further delay in the expansion timetable. In 1956, however, upon the urging of President Stegenga and the Board of Trustees, events began moving more rapidly. Plans called for offering a four-year degree only in elementary education at first; degrees in secondary education and the liberal arts would be introduced later. Even adding a limited program such as this, however, required considerable planning, particularly regarding the curriculum.

Numerous faculty and committee meetings were held to study and analyze course needs. In addition, staff members visited almost two dozen colleges and universities to seek advice on special matters, and invited consultants on higher education to the campus to evaluate what was being done. Northwestern also worked closely with the North Central Association during these years with a view eventually to obtaining accreditation for the four-year program. The result was the addition of more than sixty new courses. To facilitate matters, the course offerings were grouped under three headings, termed "Divisions": Humanities, Social Science, and Natural Science.

As finally agreed upon, the Bachelor's degree in elementary education required 120 hours of academic credit, plus four non-credit hours in physical education. The 120 hours were distributed as follows: thirty hours of professional education, thirty hours in what was called a "major area of concentration," chosen from specified courses in one of the three Divisions; fifteen hours in a "minor area of concentration," also selected from one of the Divisions; and fifty hours of general education. The purpose of the latter, according to the school catalogue, was "to help each student choose and progress in his life's work, and to help each student grow and develop as a person and as a member of society."

There were, of course, other problems besides curriculum that had to be resolved before the four-year program could be implemented. These problems, to be discussed later, were associated with such matters as staff needs and classroom space. The climax to all this planning finally came with the introduction of a third year of college work in the fall of 1959, and of a fourth year in the fall of 1960. The first baccalaureate degree was awarded in May 1961 to a class of twenty-nine students. The introduction of the bachelor's degree did not spell the end of the two-year associate in arts degree. The latter was not dropped until 1971.

Although the Junior College made steady progress during the 1950's and eventually blossomed into a four-year institution, the fate of its parent body, the Academy, was less fortunate; it closed its doors in 1961. The seventy-nine-year-old school did not disappear, however, without a struggle. Supporters for its continuance were quick to point out the contributions it had made in the past, and that it was still important in providing recruits for the ministry. It was also argued that young people in military service who had no secondary school education might desire such training upon returning home, and perhaps would prefer a school like the Academy rather than a local public high school. It was likewise claimed that abolishing the Academy would weaken the position of the Junior College.

Various suggestions were made from time to time by members of the Executive Committee and the Board of Trustees, as well as by area classes, for revitalizing the Academy. These included allowing it to have its own principal and faculty organization, and also its own budget so that it could develop separate sources of financial support. The idea of appointing a principal was nothing new—in fact, this practice had been followed from 1934 to 1943. It was reintroduced in 1953 with the appointment of Miss Clara Van Til, who was followed by Dale Hubers in 1955 and Steven Ekdom in 1959.

Other innovations were also introduced from time to time. Academy girls were given their own religious organization, called Y-Teens, as a counterpart to Hi-Y, an Academy boys organization that had been formed in the 1940's. In 1954, Academy students were given their own room in Zwemer Hall as a lounge and student union, and for a brief period in the 1950's, they were also given a special page in the *Beacon* for recording Academy happenings. As an added attraction, courses in manual training and home economics were introduced, although this was done in part to meet requirements of the Iowa Department of Education. Extracurricular activities were likewise shown greater concern than had formerly been the case. The choir, for example, which had become little more than a "music appreciation class" (to quote the *Beacon* of October 14, 1952), was reinvigorated and began giving more concerts. Similarly, the Academy boys were assigned a regular staff member rather than a college student to serve as their basketball coach.

A public relations program was also undertaken to acquaint the Reformed Church constituency with what the Academy had to offer. This is clearly brought out in President Wezeman's report to the Board of Trustees in March 1953:

Nothing [was] left undone [last year] to make the academy facilities available to those in this area who want that kind of training for their children. All eighth grade graduates from the public and Christian schools of Orange City, and other schools, too, received a letter expressing the hope they would favorably consider the Academy. Many homes were visited; an announcement appeared on several church bulletins; a public meeting was called to which interested parties were invited. . . . Again this year nothing will be left undone to arouse an interest in the Academy. If the outcome should prove discouraging, then undoubtedly a reappraisal of the problem should be made.

The efforts to revitalize the Academy seemed to bear fruit for a time. In the fall of 1954, it had an enrollment of 52 students, the largest it had in several years, and according to the registrar, "as large as many of the public high schools of our natural area." Two years later, the student body climbed to 63, and there was discussion about sectioning some classes because of their size. Unfortunately, it declined regularly thereafter: to 57 in 1957, 46 in 1958, 45 in 1959, and 43 in 1960.

Although Academy enrollment was declining steadily by the fall of 1960, it had experienced declines before, yet had always managed to revive. Moreover, the school's academic record remained high. Its students, as Principal Ekdom pointed out in 1960, were "taught by instructors whose preparation in their respective fields far [exceeded] that of the average instructors in any high school in the territory." Throughout the 1950's, the great majority of graduates (generally about 90 percent of them) went on to college. What, then, went wrong? What were the overriding causes for the closing of the Academy after the 1960-1961 school year?

In the view of many critics, the Academy was sacrificed in the interest of the College. Fear of this happening was expressed already at an early date. Note, for example, an excerpt from an editorial in the *Beacon* of 1950:

Today one would think the Academy was just running on trial as a sideline of the College. News has . . . reached our ears that word has been sent out to gain the removal of the Academy. Why? The feeble excuse is given: if we want to expand the College, we won't have the time and room to waste on the Academy.

In this respect, it is interesting to note a comment made by President Wezeman in early 1955. After praising the Academy for its scholarship and its achievements in dramatics and music, he added that the school was nevertheless considered by many as "a stepchild, unwanted, even though tolerated." As evidence that this was true, it can be noted that throughout the 1950's when Northwestern was mentioned in press releases, it frequently happened that only the qualifier "Junior College" was used—although the newspaper stories had reference to the institution as a whole.

The demise of the Academy must also be attributed to the failure of the local Reformed Church constituency to appreciate the value of church schools at the secondary level. As the principal expressed it in 1960: "The future of Northwestern Academy is in the hands of the Reformed Church." In this respect, it is interesting to note that of the forty-three students enrolled in the school during its last year of operation, twenty-seven came from Christian Reformed families and only sixteen from Reformed Church homes.

In retrospect, it can be stated that the closing of the Academy was not unique once steps had been taken to expand the Junior College program. Both Hope and Central Colleges once had academies that were dropped eventually. There had also been at one time two other preparatory schools associated with the Reformed Church, neither of which had ever been associated with a college program yet were terminated even before the Academy at Orange City was closed. These were Pleasant Prairie Academy, founded at German Valley, Illinois in 1894, and Wisconsin Memorial Academy, organized at Cedar Grove, Wisconsin in 1900. The latter was discontinued already in 1938 because of financial difficulties, but the Illinois school managed to keep going until 1958, when it, too, had to close its doors because of financial problems.

To return to the story of the Junior College, various concerns had also been expressed about it during the 1950's, despite plans for expanding to a four-year institution. Although its student body increased during the 1950's, the rate of increase was irregular and even showed a decline on two occasions. Enrollment increased from 161 to 168 between the fall of 1951 and 1952, but dropped to 153 the following year and remained the same the next year. In 1955-1956, it rose by 29 to 182, and registered a gain of 30 in 1956-1957. The following year, enrollment increased by only 14 to 226, and dropped to 204 in 1958-1959, the last year that the school functioned as a Junior College. With the introduction of the third year program in 1959-1960, enrollment increased to 245 full-time students, of whom 26 were juniors. The 1960-1961 en-

The Last Academy Graduating Class, 1961

rollment was 275, distributed as follows: seniors, 29; juniors, 44; sophomores, 71; freshmen, 119; specials, 12.

Concern was expressed from time to time about the Junior College
being primarily a local school from the standpoint of geographical representation. In 1952-1953, for example, 138 of the 167 college students
(or 82 percent of the total) came from Iowa, and of these, 42 came from
the immediate Orange City area. Of the remaining 29 students, 15 came

from Minnesota and 6 from South Dakota. The other eight students were distributed among five states and one foreign country. Thanks to the four-year program, the situation had improved somewhat by the 1960-1961 school year. Of the 275 full-time college students enrolled at that time, 179 were from Iowa, which was 66 percent of the total. This was followed by 24 from Minnesota and 21 from South Dakota. The remaining 51 students came from ten states and five foreign countries.

An evening education program was introduced in 1951. Twenty-five students enrolled in the program during the first year and interest increased steadily thereafter, reaching seventy-six in the fall of 1960. The majority of students were teachers with temporary certificates and those who were taking work to comply with the state's new requirements that public school teachers had to possess a baccalaureate degree. The teachers came from a radius of about fifty miles from Orange City. In 1959, a six-week summer school program was also introduced. Its enrollment of 119 students exceeded expectations.

As has been noted, nearly all Academy graduates of the 1950's went on to college. What about Junior College graduates? A study made by the registrar in 1955 covering the eight-year period from 1947 through 1954 shows that of the 373 students who graduated during those years, 139 continued their college education. They were distributed among twenty-four different schools. Hope College headed the list with 27, followed by Central, 21; Iowa State, 20; Westmar, 14; and Calvin, 11. Of the 234 Junior College graduates who did not continue their education, 157 chose the teaching profession. Second in importance—but far down the list—was the military with 24. The teaching profession continued to be attractive after the introduction of the four-year program. Of the 272 college students enrolled during the 1960-1961 academic year, 99 indicated teacher training as their field of specialization. This was followed by liberal arts with 79; business administration, 28; science, 24; and pre-engineering, 15. The remaining 27 were distributed among seven different fields.

Because teacher education consistently attracted a large number of students, it is not surprising that before the new four-year program went into effect, approval for it was sought from the Iowa Department of Public Instruction. This was granted with a promise to continue it for two years after the awarding of the first baccalaureate degree, following which the situation would be re-examined. Similar assurances were received from the Iowa Committee on College Relations regarding the transfer of junior and senior level credits to the state's institutions of higher education.

The increasing enrollment and expanding academic program—both of which would become more critical when the senior college was added—naturally meant that the physical plant had to be enlarged. Although there had been discussion for several years about the need for a fieldhouse and a campus chapel, it was generally agreed that priority should be given to providing additional classroom space. Particularly acute were the needs for chemistry and music. The library situation was also critical. Not only was there insufficient space for new book shelving but also for study tables.

In planning new classrooms, it was decided to build an extension to the east wall of the new Science Hall addition. Plans for this were discussed already in 1950 and approval was given by the Board early the following year, but with the understanding that actual construction would be delayed until the financial situation had improved. It thus happened that contracts were not let out until 1952. Kepp Construction Company of Orange City was the low bidder for the general contract. The new addition measured 46 by 102 feet and was built at a cost of slightly more than $200,000. Its three stories provided several classrooms, offices for instructors, chemistry laboratories, a large art room, a music room, lounges for faculty and students, and kitchen facilities that could be used for social gatherings in the Science Hall auditorium. The Executive Committee resolved to name the new addition Van Peursem Hall "in lasting memory of the longstanding generous contributions of the entire family to the community, the college, and the church."

Priority was next given to constructing a new gymnasium, which the Board of Trustees approved in 1956. Once again, the general contract went to Kepp Construction of Orange City. It was completed in late 1957 at a cost of approximately $300,000. Using the bleachers, it was able to seat about 1,400 persons at athletic events, but this could be raised to 2,200 for overflow crowds by providing additional seating in the balcony and on the stage. For non-athletic events, the capacity was approximately 3,000. Because its function was more than providing accommodations for athletic events, the new building was commonly referred to as the "Multi-Purpose Auditorium." The appropriateness of the term is seen in the following description given by President Stegenga in 1960:

The new Multi-Purpose Auditorium continues to be a wonderful addition to Northwestern's expanding campus. It is indeed amazing when one records the numerous and varied activities that have been held in the new Auditorium. [These have included] the College-Community Concert Series; Church Mass Choirs; religious services; dramatic productions; special convocations; Commencement activities; County Band

Festival; denominational meetings; [and] athletic events and daily physical education classes.

Following completion of the new auditorium, attention was given to providing additional men's housing. By the late 1950's Dykstra Hall was regularly filled to capacity, forcing a number of young men to rent private rooms in the town. This was not easy and very probably deterred some prospective students from coming to Northwestern. Construction of a new men's dormitory began in 1959 and was completed in time for occupancy in the fall of 1960. To fund it, a quarter million dollars was obtained from the federal government in the form of a forty-year loan at the modest interest rate of 4 percent. Located on the East Campus to the north of the auditorium, the new building provided quarters for eighty students and was designed so that an addition could be attached later. It was named "Colenbrander Hall," in honor of the Reverend Henry Colenbrander's thirty-three years of service to Northwestern as president of the Board of Trustees.

It was also in 1959 that construction got underway for a new president's home, located directly south of Dykstra Hall. The general contractor was Thomas O. De Jong of Alton. Following its completion, the former presidential dwelling served as housing for a faculty member until 1964, when it was converted into a residence for women students, called "Campus Cottage." A few years later, the old landmark—Northwestern's first building—was torn down.

The expansion of the physical plant and other developments involved a significant increase in the school's budget. The General Operating Fund, for example, for the fiscal year ending on July 31, 1952 was approximately $116,000; by the end of the decade, this had nearly tripled. Despite steadily increasing maintenance costs and salaries during the 1950's, President Stegenga could report to General Synod in 1961: "For the ninth consecutive year, the fiscal year was concluded without a deficit in the General Operating Fund." Credit for this must go to careful budgeting but also to the school's very able director of development, the Reverend Everett Van Engelenhoven, who took over that position in 1949.

Where did the money come from? Of the $116,000 required for the 1951-1952 fiscal year, approximately $45,000 came from tuition, $45,000 from church contributions, and $5,000 from the denominational Board of Education. This left a balance of about $21,000 that had to be raised. Acquiring this additional amount was generally a problem and was met in various ways—President Wezeman termed them "auxiliary devices." Some income came from special denominational campaigns aimed at raising money for the three Reformed Church schools. For example, $12,000 was received from the so-called "Roll-Call Campaign" in 1951-1952, and $20,000 in the following year. In 1957, Roll Call was replaced by the "Know Your College" campaign. Other "auxiliary devices" that helped meet general operating costs included special donations and gifts from churches, societies, and individuals and income from the endowment fund.

Tuition, which usually accounted for between one-third and one-half of the school's income was also raised. The basic tuition at the college level, for example, after holding steady for several years at $130 per semester, was raised annually beginning in 1956, reaching $225 by the fall of 1961. It was because tuition made up such a critical part of the school's income that so much attention was given to increasing student enrollment. This concern was clearly pointed out in his report to the Board of Trustees by President Wezeman in March 1952:

We have a . . . student deficit. Our overhead is geared to take care of twice the enrollment we now have. From the business but also [from] the professional angle we operate at a terrific loss with less than three hundred students. Classes are small, too small; income is relatively slight. College recruiting is a highly competitive business.

Two special funds—one old and the other new—must be taken note of at this point, namely, the endowment fund and the memorial chapel fund. The former dates virtually from the founding of Northwestern in 1882. For many decades, however, as has been noted in previous chapters, it increased very slowly, and in some years not at all. Although there was an occasional lean year during the 1950's, by 1961 the endowment fund had grown to nearly $240,000. The chapel fund never received as much publicity as did other efforts at fund raising. This fund was started about 1951 by two families that had each received a legacy of about $1,400. Rather than use the money for their own personal use, they gave it to Northwestern to start a memorial chapel fund. It grew slowly but steadily, and by 1961 totaled about $30,000.

Several new faculty positions were created or enlarged during the 1950's. Some of these were administrative in nature and generally called for a variety of responsibilities. For example, when a dean of women was appointed in 1951, her work also included that of dorm mother at Heemstra Hall and some teaching duties. Similarly, the responsibilities of the new director of admissions in 1953 included not only conferring with prospective students, but also serving as student counsellor, assisting in public relations work and fund raising, and occasionally teaching courses in religion. Reverend Van Engelenhoven during the first few years after his appointment as director of development in 1949 also "wore several hats." In addition to serving as chief fund raiser and public relations person, he acted as business manager and student solicitor. In 1954, a new Dean, Joe De Vries was appointed. He came to Northwestern from Sheldon where he had been dean of Sheldon Junior College and also engaged in private business. His work concerned primarily two areas: supervision of the academic program and of the physical plant, but he occasionally also taught mathematics.

The instructional staff was also increased. In requesting General Synod in 1949 to remove the restriction for establishing a four-year college, Northwestern's spokesmen acknowledged that nineteen full-time teachers would be needed as a minimum for implementing such a program. At the time the overture was made, the school had the equivalency of approximately twelve such instructors in the Junior College department. When the fourth year of college work was introduced in the fall of 1960, the full-time instructional staff of the college consisted of eighteen persons. Although it thus lacked by one member the goal mentioned in 1949, this was offset by the fact that there were eight part-time instructors on the staff. There were several weaknesses, however. For example, only two of the full-time instructors in 1960 possessed the doctorate, and five of the eight part-time persons had only baccalaureate degrees. There also was some shortsightedness with respect to staffing certain departments. Thus, although the school had two full-time coaches, it had only one full-time English instructor, and the mathematics instructor also taught physics and served as dean of men.

Teaching loads at Northwestern continued to be heavy, although there was a feeling among some Trustees that this was not true in all instances. At the annual Board meeting in March 1952, the Board's Faculty Committee reported several teachers were not carrying a full schedule of hours and that several classes had very small enrollments. It was therefore recommended that certain courses be rearranged and that the teaching staff be reduced when possible. As to what constituted a full load, the administration in 1956 stated that it was their "objective to assign from 14 to 17 hours of academic work to an individual instructor." It was admitted, however, that these goals had to be ignored occasionally because of student demands. In 1959, the Executive Committee further clarified what was considered a full work load:

The work day, Monday through Friday of the academic year is defined as beginning at eight o'clock in the morning and ending at five p.m. During this period of time it is understood that all full-time staff members of Northwestern College should be engaged in school work and activities. Any full-time employees of the college who desire a deviation from this policy and are engaged in some form of gainful employment outside of school during the above mentioned hours, must submit a written request for approval of the Executive Committee.

In 1953, a new salary schedule was adopted as follows: "Base salary, $3,000, $100 increase each year to $3,300; then $50 increase each year to the 12th year, reaching $3,750." With respect to teaching experience acquired elsewhere than at Northwestern, it was stipulated that these would be counted as half-years, and that not more than five years of such experience would be considered. For graduate study beyond the master's degree, salaries would be increased at the rate of $5 for each semester of credit earned. Because the maximum that could be achieved in this way was established at $200, it is quite understandable why some faculty members, instead of continuing their graduate study during the summer months, decided to do carpentry or house painting. In determining increases for reasons other than earning additional graduate credit, it was stated that the Executive Committee

will consider from year to year, in addition to teaching and academic usefulness, such things as research, travel, writing, participation in workshops, and other types of self-improvement utilized by the teacher during his service at the College and during the summer months.

The faculty salary schedule was revised upward from time to time. As a result, by 1958, the minimum base salary for a new full-time instructor was $3,800. In addition to increases given in accordance with the salary schedule, special circumstances were considered. Thus, an allowance of $100 per year was allowed a faculty member for each dependent child under the age of eighteen, providing no other member of the employee's home had an income exceeding $600 per year. Special dividends were also occasionally awarded, as in March 1957 when the Board of Trustees agreed to give each instructor and member of the administrative staff a bonus of $150.

In the same way that efforts had been made to increase Academy enrollment; so, too, means were sought to increase the size of the college student body. Beginning in 1953, a Career Day was held each spring, offering several hundred seniors from high schools in the area an opportunity to spend a full day on the campus as guests of Northwestern. On these occasions, leaders in various businesses and professions were available throughout the day for conferences. Career Day served as an excellent opportunity for acquainting young people with Northwestern's program and thus as a means for attracting new students. Knowledge about Northwestern was circulated in other ways too. The school became better known, for example, as its alumni increased in number and located in various parts of the country. Reformed Church ministers who had graduated from Northwestern became an especially effective means in this respect. The alumni bulletin, the *Classic*, with its news about the school and former students, served as a similar means. By 1961, each issue totaled more than 2,000 copies. On-campus dinners for school administrators and newspaper editors also helped promote the school. So, too, did widening the geographical representation of the Board. For example in 1953, a member of the Classis of Central California was elected to the Board, as was later a member of the Classis of Cascades.

Visits by the student gospel team and the newly-formed (1959) Choral Readers to churches in the area and the more extended tours of the school choirs also helped spread information. So, too, did the Junior College record in sports. In the fall of 1951, for example, the Red Raiders captured the first Northwest Iowa Junior College Conference football title. This feat was repeated in 1953, which was also the school's first perfect season in football. Similarly, in the spring of 1954, Northwestern became the state's Junior College basketball champion, an accomplishment that was repeated twice during the next few years.

With the development of the four-year college program in 1959, Northwestern participated in forming the Tri-State Conference, an organization composed of six four-year church-related colleges in Iowa, South Dakota, and Nebraska. Although inter-school athletic activities events figured prominently among the six conference members, it was designed to further the exchange of other activities as well, including drama, music, and art—thereby aiding Northwestern's total co-curricular program.

PART THREE
NORTHWESTERN AS A FOUR-YEAR COLLEGE: 1961-1982

XI

Physical Plant and Finances

References have been made in previous chapters to the fact that running a college was rapidly becoming "big business"—not big business in the sense of making profits, but in terms of expanding the physical plant and raising the ever increasing amounts of money required. At no time in Northwestern's history was this more true than during the last two decades. The feverish building activity of the 1950's was continued after 1961, with the result that the number of major facilities more than doubled in the last twenty years. This, plus an enlarged curriculum and faculty, together with inflation, naturally increased the size of the school's budget. By 1980, the latter had surpassed five million dollars.

In the fall of 1961, the college purchased two tracts of land across Highway 10 directly south of the main campus. Soon known as the South Campus, it totaled ten acres and included two homes and several other frame buildings. Plans called for developing part of the new addition into a practice field for physical education activities, with the remainder serving as a site for possible future college buildings. In the following year, the Andrew Vogel family, which had actively supported Northwestern for many years, donated a three-acre tract of land adjoining the South Campus. These additions increased the size of the campus to approximately thirty-five acres.

Construction of a library was one of the first major building projects after 1961. As has been noted, library facilities on the second floor of Zwemer Hall were becoming increasingly cramped, and makeshift arrangements had to be made repeatedly. General approval for a new library was given by the Board of Trustees at its annual spring meeting in 1962, and a committee was appointed to make preliminary plans. To assist in this, Dr. Leslie Dunlop, Director of Libraries at the University of Iowa, was hired as special consultant. The Reverend Everett Van Engelenhoven, Northwestern's director of development, was placed in charge of the fund-raising program. The initial cost was estimated at $250,000. Reformed churches and organizations as well as private individuals made contributions or pledges for the project. Northwestern's Women's Auxiliary, as it had done so often in similar situations, quickly pledged the sum of $25,000. The largest single donation came from the Henry J. Ramaker family of Sioux Center. In recognition of this and other contributions, the Executive Committee of the Board of Trustees resolved that the new building should be named the "Ramaker Library."

Ground-breaking ceremonies took place on Homecoming Day, October 13, 1962, and it was ready for occupancy in the fall of 1963. The two-story building is located on the main campus directly west of Zwemer Hall. Although the holdings of the library at that time totaled only about 25,000 volumes, there were sufficient stacks to accomodate 100,000 books. Provisions were also made for about 400 periodicals and sufficient study desks and tables to accommodate slightly more than 200 students. The library was also provided with a microfilm room, facilities for audiovisual equipment, typing rooms, conference rooms, and offices for staff personnel. It was estimated that these arrangements would care for the college's needs for about twenty years, but there was space for expansion in the basement. Moreover, the building was laid out in such a manner that an addition could be built on the west end if necessary.

A particularly unique feature is the Dutch Heritage Room for housing material concerning the history of the Netherlands and the Dutch in America as well as information on the Reformed Church. The William J. Westra family of Orange City donated $10,000 to cover the cost of construction and furnishings. As described in the student newspaper, the Heritage Room was designed and furnished with a special purpose in mind:

Wall paneling in the room is Dutch Pine Paneling, which is used extensively in libraries and studies in Holland. . . . Dutch beams support the ceilings and cupboards are built in the Dutch fashion. The room, in short, could well have been transported from any typical home in the Netherlands. The authentic atmosphere of the room lends itself well to the principle use of it: the study of the history of the Dutch people in relation to the community, the college, and the church.

A Frisian clock, presented in memory of the Reverend John D. Dykstra, principal of the Academy from 1925 to 1928, adorns one of the walls. Because many of the holdings are in the form of archival material, a walk-in, fireproof vault was constructed in one corner to store whatever was considered rare and difficult to replace.

Among the valuable historical items in the Heritage Room is a complete set of *De Volksvriend*, a weekly Dutch language newspaper issued at Orange City from 1876 to 1951, and the last such newspaper to be published in the United States. Other important and rare materials include copies of the *Sioux County Herald* dating back to 1872, old records of the Academy and Junior College, minutes and account books of various churches in the area, a complete set of the published minutes of General Synod dating from its beginning in the late eighteenth century, about two dozen volumes of published records dealing with New Netherland, letters and other memorabilia of a number of Reformed ministers and missionaries, and several old Bibles. Much of the credit for collecting and cataloguing the archival material must go to Nelson Nieuwenhuis, a former history professor at Northwestern, and Nella Kennedy, who have served as curators of the Heritage Room.

Ramaker Library also contains the "Congressman Hoeven Collection," which was presented to the college in 1965. It is named after the late Charles B. Hoeven from nearby Alton who represented Iowa's Sixth District in the U. S. Congress for twenty-two years. Located in a room at the east end of the mezzanine, the collection is made up of about five hundred books on government, history, and agriculture. It also includes letters and autographed pictures of various officials who served in Washington while Hoeven was there, and a variety of mementos amassed during his travels to other countries. Adding a more personal touch to the collection are the desk and chair the congressman used in Washington.

Simultaneously with the building of the new library, there occurred the construction of a $325,000 addition to Colenbrander Hall. Construction got underway in the early fall of 1962, and it was ready for occupation about a year later. Sands Construction Company of Humboldt, Iowa was the general contractor. When completed, it provided housing for 110 male students. It also contained dining facilities in the basement for approximately 200 persons. The basement of Heemstra Hall, which had housed the former dining room, was thereupon converted into a student union. Although the latter left something to be desired, it was understood that better days were ahead. Already in the planning stage at this time was a new combination women's dormitory and much enlarged student union.

With the completion of the addition to Colenbrander Hall, Dykstra Hall was remodeled to serve as a dormitory for housing twenty-five women. At about this same time, the old president's home was converted into a residence, called "Campus Cottage," for about a dozen women. More housing was needed, however, and discussions soon got underway for the construction of a new women's dormitory. Final plans called for sufficient space to house eighty-four women on the upper floors, with the ground floor and basement to be used for a student union. Occupancy was set for the fall of 1965. To help finance the project, a $400,000 self-liquidating loan was acquired from the federal government. The site chosen was directly north of Colenbrander Hall. Kepp Construction Company of Orange City was the general contractor.

Suggestions were solicited from the student body as to what the student union should contain. Response was immediate and included almost everything from lounges and pool tables to a bowling alley and handball courts. As reported in the *Beacon*, students felt the union should be a "place where they [could] go and talk and be with their friends—a place where they [could] forget about their studies for a little while." Not all student suggestions could, of course, be implemented, but the completed union provided a snack bar (called the "Koffee Kletz"), a book store, a large lounge with fireplace, a health clinic, a Student Senate office, and recreational facilities. Initially called "Union Hall," the new facility was renamed "Hospers Hall" in the spring of 1980. This was done to honor Henry Hospers, an early settler of Sioux County who had been a generous donor to Northwestern and served as a charter member of the Board of Trustees for seventeen years.

The new residence halls were built in response to the increasing student enrollment. This factor along with the expanding curriculum required that attention also be given to providing more classroom space. Fortunately, as with dormitory construction, federal money was available for certain types of classroom facilities. The 1963 Education Act, known as Public Law 88-204, provided for federal aid toward construction of libraries and classroom buildings intended for instruction or research in the natural and physical sciences, mathematics, and modern foreign languages. On March 3, 1965, the Board of Trustees approved plans for a building that would meet the above qualifications. A grant of $172,650 was received from the Department of Health, Education, and Welfare in Washington, and a nearly equal amount came from the Higher Education Facilities Commission in Des Moines. A long-term government loan in the amount of $220,000 was also approved. The total cost for the building was $523,000.

The new building was attached to the northeast corner of Van Peursem Hall and ran parallel to Science Hall, the three sections thus formed a U shape. The Departments of Foreign Language, Mathematics, and Physics were housed on the first floor. The second floor provided facilities for the Department of Biology, while the Department of Chemistry occupied the third floor. The total area amounted to almost 27,000 square feet of much needed floor space. As was true of several new buildings constructed since the Second World War, the architects were William Beuttler and Associates of Sioux City and the general contractor was Kepp Construction Company of Orange City. The building was

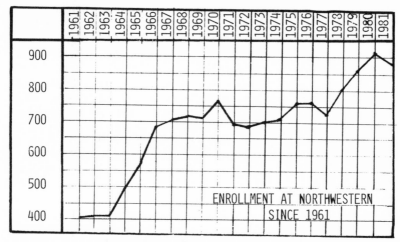

Enrollment at Northwestern Since 1961

dedicated on May 3, 1968. Its completion allowed the Departments of Art, Education, and Music to expand into those areas vacated by departments that had moved into the new addition.

The continued increase in the number of students required still additional housing. As a consequence, the Board of Trustees in 1967 gave its approval for constructing a 200-bed women's dormitory with dining facilities for seating 400. To be located on the South Campus directly across from Ramaker Library, the cost of construction was estimated at $810,000. A federal government loan for this amount was secured at 3 percent interest, and could be amortized over a period of forty years from revenue received from students occupying the facility. The new dormitory was ready for occupancy in the fall of 1968 and named Fern Smith Hall. This was done in honor of Fern Smith Rowenhorst, whose career as a music instructor at Northwestern spanned thirty-three years, 1928-1961. Upon the completion of the new dining facilities in Fern Smith Hall, the basement of Colenbrander Hall (the former dining room) was utilized in various ways. Since the mid-1970's, it has housed the Department of Business and Economics.

Two unique buildings, not involving new construction, were also added to Northwestern's physical plant at about this time. The first of these was a gift from Dr. and Mrs. A. Bushmer consisting of the old creamery building located two blocks west of the main campus. It had once been a very busy place when nearly every area farmer kept a few cows and had the milk transported to the local creamery. As the nature of farming operations changed and the dairy business was left more in the hands of large corporations, the creamery closed down. For a few years, it was used by the Maurice-Orange City High School for band activities, but with the completion of a new public high school this became no longer necessary. Donated to the college in the fall of 1969, it was put to good use. With ample space and excellent natural lighting, the building was remodeled to provide studios for painting, sculpture, ceramics, and printmaking, and appropriately named the Bushmer Art Center.

In 1970, the college came into possession of another of Orange City's historic buildings, namely, the just-vacated American Reformed Church. Located near the downtown area about six blocks north of the campus, it was purchased for $30,000 and quickly converted into a theater and named the "Playhouse." The pews were removed and replaced by old theater seats, a large stage was constructed, and provisions were made for lighting and sound control. Rooms that had formerly served as Sunday School classrooms were transformed into costume, property and dressing rooms.

The most imaginative building project ever undertaken at Northwestern was the construction of a combination student union and physical fitness center, proposals for which had been under discussion for some time. As to the need for more recreational facilities on campus, President Granberg expressed it very well in his report to the Board of Trustees in March 1967: "Orange City is a fine community for children and for married couples making a home. As a recreation center for several hundred energetic and mildly homesick young people it is less ideal." About a decade later, President Rowenhorst explained the need for a facility that would serve both as a physical fitness center and a student union:

We are giving special attention to the development of the whole person, not only academically, but spiritually and physically. . . . The concept, which I think is beautiful, is that every student on campus will have a reason to go to the facility. Most everything that happens in an extracurricular way will be centered there. It will be a beautiful opportunity for us to develop an even better community of Christian learners, not only in the classroom, but in all the other things we might participate in.

Debate about a student union/physical fitness center therefore revolved less around the question of necessity than how best to realize it. Various proposals ranged from erecting an entirely new structure to making an addition to an already existing campus building. Consideration was also given to constructing a new chapel and student center as a single facility. This was rejected in part because of the cost, estimated at over six million dollars. Moreover, it was argued that the college already had chapel facilities which, although leaving something to be desired, were adequate for the present. Also discussed was the idea of building a campus chapel first, after which Science Hall could be renovated into a student center.

The final decision involved purchasing for $325,000 the industrial building belonging to the bankrupt Agri-Quip Company, located directly west of Fern Smith Hall, and converting it into a student union and constructing an addition to the rear to serve as a physical fitness center. Approval of the plan was given by the Board of Trustees at its April 1978 meeting. Contributions were expected to make up the bulk of the funding, with interim financing to be carried out through cooperation with the town. The latter would provide Northwestern with tax-free industrial bonds, thereby permitting the college to borrow money in the open market at substantially reduced rates.

Meanwhile, the Board of Trustees at its spring meeting in April 1978 approved a capital funds drive to take place in two phases: phase one had as its goal $3 million to fund the student center complex; the goal of phase two was $2 million to fund a chapel/performing arts center. The latter, to be built east of Fern Smith Hall, was envisioned as containing a 900-seat sanctuary and a large stage, as well as the chaplain's office and adequate rooms for counseling services and for putting on musical performances. The first phase was expected to last three years, after which phase two would begin. The Board of Trustees also approved a campaign, to take place concurrently with the capital funds drive, for increasing the endowment by $1 million through estate gifts. The goal of phase one was later raised to $3.75 million and that of the endowment drive to $2 million. The various drives became known as the "Call to Commitment." The Reverend Robert Wallinga, vice-president for development and the primary overseer of the campaign, explained the reason for the name as follows:

> Northwestern has always been concerned with commitment to the biblical truths in regards to our living and learning. Now as we are faced with new challenges and the need for new facilities, the theme "A Call to Commitment" will give added meaning to the efforts of the college and her supporters as we join hands in this very exciting process.

Initial plans called for completion of the student center by the fall of 1979, with some areas in operation by January of that year. However, the first section was not opened until January 1980, and the facility did not open in its entirety until fall of that year. When completed, its 90,000 square feet of floor space more than fulfilled Rowenhorst's dreams. The front section of the building contains a 250-seat film/drama theater, art gallery, bookstore, snack bar, career counseling center, mail room, game room, information desk, and general office. All of these are located around an immense lounge area, which some observers have compared to a shopping mall or covered courtyard and others to a large hotel lobby. The rear part of the facility provides various recreational opportunities of a physical nature and is a real boon to the college's intramural program. It includes four handball/racquetball courts, three basketball/tennis courts, a volleyball/badminton area, a track for joggers, and facilities for archery, gymnastics, weightlifting, and wrestling.

The specific names given to various facilities in the center testify to the degree to which some individuals and families made significant contributions to its realization. Among the more than thirty such commemoratives, there is the Bogaard Theater, Dethmers Bookstore, De Witt Physical Fitness Center, Te Paske Art Center, and the Van Berkel Snack Bar. At a special session in December 1979, the Executive Committee of the Board of Trustees appropriately resolved to name the entire facility the "Rowenhorst Student Center."

With the completion of Fern Smith Hall in 1968, Northwestern had four main residence halls that together could accommodate approximately 600 students. Women's housing included Hospers Hall (110 students) and Fern Smith Hall (190 students); men's housing included Heemstra Hall (110 students) and Colenbrander Hall (190 students). There also was a 40' by 60' two-story structure containing eight apartments (called an "8-plex") south of Fern Smith Hall. It had been constructed in 1977 for married students. Because Mr. Rowenhorst decided to live in his present home when he became president in 1975 (a practice that was continued by his successor, Dr. Friedhelm Radandt), the house that had served previous presidents eventually became a residence for women students. It soon acquired the name of "Prexy House."

Despite these additions, the steadily increasing enrollment and a high retention rate placed a strain on campus housing by the late 1970's. To help solve the mounting crisis, forty more rooms were added to two of the main residential halls—twenty in the basement of Heemstra Hall and another twenty in the basement of Hospers Hall and on its first floor where the bookstore had once been. Later, a few lounges were also converted into rooms. In addition, two more 8-plexes (both for women) were built on the South Campus, and several mobile homes were purchased as were some family dwellings adjoining the campus. The mobile homes were located in what became known as "Raider

Village," across Highway 10 south of the football field, and the family dwellings were converted to student housing. The decision to purchase mobile homes and family dwellings had an advantage in that they could be disposed of quite easily in the event student enrollment declined. Considering these various makeshift arrangements, it is not surprising that an article in the *Beacon* referred to Northwestern's housing at this time as a "smorgasbord."

The continued housing crisis caused the Executive Committee of the Board in the late fall of 1980 to approve construction of a new residence hall to be located across the street west of Heemstra Hall. Final plans called for a structure of three floors to accommodate eighty-five women students. Funding for the new dormitory was acquired through the sale of $900,000 of industrial revenue bonds, the nature of which has been explained as follows:

In our arrangement, Orange City lends its name to us in order for this sale to become tax exempt. It in no way affects the credit of the city. NW alone is responsible for the repayment of it. The bonds permit us to construct the necessary building with money borrowed at a lower rate of interest because it is tax-exempt. These bonds are purchased from the government by large lenders like banks and savings and loan institutions.

Income from room rentals and designated gifts are expected to be the main sources of repayment over the fifteen years covered by the bonds.

The enlarged physical plant naturally resulted in additional expenses associated with the maintenance and upkeep of campus buildings. Most major repairs and improvements were made during the summer months because there were fewer students on campus. An indication of the amount of work this frequently involved can be gathered by examining the improvements made in the summer of 1975, as described in the president's annual report for that year:

During the summer, the following work was completed: Colenbrander Hall basement remodeled to accommodate the Business Administration Department; the removal of windows, installation of panels and air conditioning and humidifying units on the third floor of Van Peursem for the Music Department; a mobile home court was added on the south campus; a parking lot was eliminated south of Zwemer Hall; repair was done on the roof of Zwemer and Dykstra Halls; a baseball field was constructed on the south campus; bleachers were erected on the east side of the football field for visiting spectators; and all hallways and offices on campus were painted.

Summers were also the time to purchase new equipment. To take a single summer as an example, purchases in 1977 included microscopes for the Biology Department, a mini-computer for the Mathematics, Business, and Science Departments, typewriters for the Business Department, and a portable sound system for the Music Department.

With new construction, additions to the faculty and administration, expansion of the curriculum, and inflation, the budget increased rapidly during the last twenty years. In terms of five-year intervals, the increase was as follows:

1961-1962	$ 476,970
1966-1967	1,159,471
1971-1972	1,914,003
1976-1977	2,833,825
1981-1982	5,516,835 (estimated)

The above figures mean that the average cost per diem rose from $1,307 in 1961-1962 to slightly more than $15,000 in 1981-82. The question therefore naturally arises: Where has the additional money come from?

Tuition has traditionally been Northwestern's main source of revenue, and the last two decades were no exception, making up at least 50 percent of the institution's total annual income. Board and room charges generally accounted for another 20-25 percent. Although enrollment since 1961 has had occasional setbacks, the overall increase has been significant, as can be seen from the following figures for full-time students:

1961-1962	340
1966-1967	623
1971-1972	668
1976-1977	724
1981-1982	866

As might be expected, tuition costs have risen steadily since 1961; indeed, they rose every year with two exceptions. Looking at five-year intervals, one sees that the per-semester increase in the regular tuition charge for a full-time student was as follows:

1961-1962	$225
1966-1967	420
1971-1972	775
1976-1977	1000
1981-1982	1822.50

Fortunately, in the face of rising tuition, financial aid in various forms became available for students. Some of this was in the form of federal government aid, but for Iowa residents there also were tuition grants at the state level. Furthermore, opportunities existed for student employment on the campus. The extent to which students were recipients of these types of financial assistance in recent years can be clearly seen in the following report of March 1981:

Under the Federally Insured Student Loan program, 485 NW students receive about $700,000. Also this year, 364 NW students obtained $378,437 through BEOG [Basic Educational Opportunity Grants] grants. The Iowa Tuition Grants provided $522,291 to 320 students at NW.

In addition to grants and loans, jobs help support students through college. Campus work-study is 80 percent federally funded according to student need. NW's work-study program provides 331 NW students with $150,380. Campus employment paid by college institutional funds, involved 161 students at NW, taking in $56,850.

As an additional means for helping students deal with steadily rising costs, the number of scholarships was increased significantly during recent years.

Despite various forms of financial aid, the annual increases in tuition caused occasional complaints among the student body. From time to time, usually through the medium of the school paper, members of the administration responded to these complaints. One of the most thorough of these was made in 1976 by Paul Muyskens, vice-president for financial affairs. He noted that 38 percent of tuition income went for instructional costs, including salaries and classroom equipment; 31 percent was earmarked for administration and "general development" expenses, such as office supplies, telephone services, building and liability insurance, and postage (the latter alone amounted to $14,500); 5 percent for operating the library; and 8 percent for maintenance. Mr. Muyskens also took this opportunity to remind students that some of their tuition money (9 percent) was returned directly to them in the form of merit grants and academic scholarships. He further noted that 6.4 percent of all tuition money was returned indirectly to the students through a category called "auxiliary expenses." These included expenses associated with such activities as Student Senate, musical groups, Choral Readers, and student publications like the *Beacon* ($4,000) and the yearbook ($5,500).

Inflation has been particularly burdensome in recent years; and there

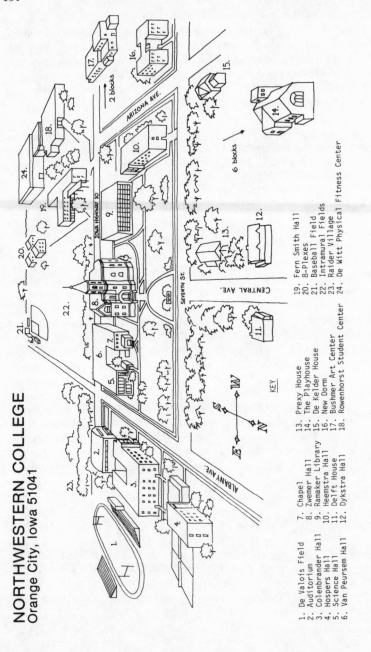

NORTHWESTERN COLLEGE
Orange City, Iowa 51041

The College Campus, 1982

KEY

1. De Valois Field
2. Auditorium
3. Colenbrander Hall
4. Hospers Hall
5. Science Hall
6. Van Peursem Hall

7. Chapel
8. Zwemer Hall
9. Ramaker Library
10. Heemstra Hall
11. Delft House
12. Dykstra Hall

13. Prexy House
14. The Playhouse
15. De Kelder House
16. New Dorm
17. Bushmer Art Center
18. Rowenhorst Student Center

19. Fern Smith Hall
20. 8-Plexes
21. Baseball Field
22. Intramural Fields
23. Raider Village
24. De Witt Physical Fitness Center

has been, especially, rising energy cost. For example, it was reported on November 3, 1973 that during the previous school year, 200,000 miles were put on school cars. This mileage was the result of class field trips, special meetings attended by faculty and students, recruiting new freshmen, and transportation to and from sporting events. Under these circumstances, it takes little imagination to see how a rise in the price of a gallon of gasoline affects the school's operating costs. The situation is similar with respect to fuel oil when, in the early 1970's, the college normally used between forty and fifty thousand gallons annually. The heating bill increased, of course, with the addition of each new building. The Rowenhorst Student Center, for example, added 90,000 square feet to the already existing 288,000 square feet.

The rising cost of energy was only one of several elements causing a rise in the budget. For example, between 1971 and 1975, the athletic budget increased by 58.6 percent. This resulted partly from the development of women's athletics and the addition of some new men's sports but was also due to inflation. Similarly, in that same period, library costs rose 41 percent, largely due to the increase in the price of books. The cost of office supplies like paper also rose significantly—33 percent in a single year between 1974 and 1975.

In view of rising costs and the subsequent increases in tuition, one sees that college administration is similar to the operation of business enterprises in that both are forced to raise "prices" because of increased operational expenses. There is, however, one important difference, as was recently pointed out by a member of Northwestern's administration:

As a non-profit educational corporation, a college is not able to deal with inflation the same way a business corporation can. NW cannot indiscriminately drop a needed course because it is losing money, in contrast to a factory which can drop a marginal product from its production line.

There is a limit, however, to the number of courses a college like Northwestern can offer, and from time to time these had to be trimmed down in an effort to help balance the budget. The need for such trimming was clearly brought out in a report of March 1971. The report stated that a college the size of Northwestern with 700-750 students should have "sixteen to eighteen" areas as a maximum. Northwestern at the time was offering courses in twenty-five different disciplines. According to the report:

To "break even" this year, three-hour courses needed eighteen to nineteen students in each class. However, such was not the case. A survey by the Academic Dean showed that nine sections had one person in the class, thirty-nine sections had five or fewer students, sixty-six sections had ten or fewer students, and one hundred fifteen sections had twenty or fewer students. This must be corrected.

To what extent this problem was corrected (or stayed corrected) is open to question, as can be judged from a similar report for the 1973-1974 academic year:

61% of teacher credit hours are spent in classes enrolling 15 students or less; 48.1% of these in classes enrolling 10 students or less. It is clear . . . that we are offering too many majors and too many course offerings within most departments. These must be reduced intelligently and carefully so as to make better use of resources.

Because of the importance of tuition and related charges in the total income of the school, financial problems naturally arose when enrollment dropped or did not rise to expectations. This is clearly seen in a report by President Rowenhorst in February 1978:

Our budget as we proposed it, was a balanced budget. But with the advent of about 49 students less than anticipated in the fall enrollment, naturally it is going to be difficult to replace the $150,000 or thereabouts. We have made some progress but it is very likely that we will not be able to operate in the black this year.

In situations like the above, "some hard and extremely distasteful steps" had to be taken, as Dr. Granberg indicated in March 1971, when a serious deficit faced the college:

After careful discussion with the dean, who had spent weeks of discussion with faculty and division chairmen, evidence pointed to the fact that we would do least harm to the program by eliminating the majors in German and Political Science, phasing out the major in Library Science and eliminating the minor in Physics. In addition, the decision was made not to replace two administrative officers who were retiring, eliminate three other administrative posts and vacate six faculty positions.

Other cutbacks mentioned in the report included such areas as secretarial help, institutional memberships, printing and advertising, staff travel, the concert and lecture series, the library budget, and expenditures for furniture and equipment.

Although tuition remained a primary element enabling Northwestern to meet its obligations, there were many other important sources of financial aid. One of these has been the generosity of the federal government. Thanks to the Higher Education Facilities Act of 1963 and the Higher Education Act of 1965, Northwestern was able to receive grants and long-term loans for constructing new campus buildings as well as financial aid for needy students who otherwise would have been unable to attend college. The federal government on several occasions also assisted Northwestern's program in special ways. The year 1980 is an example. In that year, the college received $149,000 from the Strengthening Developing Institutions program (the same program from which it had received $168,000 in federal funds the previous year) to be used, as explained in the fall 1980 issue of the *Classic*, "in four major areas; administration and fiscal management, student services, curriculum, and faculty development"—which seems to have included everything except new construction! Also in 1980, a federal grant, received through the state education agency, helped fund a course on health and nutrition for elementary and junior high teachers. In 1980, the Iowa Humanities Board, a state program of the National Endowment for the Humanities awarded the college and the Sioux County Historical Society a project grant for a four-day conference on local history.

A relatively new source of funds has been the Iowa College Foundation, to which Northwestern was admitted in 1964 as its twenty-second member. This organization, made up of non-tax-supported, regionally accredited colleges and universities in Iowa, was managed by a Board of Governors composed of the presidents of the member schools plus a number of business leaders. Its purpose was better to enable business and industry to make contributions through a single, statewide organization. Within a short time after being admitted into the Iowa College Foundation, Northwestern shared in gifts of $30,000 from the John Deere Company and $5,300 from Standard Oil. Other gifts were also soon forthcoming, with the result that Northwestern received a total of $11,853 during its first year as a member. This amount has increased steadily over the years, with the result that in 1980-1981, Northwestern's share from the Iowa College Foundation exceeded $40,000.

Gifts from individuals and families were important in helping Northwestern get started a century ago, and this kind of giving continued to be important in meeting the school's needs during the last twenty years. Gifts of money have obviously remained the most common type and these have ranged from small donations to many thousands of dollars. Gifts have come in other forms too, including—to mention only a few— books for the library, phonograph records (one such donation in 1967 consisted of 200 long-playing classical records), classroom equipment, and furnishings for offices and residence halls. Alumni giving became more important than formerly. This was due in part to a better organized Alumni Association, but also because until Northwestern developed a baccalaureate degree program, many of its graduates had a kind of a split loyalty when it came to giving to their alma mater—to the Junior College and to the colleges from which they graduated after leaving Northwestern. In recent years, a strong effort has been made to get more friends of Northwestern to include the college in their estate plans. Beginning in the spring of 1980, an annual Heritage Day was instituted to honor those who have done this by such means as wills, trusts, annuities, and life insurance policies. There were ninety-one charter members at the first Heritage Day observance.

True to its tradition, the Northwestern Women's Auxiliary continued to be in front with donations. In recent years, it developed several new and novel methods for raising money, such as the annual Hostess Suppers and the Family Fairs. As a consequence, this organization in recent years was able to renovate many of the dormitory rooms, help furnish dining rooms, assume a $20,000 debt on the Playhouse, purchase new pianos for the music department, supply the A Cappella choir with new robes, assist in underwriting the salary of a staff person in the school's development office, and purchase equipment for the Rowenhorst Student Center. In 1976, the Auxiliary paid a well-deserved tribute to its founder, Mrs. Jacob Heemstra, by establishing the "Hanna Heemstra Endowed Scholarship Fund" of $25,000, from which scholarships would be given out to needy and deserving students. In view of what the Women's Auxiliary has done for the college for more than a half century, it is not surprising that a recent article describing its work was entitled "An Incredible Group."

The Call to Commitment Campaign, described earlier, was the largest fund-raising operation ever undertaken by the school. On August 29, 1979, less than a year after the campaign began, President Radandt announced that $2,756,262 of the $3.75 million goal had been raised for the Rowenhorst Student Center, as had $944,002 of the $2 million endowment goal. The announcement was made in conjunction with a pledge of a half million dollars by Mr. and Mrs. Marvin De Witt of Zeeland, Michigan. At the time of the student center's dedication on September 28, 1980, about $3.1 million had been raised, a figure that reached $3.5 million by the close of the year. Meanwhile, the campaign for the endowment fund was also achieving success; by the close of the year 1980, $1.92 million of the two million dollar goal had been reached. By October 1981, both goals had been exceeded.

In discussing the sources from which Northwestern has received financial support, passing references have been made from time to time about the support given by the Reformed Church. Because denominational assistance has become one of the mainstays of the institution, it would be remiss to conclude this chapter without further reference to it. At the local and regional level, the so-called "quota system" of the 1960's was particularly significant. By this arrangement, individual churches in the several classes from the area surrounding Northwestern were given a kind of annual assessment. This type of assistance not only helped give continuity to financial support but helped acquaint church members in a more personal manner with Northwestern's vision and its importance to Christian higher education.

Although the quota system is no longer followed, gifts to the institution have increased substantially in recent years, including growing support from the denomination as a whole. The growth in support began to increase in 1965 when the Church provided $160,000 for operational needs and has continued through the present time with gifts from the churches totaling $495,957 in 1980. It is also worthy of note that in 1978, General Synod authorized Northwestern to solicit Reformed Church congregations to raise $500,000 for the Call to Commitment. Congregations in all Particular Synods were invited to make three-year "Faith Promise" commitments *over and above* their annual gifts to the operating budget. In addition to strong financial response from regular supporting congregations, more than sixty congregations made first-time commitments to the school.

XII

The Faculty

As might be expected, the situation with respect to the administrative and instructional staff underwent considerable change during the last two decades. Most academic departments increased significantly in size, and the administrative staff expanded to such an extent that by 1982 Zwemer Hall housed only administrative offices—which has prompted some faculty members to humorously refer to it as the "Pentagon." There were changes in staff functions and responsibilities as well, particularly at the administrative level. Finally, the faculty underwent some transformation in terms of academic training and geographical background.

The presidency changed hands several times during this period. Dr. Preston Stegenga, who assumed the office in 1955, informed the Board of Trustees at its annual meeting in March 1966 that he was tendering his resignation effective at the conclusion of the spring semester. He left Northwestern to serve as the Chief of the American Delegation at the University of Liberia in Monrovia, Liberia. More particularly, his new position was to be that of administrative director of a Cornell University project sponsored by the Agency for International Development of the American State Department. Dr. Stegenga had a long-standing interest in international education, having traveled abroad on various occasions and having spent a summer engaged in research projects at the United Nations. Dr. Stegenga's eleven years as president were among the most significant in the history of Northwestern. Not only was it transformed from an Academy/Junior College into a four-year accredited college, but the student body more than doubled during his tenure in office, and several major facilities were added to the physical plant.

A search committee was quickly appointed to make recommendations for a new president, and following a special meeting of the Board of Trustees, the position was offered in July 1966 to Dr. Lars I. Granberg. During the interim period from June when Stegenga left, to late October when Granberg officially took over, the academic dean—Dr. Thomas Ten Hoeve—served as acting vice-president. Dr. Granberg, who was born in Norway and came to America as a child, was eminently qualified for Northwestern's presidency. Educated in the Chicago public school system, he obtained his undergraduate training at nearby Wheaton College, and his masters and doctorate in psychology from the University of Chicago. In addition to excellent academic qualifications, he came to Northwestern with thirteen years' experience as a professor of psychology at Hope College. During those years he also acquired some administrative experience, at times serving as departmental chairman and as acting vice-president for academic affairs.

By his own admission, Dr. Granberg was strongly oriented toward the humanities. In an interview in the *Beacon* a few months after assuming the presidency, he outlined several of his priorities for Northwestern's future. Of immediate concern, he declared, was the need to build up the school's library collection and strengthen some departments, including philosophy, art, and music. Granberg also stressed the need to bring in more "outside voices" through the introduction of a lecture series to broaden the intellectual scope of the campus and of the community at large. The extent to which he succeeded in achieving these goals will be described in the chapter on curriculum and academic life.

Dr. Granberg's interest in the arts and humanities by no means meant that he wished to slight the sciences. He explained his position on this matter as follows:

Scientists are called on to make far-reaching decisions involving national and international problems. These decisions will call for far more than scientific knowledge; they will involve moral and social issues. To be making these decisions on technical knowledge alone could be destructive.

The new president held similar views regarding Northwestern's teacher training program, declaring that "one ought not take on oneself the responsibility of teaching without first having involved himself in the basic human questions."

It came as a surprise early in the 1974 fall semester when Dr. Granberg announced plans to resign the presidency after the current academic year. Explaining his decision in a chapel speech in early October 1974, he declared that when he accepted the call to Northwestern eight and one-half years earlier, he considered it a "mandate to give leadership to a school that was transforming from a teachers' college into a four-year liberal arts school." He explained that this task had now been "essentially completed" and that "a change in executive leadership would be beneficial." Although pleased with what had been accomplished, he expressed disappointment that "a more aesthetic and intellectual climate" had not developed on the campus during his stay—a situation he attributed in part to the failure of the faculty and students to make greater use of the library.

Soon after receiving the news of Granberg's impending departure, a presidential search committee was formed. It was made up of fourteen persons representing the Board of Trustees, the Women's Auxiliary, the administration, the faculty, the students, the alumni, and the "constituency-at-large." The committee was instructed to advertise the position and accumulate information on as many as four suitable candidates. The search committee chose Mr. H. Virgil Rowenhorst.

The new president grew up in Orange City and graduated from the local public schools. After a semester at Northwestern Junior College, he served in the Navy for four years during the Second World War. Following his discharge, he enrolled at Drake University at Des Moines, Iowa, where he received a bachelor's degree in business and finance. Following some graduate study at the University of Wisconsin, Mr. Rowenhorst took employment in the Northwestern State Bank of Orange City. Although some questions were raised about selecting a president whose academic qualifications were limited, Rowenhorst brought to the office considerable financial expertise, having served as president and chairman of the bank's Board of Directors since 1962. This kind of experience was no mean attribute at a time when colleges were demanding considerable business acumen from their chief administrators. In making the selection, the Board of Trustees undoubtedly also felt that with an academic dean of the quality of Dr. Edward Ericson, the academic side of college life would be in very capable hands.

Dr. Rowenhorst had served as president for about three and one-half years when he died on February 9, 1979, at age fifty-four. The impact that his presidency made on the school was well described in a *Beacon* editorial published a week after his death:

Rowenhorst died a week ago today; but his death was that in body only. His dreams will continue to grow, his personal leadership will long be remembered, and the college community will not easily put aside the sense of direction he gave toward the college.

He was always in the business world, not an academic one, and he never claimed to be in it. In the last four years he spent his time working for something he loved: NW. He was a people person. His face was familiar to all the college community and he was respected by the faculty, staff and students. Everyone was his friend. He loved life and he never gave up hope. He lived and made known the words: "If you have the faith, God gives the power."

Once again, the Executive Committee established a presidential search committee. The man chosen to succeed President Rowenhorst was Dr. Friedhelm Radandt, who had been serving Northwestern as vice-president for academic affairs since 1977. Born in Germany where he received his elementary and secondary education, Radandt attended Bethel College in Minnesota for one year, which was followed by studies at a Baptist seminary in Germany and at the University of Hamburg. Following graduation from seminary in 1957, he served as youth pastor for three years, after which he enrolled in the University of Chicago in 1960, where he completed his doctorate in German literature in 1967. Before coming to Northwestern, Dr. Radandt held teaching positions at the University of Chicago and at Lake Forest (Illinois) College. In 1973, he became dean of the faculty at the latter school, a position he held until 1977 when he became vice-president for academic affairs at Northwestern.

There were other personnel changes among the administrative staff besides that of the presidency. In 1961, a new position, that of academic dean, was established. As the title indicates, this office was given primary responsibility for coordinating the academic phase of the college program—a necessary step in view of the school's growing faculty and expanding curriculum. The office of college dean, established already in the late 1940's, which had been closely associated with academic matters in the past, was henceforth made chiefly responsible for business affairs at the institution. The titles of the two deans led to confusion at times, and in 1968 that of the dean of the college was changed to dean of business affairs. The title of academic dean has also undergone change and is currently known as vice-president for academic affairs. As can be seen from the list of persons who have held this office, it, like the office of the president, has changed hands several times since 1961:

Gerald F. De Jong 1961-1965
Thomas Ten Hoeve 1965-1970
V. Roy Wilbee 1970-1973
Edward E. Ericson 1973-1977
Friedhelm Radandt 1977-1979
Harold Heie 1980-

As was true of academic matters, the administration of the college in terms of business and financial affairs also gradually became more complex. As a consequence, the number of administrators involved in that aspect of college work was soon enlarged. This is clearly shown by noting the titles of some of the members of the administrative staff as they are listed in the 1971-1972 catalog:

Dean of Business Affairs
Bursar
Director of Development
Development Consultant
Treasurer
Director of Financial Aids and Athletics

The dean of business affairs rapidly became one of the chief administrators on campus. In 1971, his responsibilities were described as including "the supervision of all college business affairs, supervision of building operations, preparation of the fiscal budget, purchasing, collecting former student loans, supervision of non-academic personnel, and consultation with the [Board of Trustees] finance committee." The title of dean of business affairs, like that of academic dean, has also undergone change, and presently goes by the long-winded name of vice-president for financial affairs and long-range planning.

With increasing enrollment, it is not surprising that administrative changes also had to be made concerning matters of student recruitment and admissions and the keeping of student records. As a result, instead of having a single director of admissions-registrar, as in 1961, these duties by 1971 were divided among a registrar, an assistant registrar, a director of admissions, and three admissions counselors. The steady increase in enrollment meant that the matter of student campus life other than the academic also had to be given greater attention. As a consequence, several new administrative positions were added for this purpose. These included those of college chaplain, dean of student affairs, and director of student life and recreation, which were added in 1962, 1967, and 1969 respectively. Another office of steadily growing importance has been that of librarian.

The administrative branch has continued to expand and become more complex. Space does not permit a detailed description of this development, but an examination of the administrative organizational chart for 1981 reveals the extent to which this has occurred.

Before leaving this discussion of the administration and taking up the story of the instructional staff, a word must be said about changes that took place in the Board of Trustees. These came about as a result of revisions in the Articles of Incorporation and the By-Laws. Specific changes included a slight reduction in the size of the Board and some modification of the committee structure. Commencing in 1973, two meetings of the Board were held per year—in the spring and in the fall, with the spring session constituting the main business meeting. Under the present By-Laws, Trustees serve for a period of four years and can be re-elected for a second term. To facilitate continuity, the

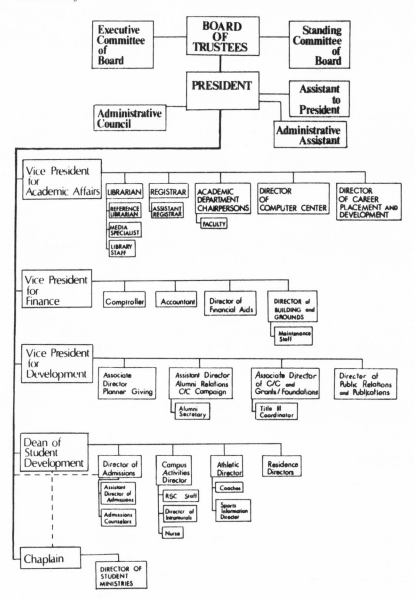

Organizational Flow Chart

Board is divided into classes or groups of approximately ten Trustees each, with one class retiring and a new one coming in each year.

In 1981, the Board consisted of forty-nine members, including the chairman, the president of the college as ex-officio member, the senior pastors of the three Reformed churches in Orange City and of the two Reformed churches in Sioux Center, and the president of the Alumni Association. Three Trustees were women. The elected members were distributed as follows: twelve from the Particular Synod of the West— one from each of the ten classes, with the exception of the Classes of East and West Sioux, each of which had two representatives; four from the Particular Synod of Chicago—one from each of its four classes; three members at large appointed by the Particular Synod of Michigan; three members at large appointed by General Synod—one from each of the three eastern Particular Synods; and twenty (excluding the five local senior pastors) elected by the Board of Trustees. A look at their geographical roots indicates that the local region continues to have strong representation. Thirteen of the twenty chosen by the Board itself were from northwest Iowa, as were the four representatives from the East Sioux and West Sioux Classes, the president of the college, the president of the Alumni Association, and the five senior pastors from the nearby Reformed churches.

Despite the reorganization of the Board of Trustees, its basic concerns have not changed from what they were when Northwestern was founded a century ago. As explained a few years ago by one of the Board members:

The Board is the policy-making body for NW and the president enforces it. . . . The Board truly shows integrity and Christian concern, love, and understanding in solving problems. [It] decides issues by considering how the witness of the college and individuals will be furthered, how the students will be benefited, and how finances fit into the picture.

Turning from a discussion of the administration to a review of what took place regarding the instructional staff, one notes that here, too, significant changes occurred. In 1961, the instructional staff was still distributed among three divisions: Humanities, Natural Science, and Social Science. Most academic departments fitted quite neatly into one of these categories, but there were exceptions, the most notable being education and business administration (both of which were placed in Social Science) and physical education (which was included under Natural Science). In 1964, a fourth division was created, that of Education, to include education, psychology, and business administration. This was followed by the formation of two more divisions in 1967 and the renaming of others, resulting in six divisions: Education, Fine Arts, Literature and Modern Language, Natural Science, Religion and Philosophy, and Social Science. In 1971, the divisional arrangement was abolished in favor of independent departments.

One of the most obvious changes in the instructional staff was its growth. For example, the 1961-1962 catalogue lists twenty full-time faculty members engaged in instruction as compared to more than fifty in the 1981-1982 catalogue. This means that the full-time instructional staff increased by more than two and one-half times in the last twenty years. This came about in part because of rising enrollment, but the introduction of new majors also had a significant effect. When the baccalaureate degree program was set up for the elementary education program in the late 1950's, there were only three majors, or "areas of concentration," as they were called, and all were of a composite nature—Humanities, Natural Science, and Social Science. The development of a secondary education program naturally required more majors, as did the decision to offer a liberal arts program. Already in the fall of 1961, fourteen new courses, mostly in the Departments of English and Business, were introduced. This was followed in 1962 by twenty new courses involving eleven different departments. The extent to which courses had to be added in order to meet the demands of new majors can be clearly seen in the case of biology. Professor Thomas Ten Hoeve of that department reported in the spring of 1963 that a "complete" biology major would be offered beginning in the fall, but to do this "will require the addition of. . .Bacteriology, Embryology, Human Anatomy, Histology, and Conservation and Field Biology." The situation for other new majors was similar.

In view of the above and the steady rise in enrollment, it is not surprising that several departments which had only one full-time person in 1960-1961, including biology, business, English, and music, had three full-time staff members five years later. Not all departments, however, showed appreciable growth. Mathematics can be cited as an example. This came about in part because of a change in the core curriculum and in part because fewer students in secondary education were selecting mathematics as a teaching field. The department did, however, hold its own because of service courses it offered other departments (such as statistics for business majors) and because pre-engineering students frequently took a two-year mathematics sequence before transferring elsewhere to complete their studies. The demand for courses in physics was even more limited than that for mathematics.

Another significant change among the staff has been in the geographical distribution of the schools from which instructors received their degrees. Of the faculty on the staff in 1961, about one-third received their undergraduate degrees from schools within about a seventy-five mile radius of Orange City. Moreover, of the sixteen instructors who possessed master's degrees, about one-third received them from either the University of South Dakota or South Dakota State University, both of which are also located relatively close to Orange City. This kind of geographical "inbreeding" has been much less prevalent during recent years. Although degrees from undergraduate schools in the mid-West continued to be dominant, the percentage of those taken in close proximity to Orange City diminished. The really significant change, however, occurred in graduate degrees. For example, schools from ten different states are represented among the twenty-seven faculty members listed in the 1980-1981 catalogue who possessed the master's degree. Because there were only four persons on the 1961-1962 instructional staff who had earned doctorates, it is difficult to make a meaningful comparison on this point, but it is worth nothing that in 1980-1981, schools from fifteen different states and one foreign country were represented among the twenty-four faculty members having degrees beyond the master's.

Despite the growth in the number of faculty members and in the geographical distribution of their degrees, the instructional staff did not change significantly in one important respect, namely, that of having received their undergraduate training at church related colleges, particularly at Reformed Church institutions. Thus, in 1961, several staff members had received their initial undergraduate education at Northwestern Junior College and about one-third of them obtained their baccalaureate degrees from either Central or Hope. An examination of the fifty-two full-time faculty listed in the 1980-1981 catalogue indicates a continuing preponderance of persons having degrees from Reformed Church colleges: Hope leading with fourteen, Northwestern with three, and Central with one. Many others graduated from colleges that would also be considered evangelical and conservative, such as Calvin, Wheaton, and Augustana, each of which had three graduates among the full-time faculty in 1980.

Northwestern in the past relied heavily on part-time instructors, and the last two decades have been no exception. Indeed, the percentage has increased. The 1961-1962 catalogue lists eight part-time instructors as compared to forty-four in 1981-1982. The increase has been the result of a number of factors. New programs in some instances have called for specialized instructors whom the school could not reasonably be expected to employ on a full-time basis. This has been particularly true in the areas of medical technology, agriculture, business, music, and library science. As a consequence, among the part-time faculty listed in the 1981-1982 catalogue eleven are in medical technology, four in agriculture, four in business, four in music, and two in library science. Also contributing to the increase in the number of part-time faculty has been the occasional practice of sharing professors with neighbor institutions, such as Dordt at Sioux Center and Westmar College at Le Mars.

There has traditionally been another group of part-time instructors who are not necessarily listed as such in the catalogues. These are those who combine teaching duties with administrative responsibilities. It is sometimes difficult to determine precisely who these staff members have been from year to year because of differences in classification, but they have always been a significant part of the instructional staff. Indeed, there was a time when even presidents did some teaching—Dr. Heemstra, for example, in 1939-1940 taught nine hours of Bible per week to 133 students. The practice of combining responsibilities has its advantages in helping administrators become better acquainted with the problems of students and with the concerns of their colleagues in full-time teaching. But there were occasions in the past when teacher-administrators were kept rather busy. In 1961-1962, for example, the dean of men, dean of women, dormitory counselor, and the division chairpersons taught full loads—this at a time when fifteen-hour teaching loads were not uncommon—and the academic dean taught six hours the first semester and nine hours the second semester. It must be added, of course, that the practice of combining administration and teaching was more possible during those years when enrollment was smaller and there was a less complex curriculum. On the other hand, administrators of those days did not have ready access to assistants and secretarial help as they have had in recent years.

A new tenure policy for the faculty was initiated in the fall of 1974. Drafted by a faculty committee and approved by the Board of Trustees, the major difference between it and preceding policy is that the awarding of tenure is less automatic. It provides that henceforth new faculty, except those specifically given short term appointments, are placed on probation for six years. To acquire tenure, a candidate has to demonstrate proficiency as a teacher through a knowledge of the subject, an ability to communicate with students, and a willingness to consider modifying his or her course presentations in the light of student reactions. It is also presumed that a candidate will show evidence of scholarship and subject interest through research and participation in professional organizations, performances, exhibits and publication. Finally, as in the past, candidates for tenure are expected to demonstrate a personal commitment to Jesus Christ as Lord and Saviour and relate their faith to all of their activities. Instructors are especially urged to integrate faith and learning in their particular academic disciplines.

During the six-year probationary period, a candidate is evaluated periodically by the Faculty Status Committee (made up of elected faculty members) and the vice-president for academic affairs. If at the end of the six years, a candidate is not considered deserving of tenure, he or she is given a one-year terminal contract. The current vice-president for academic affairs, Harold Heie, recently summarized the policy as follows: "Not getting tenure means dismissal. What tenure means, essentially, is a continuing appointment on a permanent basis. What it actually says is that we are happy enough with your performance that you can stay until retirement." Exceptions to the latter would, of course, occur in cases in which enrollment decreased to the point in which certain programs had to be eliminated.

The turnover rate among the faculty has not been excessive during the last two decades, but it did vary at times, being at its height during the 1960's and declining in the early 1970's. The difference between the two periods was perhaps due to in part to Northwestern's having a more satisfied faculty in the 1970's than in the previous decade. But there are other considerations that must be kept in mind. The decade of the 1960's was a "teacher's market," and considering Northwestern's low salary schedule and the fact that the institution had just embarked on a new venture as a four-year college, it was not always an easy task for the administration to attract good teachers of a kind who would fit into the mores of the local community. As a consequence, it was not uncommon for a new staff person to remain only one or two years. By the early 1970's, on the other hand, Northwestern had evolved to the point academically in which it was easier to attract and retain the faculty it wanted. Moreover, although salaries at Northwestern as late as 1972 were lower than the average private school, the situation was improving. Finally, the tight job market made it easier to recruit and retain qualified instructors. In recent years there appears to have been a slight rise in the turnover rate. Thus, the *Beacon* of September 5, 1980, reported twenty new faculty and staff members and that of September 4, 1981 reported twenty-three new arrivals. The latter were distributed as follows: full-time faculty, 7; part-time faculty, 6; full-time staff, 7; and part-time staff, 3.

Despite some turnover, an examination of the list of full-time faculty found in the 1981-1982 catalogue demonstrates that many have been at Northwestern for quite a few years. Of the slightly more than fifty persons on the list, over one-half had been on the staff ten years or longer, and more than one-third had been at Northwestern since 1965. Eight faculty members could be considered "veterans," having been there since the 1950's. What influenced some instructors to remain at the same institution so many years? Several answers can be given, including such factors as love for the community and hometown ties, as well as a desire to teach in a Reformed Church institution. But as Ralph Mouw, Professor of Mathematics at Northwestern since 1947 and a master at teaching, recently observed when confronted with this question, yet another answer can be given: "If you are teaching subject matter, the job might get old. But if you view the work as teaching people, there is no static situation at all. People are always different."

As in the past, faculty members were encouraged to take advantage of summer grants to attend school and work toward their doctorates. Indeed, in 1967, the Board of Trustees approved an expanded program of faculty summer grants to become effective for the summer of 1968. Increasingly, too, leaves of absence were approved for the same purpose. Thus, for the 1967-1968 academic year, four professors were given sabbaticals to work on their doctorates—two at the University of Colorado, one at the University of Iowa, and one at the University of South Dakota.

In part because of summer grants and sabbaticals, but also through careful hiring of new staff, the number of faculty with earned doctorates has increased steadily. The result has been that whereas in 1961, about 20 percent of the full-time faculty had degrees beyond the master's, by 1981, that number was about 45 percent. In making this comparison, however, certain considerations must be kept in mind. First, during those years when the number of doctorates was low, many of the faculty who did not have an earned doctorate, did have a significant number of graduate hours in their particular disciplines beyond the master's degree. Secondly, the above figures refer only to those engaged in full-time teaching; they do not include administrators who taught part-time or persons who came in from the "outside" to teach a course or two. For example, in 1961-1962, the academic dean, who had a Ph.D. in history, taught six hours the first semester and nine hours the second semester, while a professor from Westmar College, with a doctorate, came in twice a week to offer courses in German, and a local "gentleman farmer" with a doctorate from Wisconsin, taught an evening course in sociology each semester. Finally, as anyone who has taken some college work can affirm, it does not necessarily follow that a person having an earned doctorate is automatically a good teacher. In this respect, Northwestern has always been fortunate in having professors with master's degrees who as teachers could hold their own with the best of their colleagues who had doctorates.

Although leaves of absence were initially designed to increase the number of doctorates on campus, in due time sabbaticals were also granted to staff members who already had doctor's degrees who wished to broaden their education or, perhaps, research a particular topic in depth. Thus, three of the four professors who were granted sabbaticals in 1979-1980 already possessed doctorates, as did two of the four in 1980-1981.

The number of doctorates on the staff of a college is, of course, only one of several criteria for measuring the academic standing of an institution. Other considerations include the amount of original research and publishing carried on by the faculty, the size and quality of the library, and the achievements of the school's graduates. With respect to research and publishing, the fact that Northwestern's faculty for many years was not particularly known for its outside scholarly pursuits can be easily explained. Not only did most of the faculty have a marginal amount of graduate study, but the school had little or no funds to help support research. Moreover, teaching loads were exceptionally heavy and until the Academy was discontinued in 1961, many faculty members were also expected to teach courses at the secondary level. Fortunately, these conditions began changing after 1961 as teaching loads were cut and summer grants and leaves of absence became more available. Foundation awards and financial assistance from the federal government have also helped. Increasingly, too, many instructors came to realize that faculty responsibilities in a four-year college should involve more than teaching and advising students. Dr. Harold Heie, the college's current vice-president for academic affairs, expressed this point well when he recently stated:

As vitally important as [teaching and counselling] are, their sum total presents a truncated view of what it means to be a member of a college faculty. A faculty member should also be a scholar, one who is constantly learning, exploring the frontiers of new knowledge, and sharing the results of this scholarship with the larger academic community.

The situation with respect to publishing began improving gradually during the 1960's, and progressed more rapidly in the 1970's. Initially, most of the scholarly writing was in the form of short articles and book reviews, and, as might be expected, appeared primarily in religious journals. Dr. Edward Ericson, dean of academic affairs from 1973 to 1977, helped create, by his own example, an atmosphere among his faculty that placed greater emphasis on research and publishing. In addition to writing one book, *Radicals in the University,* and co-authoring another, *Religion and Modern Literature: Essays in Theory and Criticism,* Dr. Ericson published numerous articles and reviews. Upon being asked about his thoughts after finishing his first book, he replied, "it gives a person a strange feeling to hold in his hand three and one-half years of his life." Despite the tedious, time-consuming process involved, other faculty members have apparently wanted to share in that "strange feeling." In the last five years, several books have been written or started by members of Northwestern's staff. Among those published, have been works ranging from a study of the theatre and choral reading to a history of the Christian mission to the Muslims to a book of readings on the contemporary French educator and political philospher, Jacques Ellul. President Radandt himself set a good example for his colleagues with his publication in 1977 of *A German Literary History: From Baroque to Storm and Stress, 1720 to 1775.* Northwestern's faculty members have also shown a greater interest in attending meetings of professional organizations and conferences that have a bearing on their particular academic disciplines. On occasion, they have played active roles at these meetings by reading papers or serving as respondents.

There have, of course, been pursuits besides those mentioned above that have helped bring Northwestern to the favorable attention of the public. Not the least of these have been in the departments associated with fine arts: dramatic productions, musical recitals and programs, and individual art shows. Victories of the athletic department on the basketball court and the football field have also brought regional and even national recognition to the school. Some of these pursuits, especially those in the areas of music and athletics, have, of course, been a part of the Northwestern scene long before 1961. More information on faculty accomplishments in the fine arts and athletics will be found in the chapter on extracurricular activities. Last, but far from least, faculty members during the last two decades have continued to offer invaluable service to the community and the Church. For example, President Granberg reported to the Board of Trustees in the spring of 1967 that in the previous year faculty members gave more than one hundred sermons and addresses to church and civic groups. Similarly, many of the faculty have served as Sunday School and catechism teachers, as organists and choir directors, and as members of church consistories and denominational commissions.

XIII

Curriculum and Academic Life

The expansion of Northwestern's physical plant and the increase and other modifications in the staff were only part of the major changes that took place on the campus during the last twenty years. Of equal (some would say, of greater) significance were the changes that occurred in the school's curriculum and academic life. Unless a person were on campus during the late 1950's and early 1960's—years in which the Academy was gradually dissolved and Northwestern was transformed from a two-year into a four-year institution—it is difficult to appreciate the tremendous problems confronting the school during these transition years: a curriculum that allowed only the granting of a baccalaureate degree in education, a faculty burdened down with heavy teaching loads and generally possessing the minimum qualifications for teaching at the college level, a makeshift library with very limited holdings, and a need to achieve meaningful accreditation as soon as possible. Looking back on those transition years and at the situation today, one cannot help being amazed that so much was accomplished in so brief a period.

Although conditions improved only one step at a time, students by the late 1960's were already noting a significant change. Thus, an article in the *Beacon* of February 10, 1967 by a graduating senior mentioned several favorable developments that had occurred on campus since his arrival as a freshman in 1963. Similarly, an editorial in the student paper of a few months later noted that the college was making progress toward the creation of a liberal arts atmosphere although much still remained to be done:

Gradually, she is altering herself to fit a new mold—a mold which is formed by a stress on the academic; new and better course offerings enlightened faculty; interested, intellectual administrators; eager, searching students; and a physical plant which provides a place for a liberal arts atmosphere to flourish.

Without detracting from the contributions of past presidents who helped nurture the school trough trials and tribulations, a special word of tribute must go to Dr. Preston Stegenga for the guidance he gave the school during these critical transition years.

Obtaining accreditation from the North Central Association as a four-year college became one of the major tasks facing Northwestern during the 1960's. Although it had been accredited as a junior college in 1954, this was not applicable to its four-year program. A visit by President Stegenga to the Association's offices in Chicago in late 1958 resulted in setting up the following time schedule: submission of a preliminary "Institutional Self-Study" by May 1959, completion of the Self-Study by May 1960, and a visit by a team of accreditation examiners sometime during the 1961-1962 academic year. Because the Self-Study called for a detailed survey of all aspects of Northwestern, the aid of the entire faculty was enlisted to help draft it. Eleven committees, each entrusted with a particular task, were appointed to implement the project. The preliminary report was submitted on schedule, and upon receiving various suggestions from the Association office, the final draft was completed. An accrediting team of three representatives from North Central thereupon spent two days on the campus in December 1961, examining such matters as academic standards, faculty qualifications, curriculum, enrollment, finances, and physical plant.

The report of the visitation team was reviewed at the annual meeting of the Association in March 1962. Unfortunately, Northwestern was denied accreditation at this time. The reasons were several. Among the more important were the lack of a "rigorously enforced" probation and suspension system for students doing poor academic work, a shortage of professors with earned doctorates, the need for a more research-minded faculty, heavy teaching loads, and inadequate library facilities.

Although failure to receive accreditation came as a disappointment, there was a renewed determination to introduce improvements that would overcome the basic weaknesses. Moreover, North Central encouraged the college to continue the work of upgrading its program and to reapply for accreditation as soon as it seemed feasible. In fact, the "North Central Examiners' Report of 1961" indicated significant aspects of a positive nature:

the physical plant shows evidence of good planning . . . the financial situation insofar as current operations are concerned, is excellent . . . in the opinion of the examiners, the schematic arrangement or pattern of general education courses is satisfactory . . . and in general, the expansion capital assets over the past ten years has been remarkable.

In view of the various strengths of Northwesten's program, as recognized by North Central, it was encouraging that Dr. Wayland Osborn of the Iowa Department of Public Instruction granted approval for continuing the annual teacher certification for Northwestern graduates during this transitional period of upgraded accreditation.

One of the worthwhile results of the visit by the accrediting team was the opportunity to listen to outside, knowledgeable experts regarding weak spots that needed correction. Moreover, Dr. Earland Carlson, vice-president for academic affairs at Millikin University in Illinois, was officially appointed by the North Central Association to serve as a consultant for helping the college achieve accreditation. On the basis of recommendations from several quarters plus the carrying to fruition of several worthwhile changes antedating the visit of the accrediting team, Northwestern's program improved considerably during the next few years. Improvements included drafting a rigid policy on academic standards, upgrading the staff by encouraging non-doctorates to take additional graduate work, making twelve hours the standard teaching load, constructing Ramaker Library, and requesting faculty members to make a careful survey of library holdings to determine what new books should be purchased. The details of some of these improvements, such as the construction of Ramaker Library and the granting of summer stipends for graduate study, have already been discussed in previous chapters.

One of Northwestern's academic weaknesses noted by North Central's examiners was the school's retention policy with respect to students doing poorly in their course work. This problem was corrected beginning with the spring semester of 1961-1962. It was decided that on the basis of a 4.0 grading system, freshmen whose grade point averages for a semester were less than 1.50 would be placed on academic probation. The same policy applied to sophomores and upperclassmen whose grade point averages for a semester were less than 1.67 and 2.0 respectively. While on probation, a student was permitted to carry only twelve hours of course work and would be subject to the regulations of the faculty Eligibility Committee as regards participation in college-connected activities.

Students on probation who did not meet the minimum grade point average for their class rank during the probationary semester were eligible for suspension. Moreover, freshmen at the end of the second semester and other students at the end of any semester who failed in one-third or more of their course work were also eligible for suspension. The decision of whether or not to suspend a student was made by the faculty Administrative Committee. A student who was suspended had to leave school for a minimum of one semester. It was also agreed that beginning with the spring semester of 1961-1962, senior students enrolled in any course numbered in the 100's (that is, freshman level) had to obtain a minimum final grade of "C" in order to receive credit for the course. The new policy on academic standards has remained virtually intact since its introduction twenty years ago.

Although significant weaknesses still remained in Northwestern's staff and in its program—for example, the number of doctorates increased only slightly and library holdings were still small—the school was given preliminary accreditation in 1964. This came about after the submission of another Self-Study and a second visit from a North Central team of examiners. The new examiners were a unique group consisting of three college presidents and one vice-president and coming from as far east as West Virginia and as far west as Arizona. Northwestern's success in obtaining accreditation on its second attempt was significant because it meant that henceforth graduates would receive ten-year Iowa Professional Teaching Certificates. Before this, certificates had to be renewed annually.

The accreditation that Northwestern received in 1964 was labeled "preliminary." Acquiring full accreditation involved additional steps, including a new Self-Study and another examination a few years later. Moreover, the 1964 accreditation applied to baccalaureate degrees in Teacher Education only. In seeking to upgrade its accreditation, the college continued to have the assistance of a North Central consultant. In 1964-1965, this was Dr. Sherrill Cleland, dean of academic affairs at Kalamazoo College, followed by Dr. John Horner, president of Hanover College in Indiana.

Initially, it was planned to apply for full accreditation in 1967, primarily designed, as before, for the teacher training program. In 1966, however, this decision was deferred in order to upgrade the liberal arts program and seek full accreditation at that level. This by no means meant that the liberal arts program would replace teacher training. Indeed, plans called not only for preserving the latter, but for improving it by having teacher education students fulfill a set of liberal arts requirements along with those for teacher certification. Moreover, plans were soon introduced for updating the teacher education program with a view to seeking national accreditation at a later date from the National Council for Accreditation of Teacher Education (NCATE).

The task for upgrading the liberal arts program in order to award bona fide liberal arts degrees got fully underway during the early years of Dr. Granberg's presidency. The specifics of what was accomplished in broadening the liberal arts atmosphere on the campus will be discussed later. Suffice it to note at this point that the achievements were impressive, and that Dr. Granberg's own personal contributions were significant. The result was that in the 1969-1970 academic year, following one of its typical and careful examinations, North Central awarded

the college full accreditation as a liberal arts college for an initial period
of five years.

Despite this vote of confidence by North Central, some weaknesses
still remained and the examiners urged the school authorities to continue working on them. In the area of finances, for example, it was
noted that the size of the endowment should be greater and that faculty
salaries were below national norms. With respect to academic matters,
suggestions were made for enriching the program for upperclass students through more innovative curriculum planning. Criticism was also
directed at certain aspects of the library and its use, including the need
to build up the holdings further and to encourage professors to structure
their courses less around textbooks in order to bring about greater student use of the library. Questions were also raised about the excessive
number of courses offered in the Department of Business Administration
and the weakness in the physics offerings. Finally, despite significant
progress in obtaining more persons with doctorates on the staff and
expanding some of the extra-curricular activities, the examiners thought
that room for improvement still existed in both these areas.

The college took these recommendations to heart and dutifully proceeded to work on them. At the end of the five year period, the necessary steps were taken to renew the accreditation. These began with
preparing another extensive Self-Study by the administration and faculty. Like previous documents of this kind, it stated the objectives of
the college and then proceeded to explain how, through its resources
and programs, these objectives were being realized. In February 1976,
a team of five North Central examiners visited the campus for three
days once again to make an on-site inspection. The team's report was
satisfactory, and in July, North Central's Commission of Higher Education reaccredited Northwestern—this time for a period of ten years.

As noted, soon after the decision had been made in the mid-1960's
to upgrade the liberal arts program and seek North Central accreditation
at that level, plans were also made to seek accreditation from the National Council for Accreditation of Teacher Education. This was a wise
move in view of the fact that Northwestern at this time was graduating
slightly more than one hundred teachers annually; such an endorsement
would enable graduates of the teacher training program to receive automatic certification among the thirty-one states that cooperated with
NCATE. The procedures involved were similar to steps taken for North
Central accreditation. Formal application was made in 1970, and early
in the following year Northwestern was informed that its application
had been acted upon favorably, making the school one of about 475 out
of 2,500 colleges with teacher education programs to achieve that honor.

Because NCATE's initial accreditation of Northwestern was also for a period of five years, application for reaccreditation was made in 1975. The procedure was similar to the previous occasion, but this time the review board turned down the application. At a loss to understand why this had occurred, NCATE was asked to reconsider the ruling. The appeal resulted in a reversal of the earlier decision, and accreditation was extended for ten years to September 1, 1985. In commenting on this achievement, Dean Ericson stated:

This reaccreditation effort means a couple of things for Northwestern. First, it means that the college has again put itself to the test of nation-wide standards for programs in preparing teachers for elementary and secondary schools and has passed it successfully. Second, it means that the college as a whole achieves greater recognition and standing in the general academic community by virtue of having its teacher preparation program approved by a national organization.

The consultants as well as the examiners who visited Northwestern on behalf of North Central suggested on several occasions that more innovation be shown in the curriculum. The suggestions were not ignored. One of the most unique approaches to this matter was the so-called Chicago Semester. Introduced in 1974, this program enabled a student, usually in his or her junior year, to spend a full semester at the Chicago Metropolitan Center, which served primarily students from Reformed and Christian Reformed colleges. Trinity Christian College, located in Palos Heights, a suburb of Chicago, acted as the sponsoring institution. Specific credits of up to sixteen hours could be arranged in consultation with the student's advisor at Northwestern. About one-half of the credits involved a study of the humanities and fine arts as these related to Chicago, plus seminars on metropolitan problems and social research methods. The remainder of the credit hours were more in line with the student's major and comparable to an internship. The first semester that Northwestern participated in the program, seven young women enrolled in it, and all participated in programs designed to teach vocational skills associated with social work. Although interning as social workers continued to be the main interest in the Chicago Semester, students took advantage of other opportunities as well. These ranged from working in a commercial art firm to learning about some phases of a large bank to studying at first hand the intricacies of a metropolitan library.

Similar to the Chicago Semester was the Washington Semester. Introduced in 1977, this one-semester program sponsored by the Christian College Consortium, included attending seminars, meeting with government officials, and interning with some branch of the federal government. Special emphasis was placed on the role of Christians in government. Occasional government internships were also available at the state level in Des Moines. For example, in the spring of 1980, a senior received fourteen hours credit as an intern with the Iowa State Division of Criminal Investigation.

Several other unique programs, for which academic credit was given, were also introduced during recent years. In the summer of 1975, the Department of History sponsored a three-week tour to the southwestern part of the United States to study first hand the culture of the Indians of that region, while at the same time the Department of Biology supervised a group of students in the Pacific northwest to study marine life in its natural habitat. Credit was also arranged on a few occasions for trips to Europe. These included a two-week visit to England and the Netherlands in May 1974, a trip of similar duration to England and Scotland in August 1977, and a three-week visit to the Middle East in May 1979. In each instance, the students were accompanied by members of the faculty and generally received three hours credit for which they were expected to attend lectures, complete specified readings, and write a paper. Twice in recent years, Professor Stephen Cobb of the Department of Sociology accompanied small groups of students to the Bahamas for two weeks between semesters. As explained by Cobb, the purpose of these visits was "to develop a broader, more sensitive appreciation of American and Bahamanian (British influenced) social policy by examining social policy within other social, political, and economic contexts." This involved visits to churches, schools, and judicial institutions, as well as conversations with public officials and educators.

Despite such developments as expansion of the curriculum, accreditation by North Central, and the introduction of a liberal arts program, the basic goals of the school remained virtually unchanged. In a brief article in the *Beacon* of May 24, 1963, the academic dean outlined and explained three major aims of Northwestern. In ascending order of importance, he declared these to be vocational, liberalizing, and spiritual. The vocational goal was described as helping prepare students for various occupations and professions. This was justified because of the costs involved in obtaining a college education and, more importantly, because of the fact that a student, upon finishing college, was of an age when serious consideration had to be given to finding gainful employment. Along with providing opportunities for speicalized career-type training and pre-professional programs, Northwestern was described as having for its second goal the giving of a broad, liberalizing education. As explained by the dean:

Most educators . . . believe that there should be a kind of common denominator among all college graduates, no matter what careers they have chosen for themselves. Such educators believe that all college graduates should feel "at home" in certain areas of knowledge—that all college graduates ought to have an understanding of the history of man's past, an appreciation of the great masterworks in literature, art, and music, and an acquaintance with the physical and biological world.

Finally, as a third goal, he stated that Northwestern as a Christian college must seek to educate its students for service to God. To quote the academic dean again:

This goal of service to God must be inextricably linked with the vocational goal mentioned earlier. By emphasizing the former along with the latter, Northwestern is more likely to turn out teachers, businessmen, pre-med students, etc., who will . . . carry out their responsibilities toward their work and toward society in a Christian spirit. [Similarly], by linking the liberalizing view with the spiritual, Northwestern [can] give its students a meaningful education, a *wereldbeschouwing* (to use a good Dutch word which means literally "world-view-of-life") that is God and Bible centered.

Northwestern's goals as explained above were not intrinsically different from those announced from time to time before or since 1963, except that a few were more lengthy—even long-winded at times—and not all placed equal emphasis on the need for vocational and pre-professional training.

One of the most scrutinous inquiries regarding the purpose of Northwestern grew out of a special committee established in the spring of 1967, soon after Dr. Granberg assumed the presidency. This committee, known as the Steering Committee for Long Range Academic Planning, was composed of a representative from each of six academic divisions together with the president and academic dean and a member of the Board of Trustees. It met at various intervals over a five-year period from 1967 to 1972. As described later, the purpose was to set "forth for today and tomorrow Northwestern's special character as a college; its commitment, its task, and its special concerns."

During the period from 1967 to 1970, under the chairmanship of Professor George De Vries, the committee confined itself primarily to two areas of work: determining Northwestern's philosophy of Christian education and outlining specific goals based on this philosophy. Members of the committee drafted numerous position papers which they submitted to other members and later to the faculty as a whole for intensive discussion and debate. The first group of papers, some of which were scholarly and based on considerable research, examined the Biblical foundations of Christian learning and the role that the Reformed Church has played in higher education. Later papers dealt more specifically with the situation at Northwestern. Based on the papers and committee reports, together with input from the faculty as a whole, the committee on May 18, 1970 submitted a summary report entitled, "Liberal Arts for Northwestern." Although the ideas expressed in it were not particularly different from what had been stated about Northwesten's purpose in the past, they were explained in more comprehensive terms. The final report, for example, was fifteen pages in length, and even it was shorter than some of the position papers presented earlier. The essence of the summary report is in the "Prologue":

A liberal arts education for all Northwestern College students should center upon a broad non-specialized curriculum, with an emphasis on the humanities (broadly conceived—especially the history of culture and thought). Every area of the curriculum, including occupational training, should be set within this Christian humanistic approach. Our students need to grapple with the ultimate, perennial issues of life; our students need to be introduced to "the funded wisdom of the ages." We should help young Christians to develop a kind of Christian humanism, guided by the Word of God—that they may learn to think critically, to understand themselves and their world, to analyze and synthesize, to make wise decisions, to evaluate, to appreciate, to emphasize, to articulate, and in general to become conscious of their own personal Christian interpretation of life—and thereby better to serve God and man in the church and in the world.

After 1970, under the chairmanship of Dr. Lyle Vander Werff, the committee's primary task became one of revising the general education requirements for graduation. This work was closely related to what had gone on before because through such a revision it was hoped some of the newly-described goals would be realized. As explained by President Granberg: "This core program will be the chief tool in giving expression to Northwestern's special character and Christian purposes."

The result was the introduction in the fall of 1972 of a completely revised core curriculum. Consisting of three parts, or "areas," the first was labeled "Foundation Courses," and later termed "General Requirements." For the freshman and sophomores, these included the following: one hour of Orientation to the Liberal Arts, comprising mainly an interdepartmental introduction to the purposes of a Christian liberal arts program; seven hours of Biblical studies, consisting of Old Testament

Faith, The Gospels, and The Apostolic Church; six hours of Western
Literature; nine hours of Western Man, which was an inter-departmental survey of Western art, music, literature, philosophy, religion, politics, and economics from ancient times to the present; and two hours
of physical education activity courses to be chosen from a list of fourteen
(eventually increased to twenty-three) one-hour courses.

The Foundation Courses also included a Cross-Cultural Study, usually taken in the junior year, and a Senior Seminar—each for three
hours credit. The purpose of the former was to expose students to
cultures and ideologies different from their own. Besides the typical
classroom approach (involving courses like the Mind of Japan, Near East
Studies, and American Indian Studies), it was possible for students to
meet the Cross-Cultural requirements by various forms of off-campus
experiences, including work and study in poverty-stricken or minority
sections of a large city, research on an Indian reservation, or directed
study abroad. The Senior Seminar, like some other aspects of the Foundation Courses, was inter-departmental in scope. It was variously described as designed to "enable students to put their four years of college
education together into a meaningful whole," and, most recently, to
"serve as a bridge between a student's college career and future life"
and as a means to "encourage students to deal with fundamental issues
in the context of their major."

The second area of the new curriculum was initially called "Selective
Courses," but was later changed to "Distribution Requirements." In
accordance with it, a student graduating from Northwestern had to take
fourteen hours of electives chosen from at least three of the following
broad disciplines—fine arts, social science, natural science, and foreign
language. The rationale behind this requirement was to broaden the
student's scope of knowledge and interest.

The third area among the new set of requirements was the major.
This consisted of from twenty-four to forty-five hours of course work
chosen from among the majors offered by the school. In 1972, when the
new program went into effect, there were twenty-one majors from which
to choose; by 1981, this number had increased to twenty-seven. The
purpose of the major was to compel students to examine one field in
depth. Minors were eliminated from among the new requirements,
although they continued to be listed in the catalogue for students going
into secondary education to enable them to meet the teaching requirements of high schools. The total number of hours required for graduation
from Northwestern remained as before: 126 hours.

Not all students were satisfied with the so-called Foundation Courses.
This was especially true with respect to the Western Literature and

Western Man sequence. Criticisms included questions about their per-
tinency to certain majors, the different approaches used by instructors,
and the turnover among the staff members placed in charge of these
courses. Questions were also raised occasionally concerning the limited
selection of Cross-Cultural courses available on campus and whether or
not allowing a two- or three-week field trip in the summer to fulfill this
requirement was the equivalent of a semester's work in a classroom.
Criticism likewise appeared from time to time regarding the Senior
Seminar, namely, that its objectives were not being met and that juniors
were occasionally admitted into it.

The faculty was not averse to modifying the core program, and revisions and improvements were made from time to time. The one hour
Orientation course was dropped and the team-teaching approach was
refined for the inter-departmental courses. In 1976, Northwestern received a $50,000 grant from the National Endowment for the Human-
ities to be used for revising the fifteen hours in the Western Literature
and Western Man sequence. As finally worked out, the two sets of
courses were merged into a single twelve-hour block spread over three
semesters.

Students desiring to obtain state teaching certificates had to take, in
addition to the above requirements, a sequence of courses leading to
certification. Like other requirements, these, too, changed from time
to time. Some of the changes were the result of recommendations from
within Northwestern's own department of education. For example, beginning with the fall term of 1973-1974, several elementary education
courses were dropped from the list of requirements, although they continued to be offered as electives. Included were courses in art, music,
and physical education specially designed for elementary teachers, but
considered of less importance than formerly because most schools by
1973 had specialists in these areas. Some changes also came about as a
result of directives from the Iowa State Department of Education. For
example, in 1979, in accordance with one such directive, a new course,
"Human Relations," became a requirement for teacher certification in
Iowa. The purpose of this course was to develop greater sensitivity
among teachers regarding discrimination, prejudice, racism, sexism,
and similar problems. And in 1980, on the recommendation of the State
Department of Education, a faculty committee was appointed to re-
write the requirements in the elementary education program.

The new core curriculum introduced in 1972 did not include the
traditional freshman English courses among its list of requirements. This
made sense for students who had a good command of the English language, but not all students were that fortunate. Moreover, there always

were some students who wished to develop further competency. Fortunately, to meet these needs, the Skills Center was established in the basement of Dykstra Hall in 1974 and placed under the supervision of the English Department. Since its founding, the Center has developed a wide range of options for providing individualized instruction. The 1981-1982 catalog lists seven courses being offered, each carrying one hour of credit, including grammar, spelling, vocabulary development, reading efficiency, writing research papers, typewriting, and study skills. Moreover, a wide collection of individualized workbooks, tests, cassette tapes, filmstrips, and computer programs was made available to students wanting assistance. Regrettably, not all students who needed remedial work in English were taking advantage of the offerings in the Skills Center. As a consequence, there was a slight retrenchment from the new core program. It was stipulated that an entering freshman with an American College Testing score of 17 or below or Scholastic Aptitute Test verbal score below 400 would henceforth be required to take a three-hour course in Basic Writing.

In the early 1970's, Northwestern introduced several innovations that were also being followed by other colleges. For example, beginning in 1971, lower level courses in most departments at Northwestern were opened to qualified high school seniors to a maximum of six credit hours. Also in 1971, the college adjusted its school calendar so that classes would begin in late August, and the first semester would end at the time Christmas vacation began. The second semester would then begin about the second week of January and conclude in middle May. The new calendar had several advantages, including eliminating the two low-productive weeks in the first semester that traditionally followed the Christmas break, and providing an opportunity to inform suspended and probationed students about their status a week or more before the second semester began—instead of a day or two before as was the case in the past. The new calendar also enabled students to begin summer jobs a week or two earlier.

In 1972, again following the lead of other schools, Northwestern introduced the pass/fail option. By it, students were permitted to take thirteen of the 126 hours required for graduation on a pass/fail option. Courses taken in this manner counted toward graduation but did not affect grade point averages. This option was introduced in the hope it would encourage more students to take courses outside their major area of interest. With the exception of writing and tutorial courses connected with the Skills Center, the pass/fail option was not open to freshmen. Sophomores and juniors were allowed to take one course on that basis per semester, while seniors were permitted two such courses. The pass/fail option was not made available for all departments, nor was it applicable to courses in a student's major.

Also in keeping with trends in other colleges, Northwestern periodically introduced new courses designed to keep step with the changing world and with pressing social problems. For example, during the last few years new courses have been introduced in agri-business, communications, computer science, ecology, and gerontology. A change introduced during the 1970's in the grading system, however, was out of the ordinary as compared to practices among other schools. Beginning in 1974, after considerable discussion among both faculty and students, the grading system was revised to record pluses and minuses in the final grades and to use them in computing grade point averages.

In the fall of 1977, Northwestern introduced what was termed a "career concentration program." As explained in the *Classic:*

In this program a student takes a liberal arts major, such as mathematics or psychology, and then may take other courses which will train him for a specific job, like social work, journalism, or Christian education. Many career-oriented courses with on-the-job internships have already been developed—coaching, church music, music performance, recreation, Christian education, agri-business, social work, journalism, public management, accounting—professional, and accounting—industrial.

The program was described by Dean Edward Ericson as a "new curricular structure, which will be unique to Northwestern." Actually, it was not that new. Even the Academy during its early years, despite the strong emphasis placed on the classics, offered courses in business and made frequent references to the excellent teacher-education program in its efforts to attract students. None of this changed with the addition of a Junior College program in 1928. Indeed, teacher training and courses in business remained among the Junior College's most popular programs, and it was a rare school catalogue that did not devote several pages to describing the pre-professional curricula that were available. Nor did the transition from a two-year college to one offering the baccalaureate degree change matters. For example, seven of the fourteen new courses introduced in 1961 were in the Department of Business Administration, and the 1961-1962 catalogue describes fifty-two hours of courses offered in business and secretarial science. Because the 1972-1973 catalogue lists sixty-four such hours, it is obvious that this situation was not changed by the increasing emphasis placed on liberal arts. Indeed, most courses currently offered for the approximately forty career concentrations and pre-professional programs described in literature emanating from the admissions office were being offered long before the so-called career concentration program was introduced. Major exceptions to this have been courses pertaining to agriculture, computer science, and social work.

Some aspects of the program, however, are unique. For example, more career counseling is available. One of the new offices in the Rowenhorst Student Center is the Career Planning and Placement Center which is staffed with a full-time director. In addition to personal counseling, the Center is provided with a library of materials about various careers and it functions as a placement office for non-education students. (Placement for education students is handled directly by the Department of Education.) The Center also serves as a place to obtain information and guidance on graduate schools.

One of the most novel things about the career concentration program has been the introduction of internships. These were recently explained in the preface of a booklet, "Career Concentrations," issued by the college admissions office:

Significant parts of many career concentrations are on-the-job internships. Some students may spend a semester in a newspaper office, group home, or church. Others may work with a Christian theatre company, a city manager, a bank, or a recreation program. Still other job situations that interest you may be arranged. Our students have a wide diversity of experiences available to them—from working in a local business such as Northwestern State Bank in Orange City to getting experience as a hospital administrator in Omaha to a special semester in Chicago or Washington, D.C., interning in an agency and doing individualized research.

Credit toward graduation is given for these internships. For example, a senior business administration major who spent the 1980 spring semester interning at Williams & Company, an accounting firm with branches in Orange City and Le Mars, received fifteen hours of academic credit for his work. Also in 1980, a student interned for fifteen credit hours at the Sioux County State Bank in Orange City.

In the view of many academicians, the library is the nerve system of any respectable college. An account of academic life at Northwestern during the last two decades would therefore be incomplete without some discussion of this subject. Unfortunately, the library had for a long time been one of Northwestern's weakest points. Even during the late 1950's, only about 700 books were added each year. This was inadequate, and especially so in view of the fact that about one-half of these were gifts of limited value. Improvisations had to be made almost annually on the second and third floors of Zwemer Hall to make room for additional stacks and study tables, resulting in increasingly cramped quarters. Finally, adding to the library's weakness was the fact that there was only one trained librarian on the staff.

The situation improved significantly during the 1960's. The construction of Ramaker Library has already been noted, but also of great importance was the increase in the holdings. By 1968, the library had about 40,000 volumes, a four-fold increase since 1961, as well as about 2,600 volumes of bound periodicals and over 1,000 reels of microfilm. Progress continued, with the result that by 1973, Ramaker's holdings totaled 57,000 books, 4,700 bound periodicals, and 2,750 reels of microfilm. Despite this increase, the *rate* of growth declined in the early 1970's due to inflation and other financial problems. Thus, while the average growth rate in the three years 1967-1970 had been 5,500 books per year, the rate for the next three years averaged only slightly more than 1,500. The situation improved again in the later 1970's, with the result that by 1981, the library had more than 81,000 books, 5,700 bound periodicals, and 5,000 reels of microfilm.

As a member of the Colleges of Mid-America Consortium, Northwestern's students were given access to books from ten other colleges. The value of this was explained by Arthur Hielkema, Northwestern's head librarian since 1969:

It has given the library another avenue to extend its services to the students and faculty. The most important of these services is a daily inter-library loan. Each day, each college places a circuit call among the ten libraries. It requests specific titles which are not contained in the local college library. This service helps Ramaker Library fill within forty-eight hours over seventy-five per cent of the requests for materials that cannot be found in our library.

As an indication of the strength of Northwestern's library collection, it can be noted that Ramaker Library has become one of the main suppliers for this unique interlibrary loan service.

XIV

Student Life and Extracurricular Activities

Comments made during the 1960's by consultants who advised Northwestern under the asupices of the North Central Association and by visitation teams who examined the school for accreditation indicated general agreement that the intellectual climate needed careful attention. Intertwined with this was the need to create a livelier liberal arts atmosphere by promoting extracurricular activities, particularly in the fine arts, and getting students more involved in non-classroom campus life. Also important was the necessity to bring in more guest lecturers and to hold more symposiums. In all these matters, the school made giant strides.

Attesting to the progress Northwestern made during the last two decades in becoming a full-fledged liberal arts institution is the growth of the Department of Music and the increase in the number of concerts and recitals by visiting musicians. Until 1961, there was only one full-time music instructor, Lawrence Van Wyk. In addition to directing the choir and band, he taught all the music courses and was responsible for all private instruction except piano and organ, which were handled by two part-time teachers. A second full-time instructor was added in 1961, followed by others later, with the result that by 1981, the Music Department consisted of five full-time faculty (three with earned doctorates) and five part-time instructors.

Along with an expanded staff came wider opportunities for students to perform as the number of ensembles increased from a few to many, including A Cappella Choir, Chapel Choir, Heritage Singers, Men's Chorus, Concert Band, Jazz Band, Marching Band, String Ensemble, Musical Theatre, and Chamber Opera. Several of the new groups grew steadily from what they were when first organized. For example, when Professor Herbert Ritsema organized the marching band in 1961, it consisted of only 30 members; by 1981, it included about 70 instrumentalists and a 12-member flag group. It was also to Ritsema's credit that the Sioux County Orchestra was organized in 1967. Made up of Northwestern students and area musicians, its beginnings were small, but by the time of its tenth anniversary in 1977, it had grown to approximately fifty members. The status of the Music Department was greatly enhanced in the mid-1970's with the acquisition, in cooperation with the American Reformed Church, of a 3 manual, 37 stop, 49 rank organ. By making this a joint endeavor with a local church, the college was able not only to save a considerable amount of money on the cost of the instrument, but was also relieved of the expense of building an auditorium to house it.

Drama, like music, has been a part of the Northwestern scene virtually since the school was founded, but it too expanded in recent years. The expansion included an increase in staff, the enrollment of more students interested in drama, a larger budget, a wider selection of costumes, and the purchase of the Playhouse. As is often true on college campuses, one person in particular stands out to make a certain department blossom into an excellent organization. At Northwestern, such a person was Dr. Theora England, who served as chairperson of the Department of Speech and Drama for more than thirty years. The department has continued to move upward in the tradition set by Dr. England. In the last three years, for example, it has won two awards for property design and one for special effects at the regional American College Theatre Festival. This was in competition with about twenty-five colleges and universities from a four-state area.

Of the many programs put on by the Drama Department, one of the most popular for many years has been the annual Children's Theater.

Scene from Molière's "The Miser," 1981

Its roots go back to 1950 when the Academy seniors did *Five Little Peppers and How They Grew* as their class play. A few years later in 1955, the seniors did *Cinderella*. Because of the interest shown by children of the community, a children's production soon became part of the college's program and evolved into an annual practice. At first, special performances were put on only for children from the local Orange City schools, but it was soon decided to invite the Alton area children as well, and after that the list grew steadily. The result has been that in recent years as many as ten performances of a single play were attended by 7,000 to 8,000 children from schools throughout northwest Iowa.

The Choral Readers, organized by Dr. England in 1959 as one of the first such groups in the United States, quickly expanded to more than thirty members. Not only were they in demand for appearances in churches and before civic groups throughout the area, but they soon began taking extensive tours. The first of these was a two-week trip in June 1964 to the East Coast, and they have since appeared in Reformed churches throughout the United States and Canada. The nature of their program was described as follows in a report of 1971: "Bringing a message that is both contemporary and unique, the Readers make use of lights, sound and costumes. They present dramatic interpretations of Biblical passages and works by such renowned writers as Thurber, Sandburg, and Longfellow."

In keeping with the expanding liberal arts program in the late 1960's, the offerings of the Department of Art were rapidly expanded from ten courses in 1961 to nearly twice that by 1968. It was also in 1968 that a second person with the prestigious Master of Fine Arts degree was added to the staff. More student art shows were held as were exihibits by area artists and students from neighboring colleges. The Ferdinand Roten Galleries of Baltimore, Maryland, also put on occasional art displays. Established in 1952, Roten Galleries has one of the largest collections of graphic art in the country and specializes in arranging exhibits and sales at colleges and universities. Their exhibits at Northwestern have included as many as a thousand works at a single showing.

For many years, Northwestern's Art Department was handicapped by not having a satisfactory place for exhibits. The opening of the Te Paske Art Gallery in the Rowenhorst Student Center in January 1980, however, has permitted not only more regular art shows in comfortable surroundings, but also makes it easier for visiting artists to open their shows with talks and coordinate them with art films and slides. As John Kaericher, chairman of the Art Department since 1963, recently stated,

The Choral Readers, 1976

"A good gallery is like a library for visual arts students and a valuable resource center for knowledge."

The cultural life on campus was also enriched by the showing of film classics. This was initiated by the English Department to help students gain a clearer understanding of literary works they were studying—*East of Eden, Catch 22, Doll's House, Oedipus the King,* to mention a few. Beginning in the late 1960's, attention was also given to bringing in foreign films. Occasionally this was done by having a three-day foreign film festival, but generally the showings were scattered throughout the year. In 1978-1979, a series, appropriately entitled "World through a Lens," included films from Brazil, France, India, Japan, Spain, and the United States. Until the completion of the Rowenhorst Student Center, films were shown at various places on campus, including the Student Union, the Chapel, and the Playhouse.

Although there had been a time when anything having to do with movies or Hollywood was strongly frowned upon in many Reformed Church homes, this attitude was fast disappearing by the 1960's. Thus there was little or no criticism of films shown on campus when their purposes were primarily to instruct. During the past few years, however, as films became more explicit in matters of violence, sex, and language, and as more films were being shown on weekends primarily for entertainment—a development greatly facilitated by the opening of the 250-seat Bogaard Theater—some students began demanding that greater discretion be shown in their selection. Occasional questions were also raised about there being too little Christian music played on the juke box and on the intercom system.

In short, the problem was, Where should the line be drawn regarding films and music since Northwestern is a Christian college? Committees made up of faculty members and students grappled with the problem, as did several open forums. Opinions were naturally mixed, as efforts were made to strike a proper balance. As one of the reporters for the student paper expressed it in early 1980, "There are not necessarily any 'right' answers to the question [concerning] what constitutes Christian entertainment. It is really an issue which every Christian needs to resolve for himself."

Reflective of both the increase in enrollment and the growing social and cultural maturity of the campus, has been the rise in the number of student clubs and organizations—from less than ten in 1961 to more than twenty by 1981. As a result, there are now organizations that should appeal to virtually any major type of cultural or professional interest a student might have. Each of the fine arts, for example, has its own organization. Thus, for students majoring or minoring in art, there is the Art Students' League; and for those in drama, there is Alpha Psi Omega, which is associated with the national honor society for students in dramatics. The latter organization is only one of several on campus linked to regional and national associations. Other include Phi Beta Lambda, a nationally affiliated club that caters to students in business; a chapter of the Student Iowa State Education Association which is of interest to those contemplating the teaching profession; and Alpha Mu Gamma, a nationally affiliated organization for students studying foreign languages.

Some of the new organizations were given strange but nevertheless appropriate names—after one discovers their meanings. For example, Chi-Rho, a club that seeks to promote a greater interest in Christian service, derives its name from the first two letters of *Christ* in Greek. Similarly, Custos de Liber et Motem, whose Latin title connotes the idea of "Guardianship of books," is for students having a special concern for library science. The name Quintlians is also a very appropriate title for the club whose members are interested in speech education. Quintilian was a noted Roman of the first century A.D. who distinguished himself as an authority on rhetoric. On the other hand, the names of other organizations indicate their nature precisely. These include the

Language Arts and Literature Club and the International Club, both of which date back to the period before 1961, and the Physical Education Majors Club and the Fellowship of Christian Athletes, which were organized later.

Along with the *Beacon* and *De Klompen*, two new student publications appeared during this period. The first of these was *Spring Leaves*, an annual publication started in 1971 containing creative writing and art work done by Northwestern students. It caters to any literary genre, including poetry, short stories, personal essays, and research papers as well as a variety of art work. Beginning in 1972, prizes were awarded for the best entries. As an example of the contents of *Spring Leaves*, the sixth edition (1977) contained thirty-three poems and five prose works submitted by fourteen students and ten examples of art work by nine students. In 1979, a similar but smaller magazine began appearing on campus. Known as *Spectrum* and appearing about once a month, it is somewhat less sophisticated than *Spring Leaves* and focuses more on prose.

In addition to broadening the scope of the fine arts departments and encouraging greater student participation in certain extracurricular activities, other devices also advanced the school's intellectual climate and liberal arts atmosphere. Distinguished lecturers and public officials were

The International Club, 1979-1980

brought in to speak to the students and faculty, and a variety of conferences and symposiums was scheduled. The value of bringing in special speakers and holding conferences was clearly pointed out to the campus community by President Granberg in early 1969, following the appearance of Dick Gregory and several civil rights leaders who discussed the black man's search for freedom:

We bring people to the campus who represent important viewpoints, viewpoints widely held and affecting our life today, so that you will reflect, so that you will consider and weigh, so that you will discuss what you hear from these people; for it is in so doing that your grasp of the truth grows, and it is in reflection and discussion that it becomes clearer what attitudes and actions are right and good and urgent.

The fact that occasional talks by visiting lecturers challenged student thinking is apparent in the reaction to remarks made by Dr. Virginia Mollenkott, chairperson of the English Department at William Paterson College in New Jersey. A leading Milton scholar, she spent the week of February 16, 1976 on campus presenting a series of lectures on the theme, "Women, Men, and the Bible." As reported in an editorial in the *Beacon,* Mollenkott's lectures

caused much discussion among everyone on campus and forced some people to re-examine their ideas about the relationship between males and females as seen through the Bible. Some agreed with her strongly and felt refreshed by the new support she provided for their views. Still others strongly opposed what she said on the basis of their traditional interpretations of biblical texts.

Lectures and conferences took place in part under the auspices of groups and organizations on campus, including academic departments, the Student Senate, and the faculty Cultural Affairs Committee. A few national organizations also played significant roles in this respect by providing grant money to defray expenses. These included the Danforth Visiting Lecturers Program, the Thomas F. Staley Foundation of New York, and the Woodrow Wilson Visiting Fellows Program. Except for the fact that the Staley Foundation had a more evangelical disposition, the purpose of these programs was similar. That of the Woodrow Wilson organization can serve as an example. It was described as an attempt "to broaden young people's understanding of American society by bringing college students face to face with successful men and women from business, journalism, government, diplomacy, and the professions." Other organizations that assisted in bringing in lecturers and in sponsoring conferences include the College of Mid-America, the Association of Reformed Colleges (made up of Hope, Central, Northwestern, Calvin, Dordt, Trinity Christian, Geneva, and Covenant), and the Iowa Council of the Humanities. Many of the lecturers who visited Northwestern under the auspices of these organizations stayed on campus several days, during which time they addressed not only the student body but spoke in classroom situations and held small seminars.

Space permits mention of only a few of the many lecturers and scholars who have visited Northwestern's campus in recent years. Persons whose speciality was in the area of religion held particular appeal. Those of note included John Hostetler (1968), one of America's foremost authorities on the Mennonites; Ben Marais (1968), a minister of the Dutch Reformed Church and Professor of the History of Christianity at the University of Pretoria, South Africa; Thomas Banyacya (1969), a Hopi Indian spiritual leader; Nicholas Wolterstorff (1976), a professor of philosophy at Calvin College who has lectured widely throughout North America on Reformed theology; Erik von Keunhelt-Leddihn (1976), a world-renowned Catholic scholar and lecturer from Austria; David and Martha Stern (1977), prominent leaders among Messianic Jews; Rabbi Albert Gordon (1966, 1975, and 1979) of Mt. Sinai Temple in Sioux City; Christian Baeta (1980), an ordained minister of the Evangelical Prebyterian Church of Ghana; and Larry Woiwode (1980), a noted Christian fiction writer and winner of several book awards.

Visiting lecturers in the fields of literature and drama also made occasional appearances on campus. These included Robert Speaight (1967), British author, actor, and critic; Sir Tyrone Guthrie (1968), one of the world's foremost stage directors and authorities on the theater; Paul Engle (1974), considered as one of Iowa's most prominent and versatile poets; Gwendolyn Brooks (1975), a black poet and Pultizer prize-winner; and Frederick Manfred (1978), author of more than twenty novels and numerous poems whose settings are in the Midwest.

Northwestern has had a long-standing fondness for bringing political leaders to the campus, and this continued to be true during the past two decades. Included were governors and United States senators from Iowa as well as politicians from other parts of the country. As examples of the latter, there was Paul Douglass (1967), who served as a distinguished senator from Illinois for eighteen years, and Mark Hatfield (1974), the well-known Christian senator from Oregon. International political figures also made frequent appearances. Thus, in just a three-year period (1968-1970), the following visitors addressed the students and faculty: Ferenc Nagy, the last prime minister of free Hungary; Patrick Jenkin, a member of the British Parliament; Baron Rijnhard

Bernhard van Lynden, the Netherlands ambassador to the United States; and Davidson Nicol, Sierra Leone's ambassador to the United Nations and a noted African educator.

There have also been numerous conferences—variously also termed symposia, forums, or workshops. Some of them have been primarily local in nature with participants drawn from members of the faculty and the community. In other instances, distinguished personalities from outside the area were brought in as participants. During the past few years, these sessions have included "Pornography and Censorship" (1974), in which one of the participants was former Supreme Court Justice Tom Clark; "Press and Power" (1975), which included Jerald Ter Horst, who served for a brief period as press secretary for former President Gerald Ford; a conference on "Old and Aging" (1976); a "Citizens' Workshop on Energy and Environment" (1976); "The Bible as Literature" (1978); a symposium on inflation (1980), in which one of the discussion leaders was Dr. Eugene Beem, Vice-President of Economics and Corporate Development for the Sperry and Hutchinson Company of New York City; "The Role of the Church in the Third World" (1980), in which the participants included Pat Kennedy, a Woodrow Wilson Visiting Fellow and one of the first ten appointments to the Peace Corps, and Dr. Stanley Vander Aarde, a Northwestern graduate who served as a medical missionary in India for many years (1980); and a workshop on children and divorce (1981).

As might be expected, athletic activities have become more pronounced since 1961. Except for women's sports, however, developments in this area were somewhat less obvious than in most other extracurricular activities because sports had long held a prominent place at Northwestern. For example, as a Junior College in the 1950's, the school won six conference and three state titles in basketball. Nevertheless, athletics took on a new meaning when Northwestern became a four-year college. In 1961, the school joined the National Association of Intercollegiate Athletics (NAIA), and a few years later golf, tennis, and wrestling were added to the sports roster to take their place alongside basketball, baseball, football and track. The major change, however, was that henceforth the school had to compete with four-year institutions, and this involved considerable "rebuilding" in order to face tougher and bigger teams. This challenge can be seen in the 1960-1961 football season during which Northwestern lost all its conference games. Most of these games were played with only eighteen men on the squad of which only one was a senior. But the situation gradually improved, and the win column soon exceeded the loss column. In 1971, Northwestern won the Tri-State Conference football championship, a feat that was to be repeated annually during the next nine seasons. In 1973, the football team won the NAIA Division II championship title, and was runner-up for that honor on two other occasions. During Christmas vacation in 1974, the team was invited to Japan for several exhibition games.

In competing with four-year institutions, basketball got off to a better start than football. Even during the first year, it had more wins than losses and the teams were soon capturing Tri-State trophies to place alongside those won in football. In 1971, in what was billed as "the greatest basketball game in Northwestern's history," it won the District 15 NAIA championship and advanced to the national finals, a feat that was repeated the following year. Although success in other men's sports did not compare with those in football and basketball, Tri-State crowns were won occasionally in baseball, indoor track, golf, and wrestling. The baseball and indoor track teams also advanced several times to the District 15 NAIA playoffs.

As with most colleges, women's sports at Northwestern were slighted for many years. Until the late 1970's, there was the equivalent of only one full-time woman staff member in the physical education department as compared to three and sometimes four for men. Women's sports eventually included volleyball, tennis, softball, basketball, golf, and track. Despite a slow start, some of the women's teams fared rather well. For example, in 1978, the tennis team won its third straight conference title, and in 1980, the softball team won its fourth straight conference championship.

For a brief period in the mid-1970's, criticisms were directed occasionally at Northwestern's athletic program. Typical was a letter to the editor of the *Beacon* dated October 28, 1972 stating that although "athletics are an important part in one's life . . . there is also a point where they can be overemphasized." The letter went on to explain that by comparison, other activities such as music and dramatics were given little recognition. Another letter of November 9, 1974, complained about the "glorification" of sports in the latest edition of the yearbook, *De Klompen:* "It wasn't enough that there were nearly seventy pictures related to football alone (not to mention the other sports) but a football picture had to be put on the cover too. At a glance it looks like an NFL publication." With specific reference to football, an article of March 8, 1975, contributed by a Reformed Church pastor in South Dakota, referred to the sport as "a throwback of 30,000 generations of anthropological time" and as "supervised gang fights." The criticism directed at the athletic program was serious enough to prompt the president to make a reference to it in his report of April 1973 to the Board of Trustees:

Extraordinary seasons by the football and the basketball teams increased Northwestern's visibility, thrilled many alumni and enhanced the image of the institution in the eyes of many students, faculty, alumni and friends; although our remarkable success in athletics by no means engendered universal enthusiasm on campus. Some feared the college was rapidly becoming a "jock college" and that such a reputation would discourage the enrollment of serious and able students.

But athletics were not without defenders. In answer to the complaint lodged about the attention football received in *De Klompen*, a defender wrote in the *Beacon* that the sport "deserves the over-emphasis it is getting now because it, more than anything else currently stands out as a mark of excellence for this college." Similarly, in a later issue of the student paper one reads that athletics involve

an art, and if the spectator realized this and keeps this constantly in mind, he can receive great satisfaction from viewing [it]. . . . He must realize that athletics is not an end in itself, but it can be used as a way to grow and become more mature for later life. By this, we mean that a person can learn self-discipline, the meaning of teamwork, the building of character, the idea of hard work and sacrifice, etc.

By the late 1970's, the controversy regarding the question of whether athletics were being overemphasized had subsided. Thus, in an issue of January 22, 1977 one reads: "Sports are still exciting, but students are keeping sports in a better perspective in relation to their work. Students are finding movies and plays relaxing and yet stimulating. This is a big step; Northwestern can be proud of it." Henceforth, criticisms were directed more at those instances in which poor sportsmanship was displayed by the players and coaches and by the spectators.

The past dozen years have seen the development of an outstanding intramural program. In the late 1960's, there were only four such sports for men (flag football, volleyball, basketball, and softball) and only one for women (volleyball), but by 1976 this number had grown to twelve and nearly all were open to both men and women. Included were flag football, basketball, volleyball, tennis singles, tennis mixed doubles, one-on-one basketball, slow pitch softball, ping pong, foozball, pool, bowling, and minature golf. A few more were added after the De Witt Physical Fitness Area was opened in the Rowenhorst Student Center. An intramural director was appointed in 1974, as was an assistant in 1976. These persons were aided each semester by recreation and physical education majors seeking field experience or fulfilling requirements for independent study courses.

In recent years, nearly 500 students have participated regularly in one or more intramural sports. Any student is eligible to participate in a particular intramural activity providing he or she is not playing on a varsity or junior varsity team in that sport, or did not letter in it during the previous year. Until 1974, teams were generally chosen at random, but have since been selected according to living quarters, with provisions also made for commuter and faculty teams. The number of teams participating has been surprising. In 1980, for example, the number of men's and women's basketball teams were 29 and 13 respectively. There were also 30 teams entered in flag football and 32 in bowling. In 1976, a Fun and Fitness Club was organized for persons wanting to keep physically fit through jogging, bicycling, or swimming.

Two time-honored regulations, namely those against smoking and dancing, were altered in recent years. Smoking on campus had been taboo since Northwestern was founded in 1882, but this ban was lifted slightly during the 1950's to permit smoking in "a designated area in the men's dormitory." For several years, however, it continued to be forbidden anywhere else on campus—even faculty members during the early 1960's had to walk across Highway 10 or to some other non-campus "turf" if they wanted to "catch a quick smoke" between classes. But as the years passed, additional designated smoking areas were established. Although smoking is not particularly common on campus today, the privilege of doing so enjoys wide latitude that includes individual student's rooms, other designated areas in campus buildings, and outdoors.

With respect to dancing, the 1967-1968 catalogue still contained the time-honored statement that dancing was "not permitted at college functions, either on or off campus." Not all students were happy with this regulation and protests were heard during the 1960's. In support of allowing dancing on campus, it was argued that dancing would provide a form of entertainment on weekends when, as one student put it, "there was not enough activity to [even] keep a monk happy." It was also pointed out that the regulation forced students who wanted to dance to do so elsewhere under conditions that were unchaperoned and very probably at places where liquor was sold. Faced with arguments like these and in keeping with the changing times, the Board of Trustees relented and beginning in 1968, three formal dances were permitted a year, namely, for Homecoming, Winter Carnival, and May Day.

Not all students were in favor of relaxing the rules, however, and there were strong objections when a fourth dance, which was labelled as a "town dance," was scheduled in the college auditorium in the late spring of 1970 as part of Orange City's centennial celebration. A letter of protest signed by about 300 students and faculty members was sent to the administration demanding an explanation for what was considered to be a breach in college policy. When no response was forthcoming, about fifty students staged a demonstration in front of the auditorium and passed out statements expressing disapproval of the matter.

In due time, fewer criticisms were heard and dancing, like smoking, became accepted as a normal part of campus life, as can be seen in the following excerpt from the current *Student Handbook:*

Dancing is to be seen as only one of many social activities available to students. They are a part of a varied program of social and recreational activities aimed at development of the total person within a Christian residential community.

It must be added though that the conditions under which on-campus dances take place must meet approval of the Student Development Office.

The questions that were raised about restrictions against smoking and dancing were in a sense part of a larger issue, namely, a desire on the part of students to play a greater voice in determining school policies. This aim was not unique to Northwestern, as young people on campuses across the nation were raising the cry of "student power." A perusal of feature articles, student letters, and editorials in the *Beacon* indicates that Northwestern's students wanted to be heard on a variety of issues, including compulsory class attendance, more liberal visitation regulations for the dormitories, greater opportunities for non-communters to live off campus, the criteria for keeping professors on the staff, student membership on key faculty committees, the distribution proportion of merit scholarships for extracurricular activities, and Sunday evening hours for the Rowenhorst Student Center. Recommendations for change in some of these matters also emanated from campus organizations in which students had a voice, such as the Christian Life Committee, the Student Activities Council, and, of course, the Student Senate (renamed the Student Government Association in 1980).

The growing determination of students to express their views was not limited to campus affairs. This maturity was also manifested in a resolve to be heard on national issues as well. Again, one of the best sources for observing this is the student newspaper. Beginning during the mid-1960's and continuing for several years, letters, editorials, and solicited articles—some rather lengthy—appeared quite frequently in the *Beacon* criticizing or supporting American involvement in Vietnam. From an early date, too, letters and articles were published on the subject of the women's movement. Following President Carter's decision to have young men register for the draft, several communications appeared in print discussing this move, and in 1981, the pros and cons of President Reagan's plan drastically to increase the Pentagon's budget received considerable attention. To the credit of Northwestern as a church-related college, these various issues were invariably discussed in the student press from a Christian and biblical perspective. Some students also participated in occasional demonstrations. Thus, on national Moratorium Day, November 1, 1969, nearly eighty students (out of an enrollment of about 690) showed their opposition to the Vietnam war by wearing black arm bands. Similarly, on March 26, 1980, a small group of students traveled to the federal building in Sioux City to participate in a noon "vigil" against draft registration.

Of course, the students who took positions on such controversial issues as Vietnam, the draft, the women's movement, and so forth, by no means always represented a large segment of the student body. As was true of most college campuses, a significant number usually remained apathetic, no matter what the issues. It should also be noted that based on their political party preferences, the majority of Northwestern students remained politically conservative—as they had in the past. For example, in the 1972 straw poll, Nixon won over McGovern 73 to 26 percent, and in 1976, Ford received almost twice as many votes as Carter. But on this matter, too, there is some evidence of change—a "Young Democrats" club was organized on campus a few years ago!

The transition to a four-year college did not alter emphasis that had traditionally been placed on maintaining a healthy spiritual life on campus. A significant step was taken in 1962 with the appointment of the Reverend Gordon De Pree, a former missionary in Hong Kong, as college pastor. The responsibilities of this new position included planning chapel services, doing guidance and counseling in spiritual matters, teaching in the Religion Department, and serving as chairman of the Student Religious Life Committee. In an effort to keep close ties with the Reformed Church, area ministers were invited at regular intervals to address the student body. Church officials from the denominational headquarters in New York City also made occasional visits to the campus. As noted earlier, religious leaders who were not members of the Reformed Church were also invited to the campus as speakers and directors of symposia.

Interest in spiritual matters was expressed in other ways too. The administration continued to show due regard for the religious backgrounds of candidates for vacant or new staff positions, and biblical studies remained an essential part of the required core curriculum. In 1979, the Student Christian Fellowship was reorganized and renamed

Student Ministries with the avowed purpose of involving more students and widening its activities. This was done primarily through the creation of "sub-boards," such as the "Worship Board" for assisting and giving advice in the matter of chapel programs, and the "Church Ministry Board" for building a closer relationship between the college and the local churches. There also was a "Community Service Board," designed to create an awareness of community needs and developing means for meeting those needs; a "Global Issues Board" for studying certain global issues and making contacts with such organizations as Bread for the World and Amnesty International; and a "Board of Outreach" to initiate greater social interaction among people of diverse backgrounds and values on campus.

One of the centerpieces of Northwestern's role as a Christian college has been its regular chapel service, and this has been as true in recent years as it was at any time in the past. As currently practiced, chapel services are held daily and students are required to attend three per week. Although occasional voices were raised against compulsory attendance, these were of limited significance. One of the strongest arguments in support of required chapel was set forth by the Reverend Fred Buseman, campus pastor from 1963 to 1969. In his report to the Board of Trustees in March, 1969, he stated:

Human nature being what it is, the benefits of required attendance at worship would seem to outweigh the disadvantages. As long as we assume that students are not mature enough to choose their academic courses wisely, and we continue to insist on prescribed curriculum, why should we assume that in spiritual matters they are able to decide for themselves. If we believe that the Holy Spirit is present and operative in corporate worship, then we have reason to believe in the valuable and lasting impressions made upon young people in our chapel services. Maturity tends to bear this out. A number of our alumni have expressed genuine appreciation for the chapel experiences, even though while students they were less than enthusiastic about attending chapel.

In response to student opinion polls taken during the early 1970's, occasional changes were made in the nature of the chapel services. This was done to make them more appealing to the students, while at the same time keeping them meaningful. Thus, in response to complaints that chapel frequently lacked continuity—that is, on one day a topic might generate considerable discussion, but the following chapel's topic could be completely unrelated—it was resolved to plan some of them around weekly themes. These have included, to mention a few, "The Christian and Politics," "The Christian and Athletics," and "The Chris-

Chapel, ca 1970

tian and Women." There have also been chapel seminars discussing contemporary social issues. Included have been such timely topics as "Christian Faith and the Nuclear Arms Race" and "Multi-National Corporations in the Third World—A Case of Dr. Jekyll and Mr. Hyde." These novel approaches did not replace, but were in addition to the traditional procedures of having faculty speakers, student-led chapels, and outside speakers.

Northwestern's retention of daily chapel is unique. In fact, at the very time when many Christian liberal arts colleges were abandoning this tradition, or favoring only one chapel per week, Northwestern was reaffirming its practice of making corporate worship involving faculty and students an essential part of campus life. Although this might seem surprising, it must be further noted that at a time when many private colleges were moving away from their church constituencies, Northwestern, as this study points out, has maintained its close ties with the Reformed Church.

Epilogue

In 1897, on the occasion of the annual commencement exercises of Northwestern Classical Academy, Miss Henrietta Hospers, a member of the graduating class, was delegated to give the traditional class history and prophecy. In her opening remarks, as she reflected on the events of the previous four years since her enrollment as a freshman, she expressed regret she could not relive that part of her life and once again "enjoy the sweet pleasures of the past." But, she added, there was nothing to prevent her from "sitting down at the close of the day, in that sweet hour of revery, and dream of those Academy days." So, in a sense, it has been with the writer of this history. Unable physically to relive those days of yore, it has been his enjoyable task to examine the records and describe for posterity what took place since that memorable time a century ago when Northwestern was founded in 1882.

As this study has brought out, Northwestern's beginnings were very modest. It started with three part-time teachers and no building of its own. In 1883, a small structure was erected whose interior could not be finished off at first for lack of funds. Known as the Pioneer School, it became too small within a few years. An abandoned skating rink in Orange City's downtown area was thereupon purchased and partially remodeled into classrooms and a dormitory for male students. Finally, in 1894, the present Zwemer Hall was built. From these small beginnings, a small frame building on the equivalent of about a city block, Northwestern has expanded to nearly forty acres with a physical plant valued at more than eleven million dollars.

The records of the Dutch settlers of Sioux County tell us they were God-fearing people who believed in preaching and hearing the word of God and in observing the Lord's Day as a day of rest. They also believed in providing their children an education that was both academically sound and possessed of a solid Christian foundation. As Principal James Zwemer remarked in 1892 on the occasion of the tenth anniversary of the Academy, the persons responsible for establishing the school "felt that if this fertile soil were worth tilling, if this promising city were worth building, if their western life were worth living, that then, above all things, . . . the benefits of higher Christian education were worth having."

When the Academy was founded, a secondary education was rare, and especially so in a region which a short time before had been a vast expanse of unsettled prairie. With a growing need after the First World War for education beyond the secondary school, and in view of the fact that northwest Iowa and the surrounding region had the largest concentration of Reformed churches west of the Mississippi, a junior college program was added to the Academy in 1928. This was followed by a senior college program in 1961, at which time the Academy, having outlived its usefulness (at least according to the Board of Trustees), was dissolved.

One hundred years of Northwestern history have gone by in which "shadow and sunshine" frequently mingled. As has been noted, the institution from time to time faced serious financial crises and nearly closed during the depression of the 1930's. It also had to weather other problems, including those associated with two world wars and the disappointment of not achieving North Central accreditation when it was expected. There have also been times when personal tragedies struck the campus, and young lives were suddenly and unexpectedly snatched from loved ones and friends through unfortunate accidents. Particularly sad was the death by drowning in 1934 of four students and their chaperon during an outing at Lake Okoboji. Staff members, too, have occasionally passed away in the fullness of their lives, including, in recent years, President Virgil Rowenhorst and Professor Grady Holland.

But faith can ultimately triumph over adversity. As Principal Thomas Welmers remarked in his report of 1913 to General Synod, although the "shadow side" sometimes forces itself upon our attention and we become discouraged, upon reflection we find the causes for regret and sadness are mostly beyond our control and there are many things for which we may be grateful. As this study has shown, there have been many things associated with Northwestern during its first one hundred years for which we may all be grateful.

Northwestern has won for itself numerous honors in various fields— drama, forensics, music, athletics, and others—but some of its greatest accomplishments in this respect have been the achievements of its graduates. Little has been said in this study about the accomplishments of the alumni, not because of neglect but partly due to lack of space. Moreover, it is not easy to come up with criteria regarding what constitutes a distinguished alumnus. For example, what about the many "unsung heroes" who labored as dedicated elementary and secondary school teachers? Are those who instilled a thirst for knowledge among hundreds of young minds worthy of less recognition than those graduates who, generally under more pleasant circumstances, distinguished themselves as scholars in higher education?

Some names of distinguished alumni, of course, come easily to mind. To mention only a *few* of the early graduates there is Jacob Van der Zee, the first Iowan to receive a Rhodes Scholarship to Oxford University; James Muilenburg, a noted Orientalist and one of the seven translators responsible for the Revised Standard Version of the Old Testament; Alfred Popma, who did pioneer work in cancer research; and Lloyd Rozeboom, whose work in the study of malaria has been compared to that of Walter Reed in the study of yellow fever. One can also point to the many alumni who went into full-time Christian service as ministers and missionaries—and these have been many. Indeed, for years, more students went into the ministry than into teaching. By 1912 (the thirtieth anniversary of the school), about sixty alumni had gone into teaching, but nearly seventy had become clergymen. Missionary work held special appeal—for example, numbered among its earliest graduates are three men (Dirk Dykstra, Gerrit John Pennings, and Gerrit Dick Van Peursem) who between them spent a combined total of one hundred twenty-two years on the Arabian mission field. There were others who labored in China, Japan, and India and among the American Indians.

The addition of a junior college program in 1928 did nothing to alter the interest of Northwestern graduates in pursuing professional careers. Thus in 1938 (the tenth anniversary of the Junior College), 25 percent of the rural schools in the area were being supplied by Northwestern graduates. Many also continued to enter Christian service. For example, by 1958 (the thirtieth anniversary), more than sixty Junior College alumni had entered the ministry. Interest in teaching and other professional careers continued after the addition of the senior college program. Thus, upon leaving Northwestern, approximately one-fourth of the 1980 graduates entered teaching, and nearly one-fifth signified an intention to continue their education.

Emphasizing an adherence to academic excellence and fostering a love for learning has thus traditionally been one of Northwestern's goals. But, as this study has repeatedly brought out, equally significant has been the attempt to provide an education that is not only academically sound, but evangelical in its theology and distinctively Christian in its outlook. This was the goal of the school's founders, and it has been reiterated throughout the years by principal after principal and president after president. In this respect, it is worth repeating a remark made by the current president, Dr. Friedhelm Radandt, in his inaugural address—appropriately entitled, "Challenge from Our Past"—of October 16, 1979: "The direction of Northwestern College was set when those early settlers put their faith in action and pledged their meager income to make a Christian institution a reality. Nothing has changed about that basic commitment." Indeed, in the minds of some faculty members who have been at the institution for a significant number of years, there is today an even greater effort than in the past to integrate faith and learning.

In brief, the motto of Northwestern, "Deus Est Lux"—God is Light, has continued to hold sway throughout the school's long history. With that conviction, this account of Northwestern's first hundred years of service concludes with a quotation from President Jacob Heemstra's last report to the Board of Trustees before his retirement from the presidency:

Looking over the history of Northwestern . . . we must and can say, "Hitherto hath the Lord led us." It is a history of prayer and of consecrated effort on the part of many interested in her life and usefulness in the kingdom, but also one of achievements. She has sent forth in every walk of life men and women consecrated in the service of the Lord, devoted to the cause and the kingdom of our Lord and saviour Jesus Christ. She stands and lives today as an answer to much prayer and hard work, as a product of the love of the Church for Christian education, and as a living testimony to the determination of faithful men and women.

A Note on Sources

The research for this history of Northwestern has been based almost entirely on primary source materials found in the Dutch Heritage Room of the Ramaker Library. Among the most valuable sources have been the "Annual Reports" of the principals and presidents to the Board of Trustees, the "Minutes" of the Board of Trustees, the "Minutes" of the faculty, and the student and alumni newspapers, including the *Monitor*, the *Beacon*, and the *Classic*. Also of considerable help were the school catalogues, faculty handbooks, student yearbooks (*De Klompen*), "Self-Studies" made for the North Central Association, *Acts and Proceedings of General Synod*, and local newspapers, including the *Sioux County Herald* and *De Volksvriend*. Also consulted was a variety of miscellaneous archival materials in the Heritage Room that are boxed and appropriately catalogued. These include speeches, letters, financial reports, commencement programs, committee reports, photographs, and so forth. Finally, personal interviews were held with several current and former staff members of the institution.

Index